THE UNITED STATES AND EUROPE
1815–1823

THE UNITED STATES AND EUROPE

1815-1823

A Study in the Background of the Monroe Doctrine

BY

EDWARD HOWLAND TATUM, JR.

NEW YORK / RUSSELL & RUSSELL

TO
NINA AND EDWARD

Contents

Preface

ANYONE who has read the explanations which historians have given for the enunciation of the Monroe Doctrine must have been impressed with their basic similarity. There is one conventional interpretation of the background of that policy which has colored them all. However much these accounts may vary in detail, they all agree that the Monroe Doctrine was the result of two factors: the fear that the Holy Alliance would soon extend its extraordinary activities to the New World, and the threat of Russian expansion on the Northwest Coast of this continent. This simple, direct, and plausible theory has attained a degree of authority which is almost unequaled in American historiography. No one has been so bold as to challenge it directly, while most historians have been so dominated by it that they have forced their documentary evidence to fit into its arbitrary pattern.

This conventional interpretation cannot stand the test of a critical examination of American opinion regarding world affairs and of the relation of international politics to the foreign policies of the United States. These two factors, together with the trend of domestic developments within the United States, form the real foundation for a clear understanding of the Monroe Doctrine. This basis is fundamentally sound, for it is composed not of assumptions from superficial evidence but of elements which are an integral part of all international politics. It is the purpose of this study to trace their influence upon the United States from 1815 to 1823 and to indicate clearly their relation to the declaration of the Monroe Doctrine.

The thesis of this book had its inception in Professor E. I. McCormac's seminar in United States Diplomatic History at the University of California and was further developed in a doctoral dissertation written under his direction. It is a privilege to be able to express my sincere appreciation of his careful criticisms and helpful suggestions. This thoughtful and friendly assistance has done much to improve the form of this study and to make the writing of it a pleasure. My gratitude is also due to my parents for their constant interest in my research and for their careful reading of the final draft of the text.

The preparation of the manuscript for publication and the task of seeing it through the press has been a joint enterprise. Therefore I wish to record here my thanks to Finette for her invaluable assistance. Her scholarly and painstaking work on the proofs has contributed more to the readability and typographical accuracy of this book than she will admit or the casual reader will readily perceive.

EDWARD H. TATUM, JR.

Los Angeles
January, 1936

CHAPTER I

World Politics in 1815

THE MONROE DOCTRINE, as declared by the President in
his message to Congress in December, 1823, was not the
product of hasty deliberations or of irresponsible statesmanship, nor was it caused by the knowledge of new and
unexpected events. Its genesis is to be found in the deepest currents of American thought and in the experience
of the American nation. Particularly was it the result of
the conception of world affairs which the people of the
United States and the leaders of the nation gained during
the eight years which preceded its enunciation. This view
of America's place in the world was influenced by conditions within the United States, by domestic problems, by
a growing spirit of nationalism, and by a feeling of uncertainty born of untried strength. The relations of the
European states with one another and with the United
States were thus judged subjectively, and the national
policy which the Monroe Doctrine embodies reflects this
evaluation most accurately.

If one turns first to view the European Continent in
1815, there will appear a confused, almost chaotic, pattern of conflicting political, moral, social, and economic
factors. Politically, Russia was the dominant force, never
to be disregarded by the able diplomats of Austria, Prussia, and France.[1] Under the vibrant personal leadership of

[1] It would be both futile and unnecessary to attempt to document this
survey completely. Most of the facts are too well known to require proof.
This chapter deals not so much with new material as with a presentation
of old material from the point of view taken in the book as a whole. A

Tsar Alexander I, Russia stood out from the rest of the Continental Powers. Alone of the sovereigns of Europe, her ruler was a man who was not overshadowed by his ministers, and this in itself enhanced Russian influence. In a society which rigidly adhered to the distinctions of the old régime, an emperor who directed his own foreign policy had a tremendous advantage. Nor were his counselors inferior in ability to their redoubtable opponents, Metternich and Talleyrand. However, the real reason for the deference which was accorded to Russia in diplomatic circles was the unquestioned fact of her military supremacy. Once more her allies and former enemies had reason to appreciate the truth of the epigram that "Russia was a dangerous ally, for she entered the field too late, and was then too strong." Austria, Prussia, and France were exhausted and incapable of further warfare, while Alexander stood at the head of an army of a million men on a war footing.

The effect of this military power on Continental politics was immediate and profound. Russia had definite ambitions which were, and still are, the *bête noir* of European chancelleries. Although at the moment her policy was peaceful, she would certainly seek to extend her influence southward and eastward at the first opportunity. During the wars she had had to bargain for favors; in 1815 she was freed from that necessity. She could now choose the time and method without consultation. From

picture of the world situation is sketched, and certain implications which were to be of great importance as factors in the shaping of American foreign policy during these years are pointed out. Special mention should be made of the works by Artz, Srbik, Temperley, and Webster; of the *Cambridge Modern History;* and of similar books which are fundamental and whose bibliographies furnish a guide to the literature on the period.

the moment of the defeat of France it was patent that Russia would attempt to use her diplomatic and military power to further her own interests, and that Austria, France, and England would use what ability they had to block the aims of Alexander. Austria and France would use diplomacy and hope that the weakness of their position would not be exposed. England also would use diplomacy as far as possible, but she had other resources as well. Watchfulness and a feeling of uncertainty prompted by military impotence characterized the Continental situation as the fatal Eastern Question resumed its key position in the international politics of Europe.

The second element of the problem was the weakness of France. From a general point of view her complete defeat increased the power of Russia and endangered the stability of the European state system. France should be weak but not too weak, for as long as she was prostrate she could not be counted in that Balance of Power which alone would limit the danger of Russian strength. This same fact was to influence world politics in another way. France could not, and most certainly would not, remain defeated, restricted by treaty obligations, and fettered by international control. Her leaders would bend every effort to regain for their country dignity and influence in world affairs. This was necessary for their security in office and for the morale of the nation as a whole. Thus another disturbing element claimed the attention of all who viewed the European scene. One might remark in passing that these two outstanding facts were clear to all observers at the time and were especially noted in the United States by thoughtful individuals and by the press.

To these two elements, based on the individual interests of Russia and France, must be added a third which concealed but partially under its cloak of internationalism the private interests of a third state. It has been the fashion until recently to consider the superficial rather than the fundamental character of Metternich's system of policy. Metternich, who by his ability and the brilliant reputation which he gained in the years from 1809 to 1815 shared the stage with Alexander, had two purposes of which he never lost sight. To preserve the Austrian Empire from dissolution, and to maintain the Habsburgs on the imperial throne, were goals to which he subordinated all Austrian policy and for which he waged a temporarily successful war. In the process of securing the *status quo* in Austria he used all the resources of that international diplomacy of which he was a master. This fact has tended to create the impression that he was a man devoted to the propagation of a theoretical "system" of politics throughout Europe and perhaps in an even wider sphere. Nothing could be farther from the truth. Peace, the *status quo* in Austria, and Austrian dominance in Germany and Italy were his objectives, and while he looked with pleasure at the extension of his political principles everywhere, he was not concerned in taking active steps to spread them by force beyond the area indicated. To have done so would have been to weaken Austria still more and to threaten the very existence of the Habsburg empire.

It is unnecessary to review here the well-known measures which Metternich employed to promote his policy, but this survey of the political factors on the Continent should not be concluded without notice of their import. Disregarding for the moment the other elements, it should be clear that the political undercurrents gave to the international politics of Europe a character that was essentially Continental, reactionary, and unstable. Austria wished for the preservation of the *status quo,* but Russia and France would gain by a readjustment of their positions. In this basic conflict of interests lay the key to the future. Much as some men might promote the idea of European solidarity, it was in fact doomed from the start. Speeches might be made, protocols signed, and circulars published; but united action was a chimera with which few observers who were also realists allowed themselves to be deluded.

If mutually exclusive interests made the international relations of the European states uncertain, even more hostile and dangerous forces were at work within the fabrics of the states themselves. After twenty-two years of war, the states headed by representatives of the old régime had triumphed over France and had succeeded in establishing once more the order they loved so well. Exhilarated by the emotions of the moment, they imagined that they had ended revolution forever, that their power was invincible, and that they had little to fear but a rebirth of Bonapartism in France. The very words of the famous treaty of alliance of November 20, 1815, express this attitude in the clearest fashion. Article Two reads as follows:

And as the same revolutionary principles which have sustained the last criminal usurpation may be able again, under other forms, to destroy France and to menace thus the repose of other states, the high contracting parties, solemnly recognizing the duty of redoubling their care to guard in such circumstances the tranquillity and interests of their peoples, agree in case such an unfortunate event breaks out anew to concert among themselves and with His Most Christian Majesty the measures which they will judge necessary for the security of their respective states and for the general tranquillity of Europe.[2]

This false sense of security on the part of the rulers was to be shattered, but for the moment it was undisturbed.

While reaction was the accepted order of the day, the spirit of the Revolution had left its mark on all classes of society. The cry for a new order clashed with the desire to return to the ways of the past, and the result was that almost incomprehensible paradox which the liberals of the day presented. Foremost of these was the Tsar Alexander, whom the accomplished Princess de Lieven referred to as a "Jacobin." His dreams of a new basis for society had matured slowly over a period of years. From 1805 to 1815 the treaties entered into by the Tsar with England, Austria, and Prussia all bear the mark of royal idealism, and all help to explain why in 1815 Alexander was the idol of liberals the world over.[3] His advisers were equally anxious to aid the cause of a better age and did all they could to encourage their master's inclinations. One of his trusted aides wrote at this time:

My wish was that Alexander should become in some sort the arbiter of peace for the civilized world; the protector of the weak and oppressed; the guardian of international justice; that his reign should begin a new era in international politics; politics henceforth based on the general good and on the rights of all and each.[4]

---

[2] Treaty of alliance, November 20, 1815. Martens, ed., *Nouveau recueil* . . . , II, 734. This and subsequent translations are the author's.

[3] Notice may be taken of the Anglo-Russian treaty of April 11, 1805 (Rose, ed., *Select Dispatches*, 265), the treaty of Kalisch, February 16, 1813 (Martens, ed., *Nouveau recueil* . . . , III, 234), the convention of Reichenbach, June 15, 1813 (*ibid.*, I, 568), and the treaty of Chaumont, March 1, 1814 (*ibid.*, I, 683).

[4] Prince A. Czartoryski, *Mémoires*, quoted in Phillips, *The Confederation of Europe*, 43.

The liberalism which Alexander and others of high rank sought to introduce found little favor with the statesmen of Europe, who regarded it as the somewhat ridiculous hobby of irresponsible mystics. They paid lip service to it, humored the Tsar, and signed his Holy Alliance, but they never took the trouble to put any of its principles into practice. The conflict of thought caused by this liberalism on the one hand, and by the avowed reaction of the governments on the other, made liberals everywhere feel even more keenly the helplessness of their position. The emotional letdown which normally followed the war was deepened by the reactionary policies of the leaders of the states. Their failure to move in step with the times, however, was made intolerable to these high-minded, enthusiastic liberals by the expressions of progressive thought which continually emanated from high places about the court of Alexander. Metternich's own private secretary, Gentz, wrote of this phase of the period with singular keenness of perception. He declared:

Universal expectation has perhaps never been roused to such a pitch as before the opening of this dignified assembly [the Congress of Vienna]. Men had promised themselves an all-embracing reform of the political system of Europe, guarantees for universal peace, in one word, the return of the golden age. The Congress has resulted in nothing but restorations, which had already been effected by arms, agreements between the Great Powers of little value for the future balance and preservation of the peace of Europe, quite arbitrary alterations in the possessions of the smaller states; but no act of a higher nature, no great measure for public order or for the general good, which might compensate humanity for its long sufferings or pacify it for the future.[5]

---

[5] Phillips, *The Confederation of Europe*, 118.

Despair, resentment, and hatred filled the minds of those who thus felt themselves to have been defrauded by the results of the long years of war, and thus one more disturbing element was introduced into the already precarious state of Europe.

The French Revolution, in its broader sense, still moved on and extended its influence. The rulers mistook the nature of its force, but the spread of ideas could not be checked. Nationalism and liberalism were driven underground by the police measures of Metternich and those who followed his program, with the result that they spread more rapidly than ever and continually threatened to destroy the repose of the Continent. Governmental policy was helpless by itself; and, as the character of the danger became apparent, recourse was had to the only other weapon at the disposal of the rulers in this difficult situation, international action. This policy in itself was ruinous, and few enlightened observers in this country or abroad saw in it any elements of success or permanent usefulness. The moment the international organization of Europe was employed to foster schemes of reaction, all liberals were forced to throw in their lot with the revolutionaries, thus strengthening the opposition. At the same time the rival interests of the Great Powers were thrown into even sharper outline by their attempts at coöperation.

The importance of this moral or social factor in the period under discussion cannot be overemphasized. Its action was plain, its effect obvious. It revealed the fact that Europe was still revolutionary and uneasy, that she was not content with her lot, and that, given the opportunity, she would attempt to overthrow a régime that had become an anachronism. Nor were observers slow to perceive that this state of affairs had interesting implications in the broader field of world politics. An unpopular government which maintains its position only by the most rigorous police measures at home and by oppression and armed intervention in the affairs of its weaker neighbors, is not a dangerous factor in situations beyond its immediate reach. It cannot run the risk of distant war, which will be costly, long, and perhaps none too successful. In short, its hands are tied as far as world politics are concerned, and although it may use diplomacy and influence to make its views effective, it cannot push them to the point of war.

A glance at the economic condition of Europe after 1815 reveals even worse conditions than those in the political and social spheres. Decades of war had very nearly bankrupted the Continent. France was on the verge of financial collapse and was only preserved from ruin by the aid of her erstwhile adversaries. The other Continental Powers were in no more favorable positions. They had waged war for years with the help of English gold, and with the coming of peace they found it necessary to support themselves by floating large loans. It was at this time that international finance on a large scale in time of peace became an important factor in world politics. Austria, France, and Prussia borrowed extensively from the great private bankers in England, the Rothschilds and the Barings, and from such Dutch firms as that of Hope.⁶

This financial chaos in the affairs of the Continental states still further weakened their influence in Europe, to

---

⁶ This phase of world affairs deserves further investigation, for its implications are full of interest. Corti's *Rise of the House of Rothschild* throws light upon the activities of one of the most important of these private banking firms.

say nothing of the areas beyond the borders of the Continent. Brilliant diplomacy was the order of the day, but brilliant finance was sadly lacking. The inability of the states of western Europe to raise sufficient funds within their borders for their own needs placed them in a very difficult position. Steady borrowing was necessary for the expenses of government, while extraordinary ventures were almost entirely out of the question. Corti's account of the precarious financial position of the Austrian treasury at the time of the expedition into Italy in 1821 and of the whip hand held by the Rothschild family over the whole enterprise is illustrative of this phase of the economic situation.[7] Statesmen who wished to pursue an active policy at home and abroad had to meet opposition from the officials of their own exchequers and ultimately had to come to terms with foreign bankers, usually English ones. The rôle of finance in world politics is still a closed book, many pages of which will never be turned, but over a century ago the newspapers noted these loans closely and even ventured to remark that England appeared to be using them to further her commercial and political aims. Certain it is that the world knew that England was financing Continental governments and that without her aid they would be in serious financial straits.[8]

On these nations which were economically weak, and which were filled with fear, suspicion, and hatred of one another, the Industrial Revolution was begining to turn

---

[7] Corti, *Rise of the House of Rothschild*, 227 ff.

[8] This fact is pointed out, for example, in *Niles' Weekly Register*, X, 93, April 6, 1816, and XX, 74, March 31, 1821; and in a dispatch from Appleton to J. Q. Adams, August 6, 1823. Manning, ed., *Diplomatic Correspondence of the United States concerning the Independence of the Latin American Nations* (hereafter cited as Manning, ed., *Diplomatic Correspondence*), III, 2040.

its full force. Thus their attempts to re-create stable systems for themselves were infinitely complicated. With their own productive equipment in sad repair, and faced with the prospect that England's immense economic power would compete for their markets, the Continental nations turned to the weapons at hand. Napoleon had taught them the use of one of these, and before long observers were commenting upon the formation of a new and infinitely more dangerous Continental System in the tariffs which were steadily being erected against English goods. They were designed to lessen the strain on Continental economic life caused by the now familiar situation in which the world's greatest creditor is also the greatest industrial nation and possesses a tremendous productive machine creating stocks for export.

Not only must France and the other states protect their own markets and reduce their need for English goods; they must also, if they were ever to repay their borrowings, find places in which to sell their manufactured products. Thus once again interest was aroused in foreign markets, colonial and international. Colonies assumed a new importance, and all nations with an export trade began to realize the value of open markets freed from the old exclusive system of colonial regulation. This economic interest was to produce vital conflicts in the determination of policy, for such nations as France were soon faced with the necessity of supporting reaction in political circles at home and freedom of trade in commercial circles abroad, a dilemma which made clear decisions difficult. Through all these years, hostility to English enterprise the world over grew and increased in intensity. It was felt that England, liberal as she professed to be in politics, still favored monopoly and exclusion in matters economic. She had the power and the will to impose her system on any corner of the globe where her interest dictated, and the other nations saw clearly that she must be opposed at every turn if she was not to obtain complete dominance in an industrial world.

These factors, the financial difficulties of the European countries at home and the first effects of the Industrial Revolution on their economic lives, had marked effects on their foreign policies. It will suffice here to say that the first tended to limit their freedom of action in Europe and to make a vigorous policy abroad well-nigh impossible, and the second increased the friction arising from distinct sets of interests and especially tended to create a cleavage between England and the Continent. Let us examine the condition of England and her relation to the Continental Powers.

After the conclusion of the peace, England was confronted with internal problems of a most difficult kind. They did not arise, as did those of the Continental countries, so much from a conflict of political principles as from the economic difficulties in which the island was involved. While Europe had been engaged in a long and disastrous war, England had been occupied at home in building a vast industrial plant which was adjusted to the needs of a wartime world. In peaceful years this productive equipment was far in excess of her own needs, yet she faced the loss of the former Continental outlets for her goods. In addition, the Industrial Revolution brought with it conditions which entailed great hardships on the masses of the people and which lowered living standards in general. Add to these conditions the fact that England had to levy terrifically high taxes in order to pay for the war which she had waged for twenty-two years and the resultant effect becomes obvious.

Bad economic conditions were very soon reflected in political unrest and bitter hostility to the government. The elements that made the Continental situation so dangerous were absent from England, but nevertheless the demand for a policy which would improve conditions was too loud and too threatening to be disregarded. What course would a Tory government take in the circumstances? Herein lies the first of those basic conflicts of interests which had such a great effect on the course of English policy after 1815. Would the government try to keep things as they were, or to change its measures completely, or to steer a middle course? An examination of the relation of England to the Continent will elucidate English policy in this respect.

Politically, England maintained the closest coöperation with the Continental enemies of France. For nearly a generation she had manipulated alliances, coalitions, and agreements in a way that aroused the admiration even of her enemies. She had been as thoroughly enmeshed in Continental politics as France herself, and this tradition of participation in Continental affairs, on the one hand, continued to have a definite influence through the leadership of the Tories and Castlereagh, their foreign minister. On the other hand, the return of peace to a nation weary of constant war and intrigue produced a desire for isolation and freedom from foreign responsibilities. This feeling was strong in England, for it, too, was traditional and even more deeply ingrained in the English consciousness than the wartime experience with European connections.

From 1815 to 1822 these forces struggled for supremacy under the able and often brilliant leadership of Castlereagh, the internationalist, and of George Canning, the isolationist. England wished to re-create the Balance of Power on the Continent, and this involved participation in its affairs; she also desired to keep her hands free and to avoid the unpleasant features of too close contact with other nations. Here, then, is a second element to be considered in assessing the foreign policy of England.

Conservative though her government was, England was the leading exponent of liberalism in Europe. Compared with the reactionary policies pursued by the Continental states, hers was a free, progressive line of conduct. Though she had fought the French when their foreign policies threatened her interests, she still sympathized with the principles of freedom, of equal rights, and of constitutional government to which the Revolution had given impetus. The blind reaction of the Continental monarchs, their complete disregard for the rights and interests of their peoples, and the fanaticism with which the restored rulers and the nobles tried to set the clock back to 1789, aroused disgust, contempt, and outspoken disapproval throughout the island. Thus another set of opposing forces was created. Within England there was a somewhat emotional public, easily swayed by appeals to its sympathy for oppressed peoples abroad, facing a conservative government which was by no means so interested in the rights of man. At every turn these two elements affected England's foreign policy, for the question was always raised, "Should England favor the governments of Europe or the peoples over which they ruled?"

The economic situation also influenced the international policy of England. Some aspects of her position after the wars have already been observed. England's superior industrial equipment and the consequent high efficiency of her productive system made markets for her surpluses a necessity, and this required a free commercial system. Of course what England called a free commercial system might appear to her rivals to be merely English monopoly, but the fact remains that England was forced to seek open markets and this entailed the breakdown of the colonial monopoly of such nations as Spain. In addition, England was the world's greatest shipping nation, and employment for her mercantile marine was possible only if the ports of the world were open to all maritime nations. Thus she was gradually being forced into the position of supporting free trade and open competition in the commercial field. In 1815, however, this decision was still in the future, and the issue of freedom versus exclusion was unsettled. Commercial expansion was necessary as the only possible solution for her economic ills, while close relations with the Continent were desirable from a political point of view. The English government found it exceedingly difficult to reconcile these two desires. Caution was advisable, and it was a long time before England took a definite stand, for the danger of friction on a world-wide scale resulting from commercial expansion was evident.

These conflicts of interests, however, must not be allowed to obscure the real position of England in world affairs. She might be undecided as to which course she desired to follow, but uncertainty is far from being weakness. If Russia dominated the Continent by virtue of her military power, England was without question mistress of the seas. It is too often overlooked that, if any nation won the wars against France, that nation was England. *She* had engineered the combinations that ultimately wrecked the military power of France, and in the process she had swept every rival fleet from the seas, had added important bits of territory to her imperial domain, and had assumed an unchallenged position in the world. There are two corollaries to this, which contemporaries recognized and of which one must never lose sight. First, England was the only nation in the Old World that had the power in her own hands to give effect to her policies outside of Europe. She need consult no one, nor need she fear opposition. Absolute command of the sea made her independent and all-powerful. Second, no Continental Power could attempt anything beyond the shores of the Continent itself without the permission of England, explicit or tacit. Thus the converse of the use of English power for her own ends was the ability to block, single-handed, the plans of others if she so desired. The importance of sea power has often been stressed, but at few times in world history has it been so important as from 1815 to 1823. Sea power alone made England the beginning, the middle, and the end of all considerations of world policy, and it is impossible to overemphasize this fact.

Unquestioned maritime supremacy, coupled with the plain fact that England's economic life was henceforth to be based on a world market of ever-increasing proportions, did much to revive the importance of her colonial possessions and to make her solicitous for their welfare. They were to be the outposts of a commerce which touched all parts of the world. Their value as naval bases from which to protect her shipping was clear; no longer were her possessions merely parts of a closed mercantile system. Thus English policy was directed more and more to the condition of her colonial domains and was becoming increasingly jealous of the activities of other nations in adjacent areas.

These general tendencies were of great importance to an understanding of English policy at that time, and shrewd observers were quick to grasp their significance. The government of England was in no enviable position. Conservative in thought, it was faced by radicalism at home—a result of war and the Industrial Revolution. Abroad, it was inclined to maintain close political relations with the Continental Powers in order to further its own interests, but it was held back in this course by a rapidly rising popular desire for political isolation from European affairs. Inclined to favor the governments of Europe in their attempts to preserve the *status quo,* it could not disregard the unmistakable fact that the people of England were emotionally in sympathy with the oppressed peoples of Europe. Finally, the only means of bettering the economic situation seemed to be through the expansion of English export trade in free markets, and this was incompatible with close friendly relations with governments which still held fast to the old principles.

The effect of the influence of these conflicting currents on the government of England was that it pursued throughout this period a negative policy. Her leaders tried to sit on the fence and to look both ways at once, for they could not bring themselves to the assertion of a clean-cut, definite, and consistent system of policy. They were following that old, yet ever new, course of action which so many English diplomats have taken, of waiting for events to force them to make a decision. In the meantime, they sought to be both Continental and insular, conservative and liberal, with the obvious result that no one trusted them, listened to their advice, or heeded their suggestions. Thus when England's interests finally did point the way which they must follow, nothing less than open threats sufficed to make their policies effective. As is inevitably true of all negative policies, the result was negative. Being unable to see far enough ahead to gauge the course of events, and yet being not altogether blind, England's statesmen ultimately steered their country into the company of those liberalizing forces which were to dominate the nineteenth century, but they lost for her much that a long-view policy would have gained in prestige, friendship, trust, and leadership.

In the United States after 1815, internal problems required the attention of the people and of their government. That period in the nation's life during which their interest was held almost uninterruptedly on foreign affairs was drawing to a close and was to be followed by an even longer period in which they were preoccupied with domestic problems. Instead of considering domestic events in terms of the foreign scene, they were to evaluate foreign interests in terms of the domestic situation. The years under discussion saw that shift in emphasis take place. Certainly the first assertion was true in 1815, and it is equally plain that the second was valid in 1824.

The immediate difficulties that faced the United States after the war with England were economic. The return to a peacetime basis had to be achieved. The war had not been beneficial to American economic life. Business now suffered from the renewed competition of foreign goods, manufacturing was injured, and all the hardships of a period of deflation were felt with great keenness by the country as a whole. The means suggested for the improvement of the economic system—a national bank, a tariff, and internal improvements, provided great issues which required long years of bitter debate for their settlement. The postwar immigration from Europe further complicated the internal situation by swelling the tide of westward migration and thereby hastening political changes which were to cause so much sectional trouble in the years to come.

Thus the economic issues were not only exceedingly difficult to solve, but also brought in their train political questions which were well-nigh insoluble. They revived the old, basic conflicts of philosophies and individual interests, ended the era of one-party government, split the Republican party of Jefferson into factions, and realigned in a new pattern the political forces of the country. Economic and political interests together tended to absorb completely the energies of the people and their representatives. There were subjects more important than foreign affairs and issues so vital that to many it seemed as if the very existence of the Union depended upon their speedy and peaceful handling.

These complications all had their effect on foreign policy. Because of the need to apply all the energy and ability that the country possessed to their successful solution, freedom of action in the foreign field was restricted. America could not again rush into a war with some European Power if diplomacy failed to obtain her ends. She needed an interval of peace in which to develop and to organize her national life, to settle if possible some fundamental political and constitutional questions, and to recover from the dislocating effects of years of neutrality in a war-torn world followed by two years of outright hostilities. The United States could not, however, merely withdraw into herself and forget the outside world. The problem was not so simple as that. She, too, needed to develop foreign trade and commerce for the benefit of her shipping and agricultural interests. Above all, it was to be the immediate task of her statesmen to liquidate the numerous unsettled issues with foreign countries and to create as few new ones as possible. A glance at the nature of these issues will be helpful.

Foremost were the many disputed questions which the treaty of Ghent had left unsettled. These all dated back to the founding of the United States and would require wise judgment and delicate diplomacy if satisfactory results were to be obtained. Boundaries were to be determined, the fisheries question adjudicated, maritime rights discussed, the West India trade regulated, and claims adjusted. There were likewise long-standing claims against the Spanish government, and the very difficult Florida problem was becoming more and more acute. Commercial relations with France virtually amounted to an economic war in which differential duties and strangling regulations played their part. Old claims against the French nation were still pending. Besides these controversies with the leading countries of western Europe, there were numerous minor disputes with Naples and with the countries of the north. On the horizon loomed two other general issues to plague American diplomats and to harass the government. The revolutions in South America were soon to require consideration, and the problems involved in the slave trade were to be fruitful sources of trouble. Perhaps never since the American Revolution had the United States faced such a maze of difficulties at a time more filled with pressing domestic problems. The successful diplomacy which was brought to bear upon them forms one of the brightest chapters in the history of her foreign relations.

These issues were recognized as full of difficulty, but there was hope for their solution. Even those in which England was involved were susceptible of arbitration or mutual adjustment. Nevertheless, when Americans looked into the future they derived little encouragement from what they thought they saw. Relieved of the burden of war, England would again assert her commercial strength in fields which the war had left open to neutrals. In particular, the carrying trade bade fair to be a source of the closest competition. The United States did not export manufactured goods, as did England, but she counted her shipping as an important item in the balance of trade. Nor was it certain that the war for the carrying trade would be a fair fight in an open field. To America, England still stood for monopoly of colonial trade and exclusive privileges in other markets, to procure which all the tricks of English diplomacy were usually employed. The only chance for American success was to have trade completely free with no special favors or agreements by which any one nation might benefit.

A second subject which was likely to be a source of trouble with England was the slave trade. The United States was on the eve of the period when the mere mention of slavery was a sure prelude to violent discussion and debate. England, on the contrary, had become very

America was born impeach the thoroughness of their study, for, if there is one fact provable beyond doubt, it is that fear, suspicion, and hatred of England were greater in America in 1822 than in 1815, and it is only just to say that Englishmen returned the compliment. Friendship with England was yet a dream, if not a hallucination.

It is now necessary to review a very interesting historical factor in European political alignments. A Balance of Power did not exist in 1815 and therefore its influence on this period has been too little considered. It is obvious in international politics that the modern state system will either be adjusted under some form of international organization, or it will seek stability in a system of alliances which aim at the creation of a Balance of Power. The rather futile attempt to form an international organization in 1815 was doomed to failure. It was too nebulous in character and too uncertain in its form to acquire permanence, and in addition it succumbed to lack of vision on the part of the governments of Europe and to the underlying hostility and conflicting interests of the states themselves. The Continent was therefore without any effective organization and without any really binding system of alliances. Even the famous Quadruple Alliance availed little, for England regarded it solely as a guaranty against France, while the other Powers differed concerning the use to be made of it.

The key to the problem lies in the fact that England tended gradually to separate herself from Continental connections. The European Powers feared her naval strength and commercial competition. Above all, they feared the possible threat of combinations arranged by England. She had proved extraordinarily successful in this respect during the war; she might attempt the same thing in time of peace. The leading Power on the sea could be counted on to take steps to maintain her pre-eminence, and the land Powers could be relied upon to lessen the danger which confronted them.

The result was that Europe looked upon the United States as a factor in the readjustment of international relations. She had risen to the rank of a nation of some importance in world affairs and she might be useful as an element in a new Balance of Power. Russia recognized this fact at once, and Russian policy toward the United States cannot be understood unless it is realized that Russia wished to draw the United States closer to Europe and away from England. Repeated attempts were made to connect America with the European system, and at all times Russia was careful not to antagonize the United States. Her statesmen saw clearly that to push conflicts with the United States too far would be to throw that country into the arms of England (so they reasoned from their Continental experience) and to create an *entente* between the two leading maritime nations of the world. To a country situated as was Russia, dependent on foreign shipping for her trade, such a combination would have been disastrous, for her commerce would have been at the mercy of her enemies. Again sea power played its part in shaping international policy.

The conduct of France may be traced to the same sources, though in slightly different ways. She, too, manifested a disposition to prevent any break in her relations with the United States. She appointed an avowed friend of the United States as her minister, used her good offices in tense situations between the United States and other

Powers, and finally in 1822 negotiated her first commercial treaty with the United States since 1800. There were rough sides to French friendship, yet on the whole it was satisfactory; and at no time did her statesmen evince a desire to oppose the United States to the point of hostility.

England, also, may be said to have regarded the United States as a factor in the international balance. Although she pushed her own policies very far and on more than one occasion irritated Americans exceedingly, she did not wish to force America into the opposing camp. However, her attempts along this line only further convinced Americans of her treachery and duplicity, for there was no doubt that she desired to check the territorial and commercial expansion of the United States and to limit American diplomatic success as much as possible. Indeed, here is illustrated once again the negative character of English policy. England did not desire a strong United States and did all she could to prevent its growth, while at the same time she feared the effects of a complete break with America. Fight she could, and would if necessary, but the prospect of fighting a possible coalition made no appeal to her leaders.

Thus an investigation of the world situation in 1815 and of the factors which were to influence policy reveals much that bore directly on the position of the United States. It shows a Europe weakened by revolutionary unrest, by economic prostration, and by international rivalries. It shows the dominant Power, England, vacillating with respect to the direction which her policy should take but relatively strong and powerful in the international field. It shows the Old World as a whole hampered by internal troubles and by an unstable state system in which neither Balance of Power nor international organization held sway. On this side of the Atlantic was an America involved in a readjustment of her economic and political life and in the solution of most difficult foreign problems. At the same time, the European nations assumed it as axiomatic that the United States was a member of the general system of states, and this conviction profoundly affected their policy toward America. Although it was not obvious, more than one nation was bidding in a tentative way for American support and friendship in the search for a new Balance of Power. This was either active as with Russia, or passive as with England and France. Nevertheless it existed, and American statesmen were keen enough to take advantage of it for their country's good.

CHAPTER II

The American Attitude Toward the Old Régime

WHEN AMERICANS considered the Continent of Europe as a whole, they observed the progress of reaction and restoration with disgust and ridicule. The actions of the Congress of Vienna, with their disregard for national sovereignty and their high-handed rearrangements of the map of Europe, were condemned.[1] It was pointed out that Europe had freed herself from one tyrant only to become the slave of a group of despots, and that the congress, it seemed, had but restored tyranny and called it peace.[2]

In addition to noting the political aspects of the European situation, the press gave considerable space to the problem of "legitimacy" suggested by the restorations which the congress had effected. The whole theory of government based on divine right was attacked. Royal claims to power were denounced in serious articles and ridiculed in sarcastic notes, and no effort was spared to create an impression of the uselessness and the evils of such a system. Niles concluded one long article on the right of kings to rule with the remark that it is "a burlesque on common sense to suppose that so perfect an ideot [sic] as Ferdinand, or so finished a madman as George, can have a 'divine right' to govern millions of rational men!"[3] The attempts of the restored rulers to

---

[1] *Niles' Weekly Register*, IX, 23, September 9, 1815.
[2] *Ibid.*, X, 367, July 27, 1816.
[3] *Ibid.*, IX, 432, February 17, 1816.

stamp out the revolutionary spirit also drew the fire of editors;[4] and Niles, in particular, delighted in publishing all the instances of "legitimate" cruelty and barbarism which came to his attention.[5]

Europe appeared to the Americans to be sinking back into a "calm of despotism" like that of the Dark Ages. Declarations of the rulers which helped to create this conviction were occasionally printed. One of the most noteworthy examples of the effect of this type of news is to be found in the interest aroused by a speech of the emperor of Austria. Speaking to the professors of Laibach in 1821 on the function of instruction in his dominions, he declared his hostility to the new ideas which were disturbing the world and concluded, *"I do not want learned men; I want only loyal and good subjects."*[6] This dissertation on the aims of absolutism was printed in leading American newspapers and was widely commented upon as an example of the fanaticism of Old World principles.[7] All the republicanism and democracy of the United States reacted against these ideas which were so contrary to its own; and it was judged that bigotry, the inquisition, humiliation, and proscription characterized the moral state of Europe after the wars.[8]

The first manifestations of American sentiment toward

---

[4] *Niles' Weekly Register*, IX, 210, November 25, 1815.

[5] Examples of the atrocity stories related about "legitimates" are to be found *ibid.*, IX, 32, September 9, 1815; XI, 36, September 14, 1816; and XIV, 376, July 25, 1818.

[6] *Ibid.*, XX, 354, August 4, 1821.

[7] As in an article from the Petersburg *Intelligencer*, in the *National Intelligencer*, April 21, 1821.

[8] Summary of the state of Europe in *Niles' Weekly Register*, XII, 464, August 23, 1817.

the Holy Alliance express distrust and suspicion.[9] The conservative *North American Review* avowed that it placed no great confidence in this league for the preservation of peace and quoted Virgil on Greeks bearing gifts. The inconsistency of peace-loving principles and large standing armies was remarked, and the *Review* sarcastically stated that the "solemn farce of Holy Alliances will probably aggravate rather than diminish the evil [of war]."[10] The *National Intelligencer* also reflected this skeptical state of mind in an analysis of the alliance of the sovereigns. The journal asserted that it was more inclined to regard this alliance as a league for territorial conquests than for the spread of religious principles; but final judgment on the motives of its members was withheld until more information should become available.[11] The only unqualified approval of the aims and principles of the Holy Alliance appears to have come from those uncritical idealists who founded the peace societies and who, in their hatred of war, shut their eyes to the realities of the world around them.[12] The general tone of the press, however, reflected interest, apprehension of the motives of the members of the league, and a growing feeling that the vagueness of their declarations boded no good for liberty and freedom.

The events of the four or five years following 1815 con-

[9] The term "Holy Alliance" is used in this book to indicate both the treaty and the group of European Powers to which this term came to be applied, though incorrectly. The text will indicate which is meant. As the terms were used interchangeably at the time it is better to continue this practice than to resort to awkward circumlocutions and paraphrases.

[10] *The North American Review*, VI (1817), 42.

[11] *National Intelligencer*, July 8, 1817, commenting upon an article from the London *Courier* which attacked the Holy Alliance.

[12] For a more detailed account of this phase of public opinion see below, pp. 221–224.

vinced Americans that their skepticism had been justified and that their worst doubts had been well founded. The increasing reaction, the police measures of the Continental Powers, and the obvious attempts of leading statesmen to transform the concert of Europe into an alliance for their own protection, proved the case of the cynics. The Carlsbad decrees, the Congresses of Aix-la-Chapelle and Troppau, and the invasion of Italy by Austrian troops removed the veil completely. The intentions of the allied kings were now clearly manifest; their object was to keep the people in chains and to end freedom in Europe.[13] A southern paper heatedly characterized the actions of the alliance as a "war against light" and denounced the so-called deliverers of Europe,[14] and a New York journal went to the heart of the matter by declaring that the only principle which the alliance followed was its own will and power.[15]

It is interesting to observe, in passing, that the information which leading American papers received about the transactions of the European Powers was unusually full and complete. Nearly all the important documents and declarations of policy which were released to the European public found their way into such papers as *Niles' Weekly Register* and the *National Intelligencer,* where excellent articles interpreting the events were given prominence.[16] Thus Americans had an opportunity to judge for themselves the aims and policies of the European Powers,

---

[13] Editorial in *Niles' Weekly Register,* XX, 17, March 10, 1821.

[14] The Charleston *Courier,* in the *National Intelligencer,* May 12, 1821.

[15] New York *American,* in *Niles' Weekly Register,* XXIV, 364, August 9, 1823.

[16] For example, the collection of documents in *Niles' Weekly Register,* XX, 31 ff., and the article "Of the European States" in the *National Intelligencer,* November 25, 1817.

to note the difficulties which they encountered and the relative success of their enterprises. The result was that leading men and the most reliable newspapers were rarely misled in their attempts to evaluate the condition of Europe and its significance for the United States.

As thinking people in this country watched the history of Europe unfold before their eyes, the vast gulf that separated the ideas of the rulers of Europe from those of the American government and its people came clearly into view. The excitement of war and revolution was gone, and the domestic policies of restored autocrats occupied the center of interest. *The Aurora* published a long article on the "First Principles of the 'Holy Alliance' " which is typical of the Republican reaction to European ideas.[17] In 1818, after peace had been fully restored and the first sense of the injustice of the acts of the Congress of Vienna had been forgotten, this Philadelphia paper reviewed some of the writings of the Abbé de Pradt[18] in which legitimacy, the cause of kings, and the old order were defended. The Abbé admitted the conflict between royalty and the Catholic religion, on the one hand,. and constitutional government of the American type, on the other; and *The Aurora* thanked the "European high priest" for setting forth so plainly the antipathy between his principles and ours so that "we are not left at a loss to determine what he means."

In similar vein Niles contrasted the peaceful conditions in the United States to the oppression in Europe and

---

[17] *The Aurora*, in *Niles' Weekly Register*, XIV, 311, June 27, 1818.

[18] The Abbé de Pradt, once archbishop of Malines, was a royalist but not a fanatic; his dreams did not obscure his judgment. His numerous works on the state of Europe and on the American colonies received much publicity in the United States.

boldly declared that no reflective American really counted upon the friendship of nations governed by kings. There was too much divergence between the bases of their states and of America for real sympathy to exist.[19] John Quincy Adams, too, expressed this feeling when he wrote to William Plumer that

> . . . There is already in all the governments of Europe a strong prejudice against us as Republicans, and as the primary causes of the propagation of those political principles, which still make the throne of every European monarch rock under him as with the throes of an earthquake. . . . there is a vague and general sentiment of speculative and fomenting jealousy against us prevailing all over Europe. . . .[20]

Examples of this heightened sense of the difference between the United States and the Old World might be multiplied. It was the direct result of the peace of 1815 and of the reaction which followed. Nearly a generation had passed since America had been confronted with a Europe under the old régime, and even the Europe of prerevolutionary days had not been so *actively* illiberal as was the Europe of Metternich and Louis XVIII. Therefore it must be recognized that the feeling toward Europe which pervaded America after 1815 was very different from the desire to keep out of the turmoils of the Continent which characterized the Revolutionary and Napoleonic periods.

Compounded of nascent nationalism, intolerance of an alien system, and a growing consciousness that not alone the political but also the economic and social patterns of Europe were at variance with those of America, the spirit

---

[19] *Niles' Weekly Register*, XIII, 1, August 30, 1817.
[20] J. Q. Adams to W. Plumer, January 17, 1818. J. Q. Adams, *Writings*, VI, 141.

of the United States became more and more domestic and regarded the affairs of Europe with less active interest. Her complete geographical separation from the Old World was mentioned with relief on many occasions;[21] hatred of the ways of royalty and of the nobility of the old régime, which had been provoked by the Congress of Vienna, was continued by the events of the next few years;[22] and even the idea that the affairs of Europe no longer held any interest for the United States had sufficient currency to cause the *National Intelligencer* to complain of loss of subscriptions on that account.[23] One of the clearest declarations of this conviction of the social, economic, and political contrast between the Old World and the New is that of Congressman Trimble of Ohio. Speaking in the House in approval of the recognition of the South American republics, he declared

... that all civilized nations were under the dominion of two great social systems, differing widely from each other—that one was established in the *Occidental,* the other in the *Oriental* world—that the spirit of the age was against the European system. . . . It [the American system] has two aspects, two

[21] Petersburg *Intelligencer,* in the *National Intelligencer,* September 9, 1815.

[22] The Republican dislike for the manners of the *haut monde* took amusing forms at times, as when the *National Advocate* urged the withdrawal of our ministers from abroad and the substitution of chargés d'affaires, a rank that would be cheaper, more business-like, and more republican. Niles approved the idea because the consequent removal of foreign ministers from Washington would end "the grand display of monarchical splendor and equipages, . . . the dinners and rich wines to surfeit the appetite, and corrupt the principles of our country members of congress, and make them sigh after vanities which are fatal to the purity of our republic. . . ." *Niles' Weekly Register,* XXII, 273, June 29, 1822.

[23] *National Intelligencer,* September 26, 1815. Niles also deplored the same lack of interest in European affairs six years later. *Niles' Weekly Register,* XX, 145, May 5, 1821.

essential principles—one political, the other commercial. The first is known and distinguished by written constitutions, representative government, religious toleration, freedom of opinion, of speech, and of the press. The second by sailors' rights, free trade, and freedom of the seas. Contrast it with the European system. The political character of that system is aristocracy, monarchy, imperial government, arbitrary power, passive obedience, and unconditional submission. Its commercial character is prohibition, restriction, interdiction, impressment, colonial monopoly, and maritime domination.[24]

It should be remembered always that the differences between Europe and America were indeed more than political. It is true that the political phase of the situation was the most spectacular and that it aroused the interest of the country in the whole problem, but it was by no means its only or even its most important aspect.

Confronting the rulers of Europe and their ministers was the spirit of revolution and liberalism which the French Revolution had unchained and which was ultimately to cause their downfall. While their own prejudices, shortsightedness, and lack of judgment prevented the men in charge of the European governments from comprehending the nature of the forces with which they had to deal, Americans seem to have grasped their significance from the beginning. The *National Intelligencer,* reviewing the state of Europe in 1815, found that there was a general danger of revolution throughout the Continent; that the troops of Germany, of Austria, and of Russia were unreliable; and that Italy especially was restless.[25] The same paper pointed out on another occasion that the people bade fair to emulate the kings by forming associa-

---

[24] *Annals of Congress,* 17 Cong., 1 sess., House, March 28, 1822.
[25] *National Intelligencer,* June 8, 1815.

tions for their own protection; and that, with a little more organization and information, coalitions of the masses might relieve the monarchs of their responsibilities.[26]

A year later, the *Essex Register,* a journal whose estimates of foreign affairs were shrewd and to the point, discussed the instability of the Austrian régime in Italy, the centrifugal forces within the Kingdom of Holland, and the unsettled state of Germany. The conclusion which the *Register* reached was that there would be revolutions in all three countries and that Italy would probably lead the way.[27] Nor were such predictions confined to the press. The opinions of many Congressmen agreed that Europe "reposes on combustible materials; the spark is all that is necessary to light up again the flames of war."[28] As the years passed, this conviction was reiterated with increased emphasis. In 1820, Niles advised the United States to pursue a peaceful policy as the best means of gaining her diplomatic goals; for it was clear that "The peace of Europe is precarious—every nation seems to contain within itself the elements of revolution, which only want some exciting cause to give them effects more prodigious, perhaps, than any which we have seen."[29] The *National Intelligencer* generalized on this theme and said: ". . . this may be emphatically called the age of revolutions; and almost every wind brings with it tidings of some new development of the silent but irresistible operation of the 'spirit of the age.' "[30] So deep was this belief that it survived the

---

[26] *National Intelligencer,* July 18, 1815.

[27] *Essex Register, ibid.,* September 26, 1816.

[28] Barbour of Virginia on relations with Spain. *Annals of Congress,* 14 Cong., 2 sess., Senate, February 25, 1817.

[29] *Niles' Weekly Register,* XVIII, 47, March 18, 1820.

[30] *National Intelligencer,* May 8, 1821.

reverses which the revolutionists suffered in 1821 and 1823. The league of sovereigns must fail, said an article in the *Intelligencer* in 1823; the spirit of liberty can no more be checked and crushed than the forces of nature can be reversed.[31]

Even the complete defeat of the Spaniards in 1823, which so excited certain politicians, did not prevent Congressman Cary of Georgia from declaring on the floor of the House: "It cannot last, sir. That horizontal division of society . . . must and will be broken up; those glittering pageants who now appear in the upper section, rely upon it, sir, are more formidable in appearance than in reality. The materials are already in existence. . . ."[32] Thus throughout the period there was a general sentiment in America that the policies and ideals of the European rulers were very different from those of the United States, that these rulers were leagued against the peoples whom they ruled, and that the inevitable result of this antipathy would be the defeat and ruin of the despots.

With these broad ideas governing the public view of Europe, Americans looked at the series of revolutions after 1819 as so many proofs of the correctness of their judgments. The persistence and wide extent of the revolts offset the successes of the rulers and the restorations which were effected. Most of the outbreaks were predicted well in advance,[33] and the Republican press hailed them with wild enthusiasm. Two examples of the American attitude toward revolution in Europe, toward open and incipient insurrection, should be noticed. The first news of the

---

[31] *National Intelligencer*, April 24, 1823.

[32] *Annals of Congress*, 18 Cong., 1 sess., House, January 21, 1824.

[33] As was the revolt in Spain, in *Niles' Weekly Register*, XVI, 206, May 15, 1819.

revolt in Naples was greeted with approval; Naples had now become a nation worthy of respect and distinction.[34] In May, 1821, Niles, that ardent advocate of liberty, stated that the "Austrian slaves" had been beaten and that "all Italy . . . [was] in a flame."[35] Predictions were freely made that the end of the legitimates had come, and that freedom would rule once more in Europe. The reaction from this ecstasy was so complete as to be almost amusing. Reports of the utter collapse of the Neapolitan revolution produced a spirit of gloom and disgust, not because of the terrific power of the rulers, but because of the cowardice and contemptible conduct of the Neapolitans themselves.[36] They had proved unworthy of the confidence which had been placed in them, and they seemed to many Americans to deserve the slavery in which they were to live. But not even the complete victory of the Austrians could shake Niles' assurance that the "alliance has in its own nature the elements of its own destruction." In miniature, this sketch presents a reasonably accurate picture of the American attitude toward these revolts. Confidence in the certainty of the outbreak, enthusiasm at its occurrence, disgust at its failure, and unshaken conviction that the reverse was only the prelude to greater upheavals in the future, were the successive stages in the development of public opinion as the events in Naples, in Piedmont, in Portugal, and in Spain passed in review.[37]

---

[34] *Niles' Weekly Register*, XIX, 17, September 9, 1820; *National Intelligencer*, April 14, 1821.

[35] *Niles' Weekly Register*, XX, 151, May 5, 1821.

[36] *Ibid.*, XX, 177, 189, May 19, 1821.

[37] The Greek revolution presented many factors which were absent from the circumstances of revolts in the west. Their influence on American opinion constitutes a special case. For a detailed discussion see Myrtle A. Cline, *American Attitude toward the Greek War of Independence, 1821–1828* (Atlanta, 1930).

Armed revolution attracted the most attention and interest, but latent revolutionary forces were observed as well. Beginning with the restoration of the Bourbons, American journals discussed the unstable condition of French politics. The unrest and disturbances which the Bourbons combatted with severe police measures indicated that France was not entirely content and that trouble might be expected at any time.[38] Attempted assassinations of members of the royal family, which culminated in the murder of the Duke of Berri, revealed even more definitely the critical situation of the ruling house;[39] and Niles had to report on one occasion that Austria and Prussia were becoming anxious about the ferment in the political affairs of their western neighbor.[40] Americans saw that the spirit of liberalism was abroad in Europe and felt that its progress could not be halted. The great monarchs might crush it out in petty states such as Naples, or in disorganized monarchies like that of Spain; but, even as they did so, evidence was accumulating that the ground was hollow under their own feet. As long as armies were made up of men, argued one writer, so long would liberal principles spread and gain force. Even the power of despots was ultimately based on public opinion, and it was evident that sentiment everywhere was hostile to their sway.[41] So critical was the internal state of France, thought Niles in 1823, that he expressed the belief that war had been wantonly made on Spain with the hope of preserving tranquillity in France, a shrewd observation which indicates how far even emotional Republicans

---

[38] *National Intelligencer,* March 28, 1816.
[39] *Ibid.,* April 8, 1817, April 21, 1821.
[40] *Niles' Weekly Register,* XVIII, 186, May 13, 1820.
[41] *Morning Chronicle* [London], in the *National Intelligencer,* April 14, 1821.

were from being frightened by the specter of the might of European sovereigns.[42]

Thus Americans, feeling keenly the differences which separated their ideas from those of the rulers of Europe, came to regard events in the Old World with a singular calm. This was not the universal feeling, but manifestations of a different opinion appear to be the exception rather than the rule. Americans ceased to be wildly excited about the immediate reform of the world but, at the same time, they became more convinced that its reform was sure to come and that those who opposed its progress maintained a precarious position by the use of weapons which would one day prove to be their own undoing. In the words of *The North American Review:*

... the friends of civil liberty, disappointed as they are, in the anticipation of its immediate establishment throughout Europe, still indulge the idea that the way is constantly preparing for it, and that it will yet be enjoyed as universally, though not as soon as they once predicted. They have in general, however, lost a little of their enthusiasm, and no longer esteem the subversion of a despotism as equivalent to the creation of a free government, nor hail the adoption of a democratic constitution, as a complete security of the rights of the people. . . . We are continually learning therefore to look with less and less interest, upon violent and precipitate revolutions in the frame of government. . . .[43]

Since 1890, much has been written of the power of the Holy Alliance in the international field, of the world-wide scope of its policy, and of the fears which were aroused in the United States by the spectacle of its "success." The in-

---

[42] *Niles' Weekly Register,* XXIV, 17, March 15, 1823, and XXV, 17, September 13, 1823. See also *The North American Review,* XVII (1823), 370.

[43] *Ibid.,* XV (1822), 178.

nate weakness of the Powers of Europe and the fact that internal affairs were critical throughout the Continent have already been revealed. It is usually inferred, however, that, once leagued together, the autocrats might have mustered an irresistible force. It is the term "the Holy Alliance" which has so long been used to represent the Goliath which the American David outmaneuvered in 1823. An examination of the expressions of opinion on these subjects in the press and in Congress presents a different view of the problem." It would seem that it has taken more than a century for historians to discover what the American press and well-informed people in this country knew at the time to be a fact, that the alliance was weak and that its power to act was limited to Europe.[45]

The international rivalries of the Powers of Europe provided a stumbling block to any permanent and effective coöperation, and Americans knew this. The *Essex Register,* in one of its periodical reviews of foreign affairs, admitted that the fate of Europe depended on the strength of the alliance of the combined sovereigns and that the ostensible resources of this group were great.

... It is only when we begin to see the competitions of interests

[44] This discussion will cover the years before 1823. For the American attitude toward the strength of the alliance and its possible interference in the affairs of the western world in 1823, see below, Chaps. IV, VI, and IX.

[45] It should be affirmed here that no amount of research in the European archives will provide the answer to the all-important question of how much the Continental European Powers contributed to the formation of American foreign policies. The work of Messrs. Cresson, Perkins, Temperley, and Webster throws valuable light on the history of the period, but falls short of an adequate explanation of the origins of such declarations of policy as that of Adams in 1821 (see below, pp. 244–245) or that of Monroe in 1823. The origins of those policies were *American,* not European. American conditions and European conditions viewed through American eyes gave them birth.

[continued the *Register*] that we may be emboldened to consider the approaching end of the present sovereignty of Europe. Every nation is overawed by its neighbors, and having its counsels abroad, has no self direction at home. The domestic affairs of the nations are not then the first objects in the view of the politician, but the aids to the strength of the present alliance.[46]

Thus the international situation was so uncertain that it weakened European domestic policy; and lack of vision at home, in turn, threatened the existence of the state itself. The Powers were caught in a vise with possible revolution on one side and unpleasant international complications on the other.[47]

Their commercial competition, their political jealousies, and their mutual fear of intrigues led one observer to declare that the whole international organization of Europe was "pregnant . . . with the germs of self-destruction."[48] Formidable as the action of the various Powers appeared to be, both *The North American Review* and *Niles' Weekly Register* drew attention to the fact that no joint interventions had taken place and that, despite the congresses, propinquity and paramount national interest had dictated the interference of the Austrians in Italy and of the French in Spain.[49] Fear of augmenting the power of Russia had caused the other states to check the grandiose plans of Alexander for a closely knit organization; and it was predicted on more than one occasion that the Holy Alliance would "be dissolved from the nature of its own elements, just as thieves cut each other's throats to

---

[46] *Essex Register,* in the *National Intelligencer,* June 5, 1817.

[47] *Annals of Congress,* 18 Cong., 1 sess., House, January 20, 1824.

[48] Rattenbury, "Remarks . . . ," *The Pamphleteer,* XV (1819), 263.

[49] *Niles' Weekly Register,* XXV, 17, September 13, 1823; *The North American Review,* XVII (1823), 370.

acquire a greater share of the spoils of honest men. . . ."[50] It was generally felt that this antipathy would lead to war and revolution which the congresses would be powerless to prevent.[51] The Eastern Question loomed in a most menacing fashion, especially after the uprising of the Greeks, and it was thought to be only a matter of time until hostilities would begin.

Americans beheld this threatening state of affairs with equanimity. They felt that, horrible as it was, war was not the greatest of evils in the circumstances.[52] A convulsion in the Old World would probably free the oppressed peoples from the darkness of the old régime; what they had failed to achieve by revolution might easily result from the dangers of international war. The mad ambition of the royal autocrats would play into the hands of the revolutionaries—and this would benefit the United States. She had profited materially from other wars in Europe, and, as the economic crisis deepened after 1819, frequent hints were made that war abroad would not be a bad thing for America.[53] Stratford Canning stated that this view was a general one throughout the nation in 1821 and reported to George Canning that the failure of the European revolutions had hurt American business so that a general war was regarded as the only aid to recovery.[54] The

---

[50] *Niles' Weekly Register*, XX, 146, May 5, 1821.

[51] *Ibid.*, XXIII, 132, November 2, 1822.

[52] *Ibid.*, XXI, 49, September 22, 1821.

[53] For example, in an article from the *Intelligencer* [Vandalia, Ill.], *ibid.*, XXII, 321, July 20, 1822.

[54] S. Canning to G. Canning, September 29, 1821. Lane-Poole, *Life of Stratford Canning*, I, 305. Stratford Canning, English minister to the United States, 1819–1823, was a cousin of George Canning, member of the cabinet, 1816–1820, and, after the death of Castlereagh in 1822, secretary of state for foreign affairs.

same testimony was given by the Russian minister, Polética. Americans had lost interest, he wrote, in the activities of the allied sovereigns and had turned to watch the critical Near Eastern problem which seemed to be incapable of a peaceful solution. "A war in Continental Europe is the object of their most ardent desires," because of the benefits which it would bring to agriculture and shipping.[55] Niles had detected this feeling years earlier and had used it as one of the arguments for a more self-contained economic system.[56] The conclusion is inescapable that Americans sensed the delicate state of European international affairs as well as the precarious internal scene, and that they were convinced that war and conflict on that side of the Atlantic would aid both the cause of freedom and the economic condition of the United States. Certainly the implication is also plain that men who believed war to be imminent and the very institutions of the old state system to be threatened did not fear any antagonism which the old régime might feel toward the republics of the west.

A detailed study of the possible interference by Europe in the affairs of the New World as Americans, North and South, saw it at the time would be most valuable. Only such expressions of sentiment as reflect the opinion of the public in the United States can be reviewed here. In Congress and in the leading newspapers prior to 1823, the general belief was that America had nothing to fear from the Great Powers of Europe. The conditions which have

---

[55] Polética to Nesselrode, September 23, 1821. "Correspondence of the Russian Ministers in Washington, 1818–1825," *The American Historical Review*, XVIII (1913), 328 (hereafter cited as Russia, *Correspondence*, XVIII, 328, etc.). All dates are New Style.

[56] *Niles' Weekly Register*, X, 65, March 30, 1816.

been noted above were discussed at length and applied to America's own relations with Europe. In 1817 a series of articles in the Richmond *Enquirer* analyzed the situation in detail.[57] Admitting that the "legitimate" Powers of Europe disliked the spread of republican principles in the New World, the author of this review argued that they were helpless. No longer could they fight foreign wars blindly and expect the people to acquiesce without question. The struggle in Europe between the monarchs and the people still continued, and, though the people had lost their freedom, they were still so feared that Europe remained an armed camp. The least relaxation of the military force of the Holy Alliance would spell ruin. As a result, there was no danger to the United States from its hostility. The monarchs might use diplomacy and other peaceful means to further their aims abroad—force they could not use.

In 1817, of course, the freedom of South America and the recognition of the new states were the crux of the matter. Would the European Powers interfere? Let us quote the answer given to this question by *The Enquirer:*

It is impossible for any man of common capacity to see any danger from any one or all of the powers of Europe, by our taking a part with the Patriots of South America.—They cannot, they dare not molest us for such a cause.—The spirit of freedom at home *is as much as they can possibly manage &* *keep down;* they dare not go abroad, much less across the Atlantic, to grapple with the champions of liberty on this new continent. There is not one of them that has either the

---

[57] These articles were reprinted in the *National Intelligencer* beginning October 2, 1817, and were given much prominence. It may be said that they indicate the general sentiment among well-informed people at this time, and especially among those who derived their information from the leading Republican newspapers.

means or the courage to wage open war against them. The United States can have nothing to fear from Europe. . . ."[58]

That such an unequivocal statement of the real situation in Europe could be given in 1817, when the cause of reaction seemed to be completely successful and the power of the Holy Alliance unquestioned, is significant. It does not prove a rule, but it does point to a conclusion concerning public sentiment that is most interesting. Nor should the part which such articles must have had in forming public opinion be disregarded.

Almost the same opinion was voiced in the following year by Henry Clay in his great speech on South America. Notice has often been taken of the passage in this oration which refers to the grandeur of the southern continent, but little has been said of Clay's estimate of the power of the European states. Though it is granted that Clay was pleading a cause and that he wished to minimize the danger which might result from recognition of the South American states, there remains the soundness of his views on Europe and the unquestioned influence which his utterances had on the public. Conversely, account should be taken of the fact that Clay was very sensitive to public opinion and that he reflected the views of the people in his speeches and debates. Emphasizing the international difficulties of the European states rather than their internal troubles, Clay denied that they would feel their interests to be threatened by events so remote from Europe. There was no real cohesion among the allies, in spite of the brilliant appearance of the Holy Alliance. They had too many divergent interests, and while they might agree on abstract principles of government, concerted action

[58] Article No. 5, *National Intelligencer,* October, 11, 1817.

was out of the question. "But as for action, for new enterprises, there is no principle of unity, there can be no accordance of interests, or of views, among them."[59]

Europe was dominated by two Great Powers, Russia and England, Clay pointed out; and the hostility between these two in the Near East and on the sea, coupled with the incompatibility of French commercial interests with those of her European associates, relieved America of the danger of any active interference. He demonstrated clearly that England's command of the sea gave her the power of preventing any such action and he showed further how her real interests made it certain that she would block allied projects, were they contemplated. The realism of this view and the forceful presentation of it suggest that sound opinions on world conditions were current in America at an early date, when the revolutionary spirit had not yet reappeared in active form and when England was still considered to be closely allied with the Continental Powers. At the risk of repetition, it will be well to notice corresponding views expressed by two Congressmen from widely separated parts of the country. As the debates on recognition continued, the question of interference by European Powers occupied considerable time. Holmes of Massachusetts voiced the opinion that the ambitions of Russia were arousing the jealousy of all Europe and of England, and that the consequent preoccupation of those states with European affairs would prevent them from engaging in a "conflict of doubtful success, of certain danger, and inevitable loss."[60]

From the other extremity of the Union, Robertson of

[59] Clay's speech is conveniently found in his *Works*, VI, 136.
[60] *Annals of Congress*, 15 Cong., 1 sess., House, March 27, 1818.

Louisiana summed up in conclusive fashion the circumstances in which the alliance found itself.

Mr. Chairman, the combined despots of Europe cannot, as formerly, indulge themselves in the royal sport of arms; they cannot wage wars of amusement or ambition; they are sufficiently employed in keeping their own subjects in subordination. Admirable as their Governments may be, something like coercion seems necessary to impress that opinion on the minds of their people. The armies of Europe are not now intended to guard against, or to make foreign conquests; they are to keep their inhabitants in slavery, and the kings on their thrones; three millions of soldiers in arms are all necessary for that purpose; they have no occasion to look abroad for employment; they need not come across the Atlantic. Sir, the impulse given to the human character by the American and French Revolutions still survives; the principles of despotism and superstition are dead—they do not suit the age; they may be sustained a little longer by the force of bayonets, but the love of liberty lives in the heart, will again before long have utterance, and ultimately succeed and triumph. Blind, indeed, must that man be who does not see in the large standing armies of the Governments of Europe, the fear—the just fear—in which they stand of those whom they rule and oppress. Sir, we may manage our own affairs in our own way, without the fear of kings before our eyes. They have enough to do to keep things in order at home; their vigilance is more and more necessary every day; if they relax, they are hurled from their usurped dominion. . . .[61]

Robertson was correct in his analysis of the European scene, and the events of the succeeding years proved to his countrymen the truth of many of his conclusions.

Thus from all sections came affirmations that, whatever the difficulties of the United States might be in the foreign field, danger of interference was not one of them.

---

[61] *Annals of Congress*, 15 Cong., 1 sess., House, March 26, 1818.

Even Calhoun[62] and Jackson[63] agreed that there was nothing to fear from Europe at this time. Their opinions will be discussed in more detail later, but it is worth observing here that fear of the Holy Alliance was not a deep-seated conviction of either.

The press, as well, voiced a calm and reasoned opinion of the European alliance. Discussions of this subject in the *National Intelligencer* expressed the view that America was fortunately beyond the reach of Europe.[64] In 1819 in one of his political surveys Niles declared to his readers: "Although our interests demand a cautionary course of policy, . . . no one will admit that this policy emanates from a fear of the power of Spain, or of that of the *holy alliance*. Our safety does not depend upon an acquiescence in the dictation of European sovereigns."[65] A year later, after the Spanish revolution had been condemned by Alexander, Niles repeated his assertion that America might scoff at the idea that her destinies were involved in any European affairs. She has a general interest in Europe, but that is all.[66] The New World is outside the sphere of Continental politics. Niles did not always express this confident view, however. The events in Naples gave him momentary qualms,[67] but he soon recovered his poise and after the failure of the revolt declared that the alliance was doomed.

Not even the events of 1821 and 1822 shook the con-

---

[62] Calhoun to Jackson, September 8, 1818. Jackson, *Correspondence*, II, 393.

[63] Jackson to Monroe, March 18, 1817. *Ibid.*, II, 282.

[64] *National Intelligencer*, October 3, 1818.

[65] *Niles' Weekly Register*, XVII, 181, November 20, 1819.

[66] *Ibid.*, XIX, 67, September 30, 1820.

[67] *Ibid.*, XX, 129, April 28, 1821.

viction of the editors of the *Intelligencer* that America was safe from the sovereigns of Europe. After the recognition of South America, they stated in an editorial that, whatever might have been true years before, in 1822 the United States incurred no danger.[68] She stood on safe ground in all her foreign relations. Finally, in October of this year, when plans for the Congress of Verona were being discussed, this paper advocated a policy of noninterference in the Greek revolution. It took this stand not because of fear of the Holy Alliance, for the United States could and would defy the world in defense of its own rights. Caution was advisable in order to prevent the stirring up of antagonism among the Powers which would injure the cause of the Greek patriots.[69]

From 1815 to 1822, therefore, the American attitude toward the European Continent was plainly one of interested aloofness. Americans hated the principles which were being put into practice by the governments; they sympathized heartily with the attempts of the masses to set up a new order in society and they watched the passing events with keen attention. At the same time, they became more and more conscious of the great differences between the Old World and the New, and saw in the involved condition of Continental politics the opportunity for the United States to pursue an independent course with impunity. The United States had many domestic problems to solve, while Europe appeared to be upon the verge of war and revolution. It seemed obvious that in these circumstances neither party could waste its energies in meddling in the affairs of the other.

[68] *National Intelligencer,* March 19, 1822.
[69] *Ibid.,* October 26, 1822.

CHAPTER III

The American Attitude Toward
the Great Powers

IF ATTENTION is now directed to the opinion of Americans toward France, Russia, and England, light will be cast upon some very interesting aspects of the topic, particularly as it applies to England. Dr. Elizabeth White has presented the results of an investigation into the American attitude toward France in a most satisfactory manner,[1] and it is unnecessary to traverse the field again, except to point out certain of its more pertinent features.

In common with the other restored rulers in Europe, the Bourbons were hated by Americans, and their downfall was desired. The institutions which they attempted to reëstablish aroused the ridicule of the American press,[2] and the "legitimacy" of the royal court and the priesthood were condemned without reservation. The remnants of pro-Napoleonic sentiment in America heightened this feeling and caused considerable friction between the two governments.[3]

[1] See her *American Opinion of France from LaFayette to Poincaré*, Chaps. II and III.

[2] *Niles' Weekly Register*, IX, 283, December 16, 1815, and XIII, 28, September 6, 1817.

[3] The best example of this is the toast of the postmaster of Baltimore to "the generals of France in exile," *ibid.*, XI, 169, November 9, 1816; and a complete account in White, *American Opinion of France*, 42–44. Gallatin told the Duke of Richelieu that even this spirit was only a result of the "hatred of Great Britain or apprehension of her enormous power." Gallatin to Monroe, July 12, 1816. Gallatin, *Writings*, II, 2. Albert Gallatin was minister to France, 1816–1823. The Duke of Richelieu was prime minister of France, 1816–1820.

These currents of thought, together with incidents connected with commerce, the slave trade, and spoliation claims, contributed to create bad feeling between France and the United States, which increased as reaction in Europe progressed. There were, however, elements in the situation which altered this superficial appearance of Franco-American relations. Practically all the criticism of France was directed at the restoration government and not at the French people.[4] Much as the Bourbons and their policies were despised, the tradition of friendship for France continued to influence the American outlook. The most violent critics of the restored régime had good things to say about the country itself. In an article on "France and the Bourbons" Niles reviewed this attitude and concluded that, much as they disliked royalty in general and the Bourbons in particular, the people of the United States still wished France all the good fortune in the world.[5] In addition, the able diplomacy of the French minister, Hyde de Neuville, contributed much to improve relations between the two countries and to limit the effects of divergent principles.

As a result of the position of France after the wars, Americans came to feel a sort of indifference toward her. Her interests did not touch theirs very closely, and, while they watched and condemned the activities of the conservatives in that country, they regarded her affairs with much the same aloofness with which they viewed all Continental politics. Their attitude was plainly negative, colored by a traditional friendship. The *National Intelli-*

---

[4] Ample evidence of this dual nature of American opinion of France is furnished by Dr. White, but the obvious inference is not clearly drawn, nor is its significance emphasized.

[5] *Niles' Weekly Register,* XI, 33, September 14, 1816.

gencer once declared: "France is the same to us, whether ruled by Napoleon or Louis, by a King or an Emperor.— We owed no enmity to Louis; we owe no debt of gratitude to Napoleon . . . ;"[6] and *The North American Review* asserted, in the middle of the postwar decade: ". . . we have become almost indifferent to France, and it does not enter any body's imagination to like or to dislike her."[7] Americans did not regard France as innately hostile, nor, did they count upon her friendship as long as the Bourbons ruled her destinies.

The relations between the United States and Imperial Russia form a strange chapter in history. The personality of the Tsar Alexander and a variety of almost fortuitous incidents created a sentiment of friendship which is as difficult to explain as some of the national hatreds of which historians must take account. Though there were few points of contact between the two, and though it could be said that

The government of Russia is integral, ours confederate. That government is the most despotic in Europe; ours the most free. The people of Russia, except the sovereign and nobles, are the most ignorant; the people of America the most generally enlightened . . . ,[8]

nevertheless Americans did not exhibit the violent dislike for Russia that they did for the countries of western Europe. Despotic the government was, but the ruler was almost universally regarded in America as an enlightened liberal and leader of ability. Adams confessed that he had confidence in nothing in Europe but the "moderation,

---

[6] *National Intelligencer*, May 4, 1815.
[7] *The North American Review*, X (1820), 335.
[8] *National Intelligencer*, July 12, 1817.

equity, and humanity of the Emperor Alexander,"[9] and Jefferson remarked on the good effects which might be expected from his leadership.[10] The press, too, voiced approval of the ability and wisdom of the Tsar. So much was he admired that his despotism was forgotten and the nation which he ruled was complimented on its good fortune.[11] Even Niles admitted that, if kings were to prevail, he would prefer to see a man like Alexander dominate the scene than any other monarch in Europe; for "He has more sense and virtue in his own person, perhaps, than the whole stock of all the rest of the legitimates . . . would amount to, collected."[12]

This respect for Alexander's ability, intelligence, and princely virtues, which the members of the peace societies carried to a ridiculous degree,[13] was enhanced by the events of the first years after the Congress of Vienna. Americans believed that the Tsar was responsible for the moderation with which France was treated at the congress, and they credited him with influencing the Great Powers along liberal lines.[14] The *National Intelligencer* recognized that he was wisely and cleverly pursuing policies which would redound to the benefit of his empire,[15] but affirmed also that his actions with respect to this country were "evidence of the continuance of the disposition, which . . . [he] has always shewn, to maintain amicable re-

---

[9] J. Q. Adams to Abigail Adams, his mother, May 12, 1814. J. Q. Adams, *Writings*, V, 43.

[10] Jefferson to Dr. Logan, July 23, 1816. Jefferson, *Writings* (Mem. ed.), XV, 47.

[11] *National Intelligencer*, July 9, 1816.

[12] *Niles' Weekly Register*, XII, 345, July 26, 1817.

[13] See below, p. 222.

[14] *Niles' Weekly Register*, IX, 258, December 9, 1815.

[15] *National Intelligencer*, July 17, 1819.

lations with the United States."[16] Again there occurs an instance of a peculiar manifestation of American feeling. Swept away by a sentimental admiration for a romantic figure in world politics, for a man whose magnanimity and friendship for the United States seemed real, Americans persisted in thinking of Russia as a friendly Power.

The factors which conditioned the American view of England were very different from those which applied to Russia and to France. In place of vague sentiments of friendship, or at least of lack of hostility, was an active hatred which was also the product of tradition and unreasoning instinct. One finds it difficult to give a specific explanation for this attitude. It is, indeed, implicit in the history of the American nation, and this fact was recognized by contemporary English observers. Henry Fearon declared in 1818 that

... the American hatred of our country is not bottomed upon causes which *reason* would have dictated: its component parts cannot be denominated to be either rational or reflective:—it is, in source, and in mode of expression, an exact parallel to that of our most uneducated classes concerning the French people, who always dislike Frenchmen, and the only reason that they can give for such feelings is, because they *are* Frenchmen—and because the newspapers say Frenchmen ought to be hated.[17]

Fearon was right; there *was* a parallel between the American attitude toward England and the English attitude toward France: both were predicated upon traditions of conflict which had their roots in the past.

The undercurrent was there; the doubtful nature of the peace of 1814 did much to continue its force. The

---

[16] *National Intelligencer,* March 22, 1817.
[17] Fearon, *Sketches of America,* 369–370.

war had sharpened the ill feeling between England and America, and, while the treaty was hailed as ushering in an era of peace and possible friendship,[18] little hope was expressed that England would exert herself to make it an instrument of good will. The *National Intelligencer* predicted that since "natural hatred of republican government" had reached such a pitch in England the treaty of Ghent would probably be the most unpopular act of the reign of the Prince Regent.[19] The pride which the United States felt in its "victory" over the mistress of the seas, and the undoubted chagrin which existed in England were recognized as stumbling blocks in the path to reconciliation. The Boston *Patriot* remarked, "Beat them as we may, Englishmen will be Englishmen still; they will boast . . . ;"[20] and the *National Advocate* noted with pride that the mortification of the English was increased by their repulse at the hands of a nation which was still young and immature.[21] How can we fail to express resentment at the acts of England, asked Niles, when she is continually exciting it by new acts of a provocative character?[22] Thus at the very beginning of this period men were doubtful of the future of Anglo-American relations. America, self-

---

[18] *National Intelligencer*, February 16, 1815.

[19] *Ibid.*, May 27, 1815. For an Englishman's expression of the same view see *The Colonial Policy of Great Britain*, 18, where the treaty is "termed one of the most unfortunate acts of diplomacy in which Great Britain ever engaged."

[20] *The Patriot* [Boston], in the *National Intelligencer*, May 30, 1816.

[21] The *National Advocate*, in the *National Intelligencer*, January 28, 1815. See also the *Republican* [Savannah], in *Niles' Weekly Register*, XIII, 431, February 21, 1818.

[22] *Niles' Weekly Register*, X, 418, August 24, 1816. A complete program for English commercial and colonial expansion in the New World was presented by the author of *The Colonial Policy of Great Britain*. This work was reprinted in Philadelphia in order to acquaint Americans with the possible course of English policy.

conscious and proud of her achievements, felt that English antagonism was inevitable because of much that had occurred in the past.

What might occur in the future only added to the apprehensions which already existed. The coming of peace renewed commercial competition between the two countries. Deprived of the wartime carrying trade and of freedom from rival merchants, America would be compelled to seek new markets and new outlets for her commerce. Mutual interchange of goods must succeed the risky monopolies which had been enjoyed previously, and the capital of the country must be diverted into other channels.[23] The probable decline of American shipping was admitted;[24] but even such advocates of a self-contained economic system as Niles recognized that the danger of commercial collisions with England was bound to increase. The United States differed from England on such vital issues as form of government and principles of trade and navigation, and if she would maintain her fair share of the commerce of the world, she must guard against English influence with especial care.[25] As Niles pointed out in 1816 and as the *Franklin Gazette* reported a few years later, not only was the preponderant naval power of England a menace to the freedom of world commerce, but her wealth, her merchant marine, and her system of colonial possessions gave her advantages in the fight for world markets.[26] American merchants must be watchful

---

[23] The general view of the economic future of the United States abroad is well expressed in an editorial in the *National Intelligencer*, April 17, 1818.

[24] *Niles' Weekly Register*, IX, 1, September 2, 1815.

[25] *Ibid.*, X, 3, March 2, 1816.

[26] The *Franklin Gazette* [Philadelphia], in the *National Intelligencer*, September 11, 1822.

at all times lest English dominance in commerce injure their business. A sense of impending commercial conflict with England was thus added to the more deeply ingrained feelings which strained relations between the two maritime Powers.

Republicans were also especially alive to what they conceived to be English influence in America after 1815, and they attacked it with fully as much bitterness as the Federalists had ever employed against supposed French influence àt Washington. It must not be forgotten that, in America, praise of England was tainted with treason, and this in itself made the resumption of normal relations difficult. *The North American Review* was subjected to a most unmerciful castigation by the *National Intelligencer* for that reason. "Its politics [averred the *Intelligencer*] are Essex Junto politics; its religion Sectarian; its morals those of Oliver Cromwell . . . and its patriotism that of the renegade who is false to his own country without being true to any other."[27] In the same spirit, Niles declared that his hostility to England was purely defensive and was directed against the English party in America.[28] From this conviction on the part of the Republican press and those who hated the spirit of New England Federalism, arose part of that sensitiveness to English opinion of America which so embittered the relations between them.

Finally, another intangible èlement had great influence on the American attitude toward England. This was the conviction on both sides that armed conflict between England and America was inevitable. The Albany *Argus* pessimistically wrote in 1815 that no doubt there would be

[27] *National Intelligencer*, July 18, 1815.
[28] *Niles' Weekly Register*, XI, 1, August 31, 1816.

war again;[29] and in a leading article a year later the organ of the administration expressed itself as follows:

... It has been predicted by our most perspicacious statesmen, that future wars of a sanguinary character are to take place between Great-Britain and the U. States.—These are events which, though perhaps as certain as mortality to man, it is agreeable to be enabled to believe are placed at a remote distance from us.[30]

This gloomy prediction by a rather sane newspaper was not encouraging, but it agreed with the sentiment of Niles, that "If there be such things as a 'natural enmity' between nations ... Great Britain must be such an enemy to this republic ... ,"[31] and with that of John Adams, that "Britain will never be our friend till we are her master."[32] These views reflect a general feeling which may be observed throughout the entire period under discussion. It grew stronger as time went on[33] and was especially encouraged by similar declarations in the English press.[34] As Fearon said, there was no specific cause for this and other apprehensions on the part of Americans, or of English-

---

[29] *The Argus* [Albany], in the *National Intelligencer,* August 31, 1815.

[30] *National Intelligencer,* April 27, 1816.

[31] *Niles' Weekly Register,* X, 3, March 2, 1816.

[32] J. Adams to Jefferson, December 16, 1816. Jefferson, *Writings* (Mem. ed.), XV, 87.

[33] In January, 1824, the declaration was made in Congress: ". . . they [the English] cherish a deadly hostility against you; . . . they are jealous of your rising greatness; . . . they remember well your naval triumphs, and ... war will one day be the issue." Cuthbert on the Greeks. *Annals of Congress,* 18 Cong., 1 sess., House, January 22, 1824.

[34] See articles from *Cobbett's Register,* in *Niles' Weekly Register,* IX, 144, October 28, 1815; from the *Observer* [London], *ibid.,* XI, 99, October 12, 1816; and from *The Times* [London], *ibid.,* XII, 230, June 17, 1817. Rattenbury's pamphlet, which received considerable publicity in America, expressed the same view. See *The Pamphleteer,* XV (1819), 277. Four years earlier the anonymous author of *The Colonial Policy of Great Britain* predicted that "wars will be the consequence."

men either; but they existed and their corrosive effect on public sentiment cannot be overlooked.

A Frenchman whose views usually found little favor in America because of their monarchical bias, but who was an observer of ability, wrote that four distinctive American conceptions had to be taken into account whenever attempts were made to estimate her policy. Americans were convinced, according to the Abbé de Pradt, that the western world was the natural inheritance of its inhabitants; that all parts of it which broke away from Spain were so many natural aids against European domination; that commerce was to be the new cause of conflict, and that South America was to be the scene of the struggle; and, finally, that England was the archrival to be fought in the future.[35] These beliefs were, indeed, strongly held by Americans; and the student should never forget that their attitude toward England after 1815 was conditioned by an uncertain peace, by an impending commercial conflict with a stronger rival, by a jealousy of English influence in their national life, and by a deep, almost involuntary, hatred of England as their most persistent foe in the past and their most certain enemy in the future.

The immediate manifestation of American sentiment toward England after the war took the form of criticisms of her institutions and ways of thinking. In part these denunciations were the American answer to English observations on America, but it is safe to say that many of the strictures on England would have been made anyway, irrespective of her attitude. The very spirit of English policy was singled out as a perfect example of selfish-

---

[35] Parts of his work, *On Colonies*, were translated and reprinted in the *National Intelligencer*, June 7 ff., 1817.

ness and sordid commercialism. Everything was subordinated to speculation and trade in England, and even political usurpation could be justified on that score, declared Niles.[36] This narrow meanness was especially revealed, so Americans thought, by the treatment which was meted out to Napoleon by his captors. Both the leading Republican papers scored the English for acting in a manner contrary to all principles of magnanimity to a fallen foe.[37] The Boston *Patriot* concluded that Americans should learn to know the English as they really were, so that their example might be avoided—"The English are, generally speaking, a wrong-headed people, and uncharitable in proportion to their bigotry, and their bigotry commonly operates against the welfare of all mankind beyond their own island."[38]

Interest warped the English mind, but tradition produced even more ridiculous results. The "trappings of monarchy," which covered the entire English social system, were favorite targets of the American press. The expenses of the court and the injustice of a system which lavished millions on dissolute royalty while men starved in the streets, evoked condemnations which fully equaled those which Americans directed at the Bourbons.[39] The interest which the English have always had in the activities of the court and of the aristocracy was regarded as the essence of servility, and the most scurrilous articles in *Niles' Weekly Register* and in the *National Intelligencer* are those which deal with this aspect of English social

[36] *Niles' Weekly Register*, XIV, 228, May 30, 1818.
[37] *Ibid.*, IX, 70, September 30, 1815; the *National Intelligencer*, September 23, 1815.
[38] *The Patriot* [Boston], in the *National Intelligencer*, May 17, 1817.
[39] *National Intelligencer*, August 1, 31, 1815.

life.[40] Other English customs which Americans considered to be degrading and immoral received appropriate comment under such headings as "British Piety," "British Charity," and "British Magnanimity."[41]

To disapproval of English selfishness and English society were added unfavorable observations on the English political and economic system. The injustice of the political arrangements in England had long been the subject of American oratory and journalism. After 1815, however, prophecy was added to criticism. Americans were quick to notice evidences of the economic difficulties which undoubtedly existed in England,[42] and to point out that peace bore more heavily upon the nation than did war.[43] England was fast approaching an economic *impasse,* thought some Americans, which would have revolutionary consequences.[44] These economic troubles were made worse by

[40] *National Intelligencer,* January 31, 1818. The best examples of the slanderous notices of English royalty are those in *Niles' Weekly Register,* XI, 10, August 31, 1816; XI, 190, November 16, 1816; and XVI, 220, May 22, 1819.

[41] As in the *National Intelligencer,* September 23, 1815. It is amusing to notice that one of the most universally condemned activities was the custom of prize fighting. It was regarded as a manifestation of the barbarism of a degenerate society.

[42] Typical articles on the economic outlook in England are those in the *National Intelligencer,* August 10, 1816; and in *Niles' Weekly Register,* XI, 209, November 30, 1816, and XII, 294, July 5, 1817.

[43] *Niles' Weekly Register,* X, 40, March 16, 1816.

[44] Those who are interested in historical parallels will find a comparison of Niles' analysis of the English situation in 1816 with a similar statement of the Russian crisis of 1904 full of interest. Different as the two countries are, the causes of the English economic tension in 1816 and of the Russian crisis nearly ninety years later were the same, and England came closer to experiencing the same result—revolution—than is usually supposed.

Niles wrote in April, 1816: ". . . it appears impossible that the present taxes in Britain can be paid, and it seems equally impossible to reduce them, without doing something that will amount nearly to a revolution,

the attempts of the ruling classes to preserve their power. The *Democratic Press* declared that this was not the first time that an English ministry in a critical position had been forced to use high-handed measures to maintain its power,[45] and Niles decried the "miserable shifts of the British ministry to keep up 'their system'" by repression.[46]

Reaction and despotism were not confined to the continent of Europe, in the opinion of Americans. The picture of English institutions which Americans saw in the postwar years created the impression that, while some of the worst features of Continental obscurantism were absent from England, the same forces were operating there that were at work in other European countries. It was felt that revolution was as likely to result in England as elsewhere.[47] One may venture the opinion that American dislike of monarchy and Old World institutions was derived fully as much from the example of the English rulers as from that of the Holy Allies.[48]

While public opinion in America was thus instinctively hostile to England and ready to criticize things English on the least excuse, or on no excuse at all, the English them-

---

to shake off the leeches, ecclesiastical, civil and military, that have fastened themselves on the laboring classes of the people." *Niles' Weekly Register*, X, 96.

Of Russia in 1904, a minister of finance is reported to have declared: "1. It is impossible to diminish the taxes. . . . 2. It is impossible to increase the taxes. . . . 3. It is impossible to abolish [the land system]. . . . 4. The intellectual situation is such as to prevent any increase of the national welfare. Thus, it is evident that . . . no reform at all is possible under autocratic or bureaucratic government." A report attributed to Count Witte, quoted by Alexander Ular in his article, "The Prospects of Russian Revolution," *The Contemporary Review*, LXXXVII (1905), 172.

[45] *Democratic Press*, in the *National Intelligencer*, April 10, 1817.
[46] *Niles' Weekly Register*, XIII, 3, August 30, 1817.
[47] *National Intelligencer*, November 22, 1816.
[48] *Niles' Weekly Register*, X, 113, April 20, 1816.

selves proceeded to aggravate it in every way possible. The part played by the English reviews in increasing American hatred of England has not often been emphasized. Yet it is difficult to name any agencies which did more in this respect than those publications. Taking as their texts books written about America by English travelers or by Americans themselves, *The Edinburgh* and *The Quarterly Review* from 1814 to 1823 filled their pages with essays in which America was attacked and criticized with all the pontifical certitude, the lofty condescension, and the biting wit of which they were capable. Whatever one may think of the politics or critical standards of Jeffreys and his clan, no one can deny their ability to write in a vein worthy of Swift himself. They sought out the most sensitive parts of the American character and drove home the shafts of their criticism until their victims were frantic with rage and pain. So violent did the reviews become in the course of these years that Americans very nearly forgot to notice the slanders and unfavorable comments of the travelers themselves. The reviews of the books were more consistently critical, more ably written, more devastating in their thoroughness than the books which they discussed—and they were more widely read in America.[49] The rest of this chapter will, therefore, be given up to a consideration of the attacks of the reviews, the American replies to those attacks, and the results of this interchange on American public opinion.[50]

---

[49] A good summary of the opinions and comments of English visitors to America will be found in Mesick, *The English Traveller in America, 1789–1835*. See also the criticisms of the Americans contained in *The Colonial Policy of Great Britain*, 8 ff. This work anticipated the plan of attack which the reviews later employed.

[50] Chap. XLVIII of J. B. McMaster, *History of the People of the United*

Sooner or later the reviews managed to condemn nearly everything in America, sacred or profane, but certain subjects attracted their attention more regularly than did others. The Tory *Quarterly Review* delighted in praising the respectability and conservative political views of the Federalists and in characterizing the Republicans as a "majority composed of the lower classes...and the paupers existing on charity. . . ."[51] Such statements had anything but a favorable effect on the temper of the "majority" of the people, and much of the hostility to so-called English influence in America may be traced to the fact that certain parties and periodicals were complimented by the English reviews.[52]

English diatribes on the institution of slavery in the United States were particularly bitter and persistent. Sentiment against slavery was increasing in England, yet the American government declined to join England in suppressing even the slave trade. The fact that actual defense of the institution had already begun in America at this time made criticism from the outside even more galling. Both the English reviews named, however, chose these years to condemn slavery unmercifully and to taunt Americans with charges of hypocrisy, inconsistency, and immoral principles in a way that made reply difficult. On

States from the Revolution to the Civil War, consists of extensive extracts from the articles in the reviews. As the chapter does not point out the implications of the material presented or draw the obvious conclusions, it is necessary to consider the subject anew.

[51] *The Quarterly Review,* XXI (1819), 19. This opinion of Republicans was rather generally held in England. See, also, *The Colonial Policy of Great Britain,* 17.

[52] This fact undoubtedly helps to explain the unpopularity of *The North American Review.* It was regarded in England as the best publication in the United States.

one occasion, *The Edinburgh Review* attacked the institution and observed:

That such feelings and such practices should exist among men who know the value of liberty, and profess to understand its principles, is the consummation of wickedness. . . . the existence of slavery in America is an atrocious crime, with which no measures can be kept—for which her situation affords no sort of apology—which makes liberty itself distrusted, and the boast of it disgusting.[53]

The Quarterly Review also emphasized the fact that slavery was a great vice and used much the same arguments as did its northern associate.[54] The temper of the American people was not ready for abolitionist propaganda, and the result of these repeated thrusts was to provoke recrimination and violent national sentiment.

The attacks of the English were not confined to political and social institutions. In their remarks on American culture, their contempt for the "barbarians" became unbounded. Nothing admirable could be found in the spiritual life of America. The simple tastes of such retired statesmen as John Adams were derided as affected,[55] and the manners of the mass of the inhabitants were classed with those common to all "vulgar" people.[56] One English newspaper came to the aid of the reviews by informing its readers that England would have to retrograde four centuries and lose all her culture before she could hope to equal America in the realm of the spirit.[57] No one in England but a disgruntled traitor would be so foolish as to

[53] *The Edinburgh Review*, XXXI (1818), 148.
[54] *The Quarterly Review*, XXI (1819), 124.
[55] *Idem.*
[56] *The Edinburgh Review*, XXXI (1818), 140.
[57] *The Courier* [London], in *Niles' Weekly Register*, XXIII, 116, October 26, 1822.

range the peoples of England and America on the same plane. The shifting and mixed nature of the population of America made it vain, declared *The Quarterly Review*, to search there for "the arts, the elegances, the refinements, and general intelligence of . . . [England]."[58] The English also had the temerity to predict what the future held for America. This was a particularly vicious mode of attack and one which the Americans could only answer in kind; a lie could be proved to be a lie, a prophecy could only be demonstrated to be false by the passage of time. Thus one journal asserted that the Americans not only were not civilized but that they never would become civilized. In words which touched Americans to the quick, it was observed that "they may become the Goths of the Western Continent, but they can never become the Greeks," and that, being both stubborn and conceited, "they bid fair to retain their *barbarism* from mere regard to consistency."[59] These estimates of the culture of Americans are typical of the statements which are to be found in reviews of books on America; examples could be multiplied almost indefinitely.

What gives significance to these bold condemnations of the Americans is the proof which they contain of the inability of the English to understand the people of the United States. Reviews of the type of *The Quarterly* had tremendous influence in England and they had great weight in forming public opinion. It is axiomatic that lack of understanding between the peoples of democratic countries is fatal to friendly relations. Rough, America

[58] *The Quarterly Review*, XXVII (1822), 98.
[59] *Critical Journal* [London], quoted in Walsh, *An Appeal from the Judgments of Great Britain*, 292.

was; she was different from England in aims and ideals; but she was not barbaric. What shall be thought of criticisms of John Quincy Adams's literary style as a "spurious dialect" which would probably be current in America until classes should become stratified as in England and permit the leisured few to develop a true culture?[60] Statements like that had definite effects in America at the time, but they are also eloquent of the fundamental cause of the bad state of Anglo-American public opinion—lack of sympathy and understanding. Indeed, the dogmatic words of *The Edinburgh Review* in 1818, "Literature the Americans have none. . . . Prairies, steam-boats, grist-mills, are their natural objects for centuries to come,"[61] arouse wonder at the Providence which kept the two nations from drifting into war.

It is true that at this time Americans felt great pride in their country, its institutions and achievements. No doubt this spirit of pride, or vanity as the English would have it, went to extremes at times. It availed little but to increase that spirit, however, for the high priests of Scottish criticism to remind their readers "that vulgar people of all countries are full of gasconade."[62] The English emphasized the character and effects of the national vanity of the Americans with the same sneering air of superiority with which they evaluated American politics, American slavery, and American culture. England could never make America her friend, said *The Quarterly,* so long as Americans assumed it "as a self-evident fact, that . . . [they] surpass all other nations in virtue, wisdom, valour, liberty,

---

[60] *The Edinburgh Review,* quoted in Walsh, *An Appeal . . . ,* 222.
[61] *The Edinburgh Review,* XXXI (1818), 144.
[62] *Ibid.,* XXXI (1818), 140.

government, and every other excellence [and] . . . despise [all Europeans] as ignorant paupers and dastardly slaves."[63] This was one of the favorite modes of attack and one in which the qualities of the English writers that most irritated Americans came into play. They scored this spirit as evidence of national immaturity, of native crudeness, and of bombastic patriotism. They undertook to give the adolescent Americans paternal advice and to point the way to saner living. Their style cannot be paraphrased with effectiveness; the type of criticism which sensitive Americans faced may be comprehended better from a characteristic quotation.

At present, too [wrote *The Quarterly*], America is rioting in the first delicious intoxication of national vanity, and reveling in extravagant speculations of future greatness. The late war lasted just long enough to give her an appetite for the pomps and vanities of military glory, and not long enough to make her feel the inevitable consequences which must ensue, if this appetite should grow into a confirmed taste. The creation of a navy is now the darling object of her care; and the spirit which displays itself at the launch of every ship gives a sufficient indication of the confidence with which she looks forward to the realization of her ambitious day-dreams. *Time and the hour* may, perhaps, sober this calenture of the national brain; and when she shall have bought wisdom at the usual price of experience, by passing through the ordinary career of hope and disappointment, she will perhaps subside into a state of mind more propitious to the growth of good taste, and the advancement of literature.[64]

The reference in this quotation to the late war between England and America suggests a consideration of the

---

[63] *The Quarterly Review*, XXI (1819), 24. The same opinion was voiced in this year by Rattenbury in his essay in *The Pamphleteer*, XV (1819), 274.

[64] *The Quarterly Review*, XXV (1821), 51.

weapon which the reviews took up after five years of attacks on American institutions and characteristics had very nearly exhausted their stock of commonplace invective. Americans had begun to reply to the earlier articles in books and in the press, when their English adversaries descended from the level of criticism and employed the tactics of the irresponsible section of the press in holding up to scorn the war record of the Americans. It was pointed out that the only successes which they had won in that struggle were the result of overwhelming superiority of force and that these furnished no real test of the relative merits of English and American seamen. Man for man, gun for gun, there was no comparison between the gallant tars of old England and crews composed of deserters, jailbirds, and traitors.[65] After all, England's war with America was a series of petty skirmishes to which she could not turn her full attention while empires were at stake in Europe. Yet despite the "victories" which the Americans said they had won, they had suffered "the capture of their armies, the ravages of their coasts, and the insult of their capital, [and] they were finally reduced to negociate a peace, which left our possessions uninjured, and omitted all mention of their original pretensions."[66] These thrusts touched Americans deeply, and the repetition of similar criticisms brought opinion in this country to the verge of hysteria.

Nothing was too low or too ridiculous for the reviews to print. If an item damned Americans as beasts, the edi-

[65] Rattenbury, "Remarks . . .," *The Pamphleteer,* XV (1819), 277. Englishmen agreed with Irving's view that similarity of language furthered hostility between England and America. *The Colonial Policy of Great Britain,* 5, 208.

[66] *The Quarterly Review,* XXVII (1822), 405.

tors noted it. In 1822 the climax was reached when *The Quarterly Review* began to print stories of atrocities alleged to have been committed by Americans in the course of the war. It is hard to believe that a journal of standing in London could have stooped so low or have so completely lost the critical sense on which it prided itself as to relate that in the prosecution of hostilities a group of the "choicest sons of Kentucky . . . seized a party of Indians . . . , the greater part of whom they not only *scalped,* according to their common practice, but cooly and deliberately amused themselves *by cutting razor-strops from their backs* while alive!"[67] This unpleasant bit of journalism is not related for its own sake, but as an illustration of the length to which the blind hostility of English criticism of America could go. There were no limits to its violence and no bounds to its indecency.

It is highly probable that the effect produced in America by these English writers was as much the result of the tone assumed and the style employed as of what they said. The air of sovereign contempt and unquestioned superiority which pervaded the writings of these reviewers was intolerable to Americans at the time, and it still carries a sting. For example, it is the form of the statement as well as the content which gives this sentence its lash:

. . . We can smile at the bloated vanity which proclaims a Solon and Lycurgus to be mere simpletons in legislation compared with a Jefferson; and Hannibal a bungler by the side of a General Jackson, whose most glorious achievement, we be-

[67] *The Quarterly Review,* XXVII (1822), 74. That this was no chance slip of the editors is indicated by the fact that this same story was reprinted twice within the same year, with certain picturesque embellishments. Cf. *ibid.,* XXVII (1822), 431.

lieve, (before his unparalleled campaign in the Floridas,) was that of the murder of two unarmed Englishmen. . . .[68]

Matters were not improved by the more or less honest feeling of some Englishmen that they had made no statements about America which were not undeniably true.[69] Sarcasm and condescension were especially irritating, and, if the testimony of a Federalist who admired England may be accepted, "their pens . . . [were] dipped in gall; and their representations . . . [were] a mixture of malevolence and falsehood."[70] Their "haughty airs and . . . imperious style," coupled with a language characterized as "brutal Billingsgate,"[71] produced as much ill feeling in America as the ideas which they expressed.

The reviews thus played a great part in the formation of American public opinion at this time. English policy had its effect too, but these journalistic attacks were direct, unqualified, and inescapable. Nothing was spared. Politics, institutions, culture, national characteristics, and past history were held up to ridicule and scorn with a lofty air and a basic lack of understanding which made the criticisms even more galling to Americans.

Both *The Edinburgh* and *The Quarterly Review* were reprinted in America, and other English periodicals enjoyed an extensive circulation. The effect produced in America by this persistent journalistic abuse, therefore,

[68] *The Quarterly Review*, XXVII (1822), 73. Parenthetically, it may be observed that this statement was of the type which could not fail to produce the most violent recriminations. Few Americans outside of New England could have read it in 1822 without a howl of "New Orleans" rising to their lips.

[69] The clumsy effort of *The Edinburgh Review* to be conciliatory by giving this as an excuse for its articles would be amusing if it were not a bit tragic (XXXIII [1820], 395).

[70] Dwight, *Remarks . . .* , iv.   [71] *Ibid.*, 26, 273.

was striking. Since these attacks were printed in American publications, every word relating to America was noticed and discussed.[72] The very closeness of the two countries in language and tradition served to drive them apart. Americans read the journals and newspapers with eagerness, and this habit gave to the reviews their power to create hostile opinion. In his genteel way, Washington Irving explained this to his English friends.

> Over no nation does the press hold a more absolute control [he wrote] than over the people of America; for the universal education of the poorest classes makes every individual a reader. There is nothing published in England on the subject of our country that does not circulate through every part of it. There is not a calumny dropped from English pen, nor an unworthy sarcasm uttered by an English statesman, that does not go to blight good-will, and add to the mass of latent resentment.[73]

Americans read the reviews and took their observations seriously, not only because the reviews reflected English public opinion, as Dwight remarked,[74] but also because they were sure that the attitude expressed was that of the government of England. *The Quarterly Review* was held to be the mouthpiece of the Tory party, and the continuance of its assaults was accepted as evidence of official approval.[75] Niles raged at the "jealousy, malignity, and insolence of those pensioned reviewers,"[76] and the organ of the *American* government declared that these articles were published in "Reviews and newspapers generally understood to receive the patronage of the [English] gov-

---

[72] Dwight, *Remarks . . .* , v.
[73] Irving, "English Writers on America," *The Sketch Book.*
[74] Dwight, *Remarks . . .* , v.
[75] *National Intelligencer,* June 29, 1816.
[76] *Niles' Weekly Register,* XXIII, 7, September 7, 1822.

ernment.'"[77] This opinion was rather widespread and it had more than mere rumor as its source. On one occasion in 1819 Richard Rush, the American minister to England, wrote to his chief that all parties there were united in hostility to the United States. While his official reception had been courteous, it had been more than offset by the "cautious incivilities" of the Prince Regent himself. Hatred and envy of the United States, wrote Rush, were equally felt "by Whigs and Tories, Ministerialists and Reformers."[78] Is it strange that the attacks of the reviews were thought to represent the true attitude of England?

Two other beliefs of the Americans contributed to make it impossible for them to disregard or to minimize the importance of the English press. With that extreme sensitiveness to criticism which has been discussed, they felt that America was being singled out for particularly bitter denunciation. Had the English been more impartial in their selection of targets, everything might have been ascribed to English peevishness and the matter dismissed. "It is the attribution of these iniquities to the *Americans,* with an intention to make them a characteristical disgrace peculiar to *them,* of which I complain," wrote a man whom no one ever accused of hating the English.[79] Federalists and Republicans alike reacted violently

[77] *National Intelligencer,* May 20, 1817. Further proof of this conviction is adduced from the very title of Dwight's book. His reply to the reviews was addressed to *George Canning.*

[78] Rush to J. Q. Adams, received March 22, 1819. See J. Q. Adams, *Memoirs,* IV, 310.

[79] Dwight, *Remarks . . . ,* 81. Unusual weight can be given to his judgments on the subject of American opinion of England and to his criticisms of the English. He was, of course, a Federalist, an admirer of England, and a man who hated Republicans as much as did any Englishman that ever lived. He wrote at the very beginning of the years of journalistic abuse of America and before the extremes of condemnation had been reached.

to this unfairness, and as the years passed more and more complaints were heard that no nation received as much abuse at the hands of the English press as did the United States. In addition, the Americans were unaware that the English were used to this type of heavy-handed criticism of things liberal, and that it was meted out to Englishmen as well as to Americans. Feeling that they were the sole objects of abuse, they feared the effect that would be created in England.[80] The need for defense was apparent.

Because Americans did read the attacks on themselves, because they honestly believed that the English government and people were unfairly emphasizing the alleged faults of the Americans, and because they did not understand the methods of English criticism, replies and counterattacks were inevitable. The American press abounded with the most scathing indictments and ribald witticisms directed at English institutions. Comparisons between the free life of America and the base slavery of England were common, and all the proud nationalism which was so condemned rose to assert American greatness in no uncertain fashion. The reviews were accused of the basest motives for their statements about slavery in America;[81] the atrocity stories were matched; and, however base the allegations of the English, their charges were hurled back at them with interest.[82] The *National Intelligencer,* for example, regretted that a war of accusation and recrimination was being waged, but printed in the same issue three and a half columns of choice invective in reply to two particularly cutting reviews.[83]

---

[80] *National Intelligencer,* April 8, 1819; *Niles' Weekly Register,* XX, 409, August 25, 1821.   [81] *National Intelligencer,* May 22, 1819.
[82] *Ibid.,* March 18, 1823.   [83] *Ibid.,* November 3, 1819.

In books, as well as in the press, Americans defended their own country and derided England. Timothy Dwight and Robert Walsh produced the most complete and characteristic works, Washington Irving the most polished and even-tempered.[84] Both Dwight and Walsh wrote replies to the reviews which condemned the English publications completely, and which either refuted all the specific allegations against America or palliated them by citing examples of worse conditions in England. It was easier and more satisfying to praise American ways by comparison with English baseness than to argue about abstractions. "The *painting,* which is intended to prove your superiority [wrote Dwight], and our degradation, *has hitherto been done by you.* It is time, that the pencil had changed hands; and that justice should ... be done to us."[85]

One can hardly imagine anything that could bring a man like Dwight to the point of defending the characters of Thomas Jefferson and James Madison; but *The Quarterly Review* so aroused his Americanism that he declared that the life of Jefferson, "with the utmost enormities attributed to it, cannot be placed by the side of that brute in human shape Charles the 2d."[86] In similar fashion Dwight and Walsh condemned English slavery in the West Indies and English barbarity in India and at Copenhagen, and told stories of English inhumanity that equal

[84] Dwight, *Remarks on the Review* ... ; Walsh, *An Appeal from the Judgments of Great Britain;* Irving, "English Writers on America," *The Sketch Book.*

[85] Dwight, *Remarks* ... , 140.

[86] *Ibid.,* 25. Of Madison he wrote: "It is true, he makes no pretensions to the character of a religious man. But, I believe, he never swears, gets drunk, frequents the gaming table, nor keeps a mistress. How small, Sir, do you think, is the number of your princes, of whom this could be said with truth?" *Ibid.,* 22.

the worst of the Tory libels.[87] The brute character of the editors was asserted, and, when all else failed, Dwight declared:

Amid all the base reflections, cast upon the people of the United States, for their destitution of understanding, and worth, in these dirty-minded effusions of spite and ribaldry, there is not one, half so humiliating, as the fact, *that the Edinburgh and Quarterly Reviews are republished in this country.*[88]

To turn from the long indictments of English perfidy and political, social, and moral rottenness which fill the pages of these two books, to Irving's urbane appeal for better understanding between the two countries, is to experience a distinct feeling of relief. In the space of a few pages the character of the English writers is sketched and the effect of their work on American thought is analyzed. Irving stated the facts and revealed the faults of the English without resorting to defamation and slander. In the tone of one who regretted to see a man who should be his friend insult him, Irving presented his case quietly, but it lost nothing by its style. In a way it confirms all that Walsh and Dwight had said. Irving did not hate the English, and when he protested against the effect which was being produced in America by English writers, it is easy to understand how universal was the sentiment which he deplored. When he recalls the friendship that remained between England and America and asks,

Is all this to be at an end? Is this golden band of kindred sympathies, so rare between nations, to be broken for ever?— Perhaps it is for the best—it may dispel an illusion which

---

[87] See especially Dwight's tales of the actions of English slaveholders in the West Indies. *Remarks . . .*, 84.

[88] *Ibid.*, 159.

might have kept us in mental vassalage; which might have interfered occasionally with our true interests, and prevented
the growth of proper national pride,[89]

it seems clear that all that had been said against England
was true. Whether it was with Walsh's bludgeon or with
Irving's rapier, the counterthrust was made. If men who
loved England, as did Dwight and Irving, were so deeply
impressed by the "waywardness of the parent," what must
have been its effect upon the mass of the nation?

The primary effect was to increase the self-conscious
nationalism of America. The natural result of such attacks was to make the people all the more loyal to their
own ways of doing things and all the more desirous of being free from contact with people who hated them. Irving
expressed an almost involuntary wish to end any "mental
vassalage" to England, and Niles regretted more than
once that emancipation from her ways had not been accomplished.[90] America tended to separate herself from
Europe because of many geographical and political factors; the experience of these years convinced her that
nothing was to be gained from close cultural relations.
Dwight defined the issue clearly:

> If we can be connected with *Great Britain* on terms of mu-
> tual good will, and mutual respect; I shall hail the connexion
> with the most sincere pleasure; but, if the people of that coun-
> try are to regard us with malignity and contempt, and to treat
> us with abuse and slander; the sooner, and the farther, we
> are separated, the better.[91]

It was accordingly suggested that Americans cease being
so hospitable to travelers who came here to be guests and

[89] Irving, "English Writers on America," *The Sketch Book.*
[90] *Niles' Weekly Register,* XIV, 241, June 6, 1818.
[91] Dwight, *Remarks . . .* , viii.

left to revile the United States,[92] and that they cease to read English magazines and papers which had "had too long and too extensive a circulation in this country."[93] In many other ways, the desire for complete independence was increased. English hatred of America was used as an argument for national defense and for a more self-contained economic system.[94] In all these ways the spirit of nationalism was fostered and aided in its growth. It was bound to increase and develop as the nation grew and prospered, but the English reviews hastened its development and gave it its peculiar anti-English bias.

The most far-reaching and permanent result of the bitterness of the English press was the consolidation of public opinion in America and the direction of it squarely against England. How well this was done is attested by the ingrained lack of cordiality between the two peoples, which more than a hundred years of peace has not wholly eradicated. Dwight predicted this result in 1815. He told the English point-blank that nothing would alienate the people of the United States more quickly than criticisms in the press. He warned them that they were creating a permanent feeling of hostility. Contempt and ill nature were best adapted to this end.

No alienations are more absolute [he wrote] than such, as are produced by these means. The sting may be extracted; but the poison will be left behind, and will there rankle for a time. . . . This ill nature, this contempt, have been poured upon the *American* people for several years in torrents of abuse and falsehood. . . . If you wish us to be your enemies,

---

[92] Dwight, *Remarks* . . . , vii.

[93] *National Intelligencer*, March 18, 1823.

[94] *Niles' Weekly Register*, XX, 409, August 25, 1821, and XXIII, 116, October 26, 1822.

proceed. The task to a spirit of bitterness will be easy; and the success certain.[95]

Dwight did not err. An admirer of England, he saw truly the destination toward which she was proceeding. His advice was not heeded, however, and the progressive increase in the violence of the English reviews[96] enabled Walsh to declare, in 1818: *"Anglo-mania* has . . . almost universally subsided. . . .'"[97] Even the Whigs, whom Americans had believed to be friendly, had proved false. During the war they had favored the United States because they opposed the Tories; now that peace had returned, *The Edinburgh Review* led the way in defaming American character.[98] Both Englishmen and Americans of high standing admitted that four years of abuse had so roused the country and consolidated public sentiment that party lines were forgotten when England was discussed; ". . . whether Federalists or Democrats, the people of the United States are all equally hostile to Great Britain, and the spirit of party, as if influenced by a magic spell, subsides into quiescence whenever she becomes the subject of debate.'"[99] The *National Intelligencer* discussed the situation at length and revealed the progress of American public opinion after the war.

We have observed, for the last three or four years, the progress of a silent but certain change in the opinions of that por-

---

[95] Dwight, *Remarks* . . . , 165. Irving repeated this advice in 1819.

[96] This fact is also worth noticing. The most libelous stories and charges in the reviews are the ones published in 1822 and 1823. Instead of declining from its wartime level, dislike of Americans increased throughout this period.

[97] Walsh, *An Appeal* . . . , xlix.   [98] *Ibid.,* xiii.

[99] Rattenbury, "Remarks . . ," *The Pamphleteer,* XV (1819), 274. The same view was expressed a year later by *The North American Review,* X (1820), 334, when it noted the "unusual unanimity" of American sentiment against England.

tion of the People of the United States, who had hitherto clung, with something like a filial attachment, to the character and government of that country from which most of us have descended. . . . It was only during the war, that many of the intelligent citizens of the Federal party began to perceive that the identity of language and community of parentage constituted no affinity of disposition or character between them and the trans-Atlantic People. At the close of the war, when Columbia extended her hand to her late enemy, in all the frankness of generous amity—when her public men and public writers, with very few exceptions, inculcated sentiments of conciliation and oblivion of injuries—they have found their advances repelled by a course of cold-blooded and systematic depreciation and vituperation by the leading journals and periodical literary works of England, indicating a settled determination to excite and foster perdurable animosities against our country and its institutions. . . . The latest numbers of those works, which ought to have been sacred to science and to truth, have contained articles as full of spleen and jealousy towards this country, as was to be found, in regard to Great Britain, in the most vindictive moment of hostilities in the pages of the most loosely conducted paper in our country. This outrage has touched the feelings of the People of this country to the quick; it has dispelled the charm of British generosity, of British magnanimity—of British infallibility. The strongest attachment is not proof against meditated insult. The attachment hitherto existing towards England is dissipated with a breath; it is in danger of turning into a feeling still worse—into that feeling which the Reviewers write as if they wished to provoke—into *hatred*.[100]

The next few years were to see this spirit continue to grow in bitterness. Stratford Canning remarked that the

---

[100] *National Intelligencer*, October 9, 1819. This was the *avowed* aim of certain English writers. The author of *The Colonial Policy of Great Britain* hoped to "teach Englishmen to regard Americans in the same point of view in which they themselves are considered, that is, not in the light of *kinsmen, but of foreigners, aliens, enemies, natural-born foes*."

feeling of the American nation was pacific, "but so is gun-powder till the spark touches it." And it was not the mere acerbity of Adams's wit that led him to declare to the English minister in 1821, "Sir, it took us of late several years to go to war with you for the redress of our grievances: renew these subjects of complaint, and it will not take as many weeks to produce the same effect."[101] By the interaction of the forces of tradition, of misunderstanding, and of ignorance, the worst elements in the national characters of the two peoples had been brought to a point where only an "incident" stood between peace and war. The "incident" did not occur, chance as much as wise statesmanship prevented another armed conflict; but a spirit had been conjured up in America which was to drive England and the United States to the verge of hostilities more than once in the future.[102]

The main elements in the formation of the state of mind in which Americans looked at the outside world from 1815 to 1823 have now been analyzed. They felt that the Continental Powers constituted a different political and social world from theirs. European rulers did not agree with American principles and they opposed them in their own countries, but they did not go out of their way to express virulent hatred for everything American. Their interests did not touch those of the United States very closely, and they were not regarded as competitors. Indeed, there were men in Europe whom Americans rather liked and admired as gallant gentlemen and gracious sovereigns. Europe was not feared, and it did not

---

[101] Lane-Poole, *Life of Stratford Canning*, I, 302.

[102] It is probable that popular hatred of England, which flared up over Oregon, the Civil War, and Venezuela, for example, had its roots in the events of this decade.

occur to Americans to hate the Old World. After all, even Bourbon France had aided them in a crisis once, and there was much to thrill them in the name of Alexander.

With respect to England, sentiment was very different. The traditional view had been made worse after 1815 by active manifestations of ill will on her part. Similarity of language and the consequent close contacts between the peoples made it certain that they would be either friends or enemies. One could assume nothing about England; if her views were hostile, America knew it and responded accordingly. Their paths crossed too often in the economic world for either to become indifferent to the sentiments and actions of the other. They were forced to associate with each other and to get along together or to fight it out on the sea. Americans realized this, feared it, and yet were not of a mind to avoid the issue—they were too young and optimistic a people to admit helplessness. Therefore, the United States faced England convinced that she was the one country in the world that was really hostile. Hurt by her attacks and chagrined at her refusal to treat them as equals, yet withal a bit self-conscious and defiant, Americans entered upon the year 1823.

CHAPTER IV

French Policy and the United States

FRANCO-AMERICAN relations and the factors involved in their determination have already been touched upon. They may be grouped as moral, commercial, and political. The wide divergence of the political thought of the French government from that of America has been mentioned. There was almost nothing upon which they agreed, and there was much that produced the most determined opposition. This was recognized by keen thinkers on both sides, and there was a mutual desire to minimize its effect.[1] Americans might differ from the French on many points of theory and yet be tolerably good friends in the realm of international diplomacy. However, the growing nationalism of each country and the need of France to recover the prestige which she had lost were to bring about uncertainty and apprehension and to make association with her quite difficult.

In the commercial field, French interests demanded rehabilitation and the creation of an independent economic system. Her financial situation and her international obligations made necessary the expansion of trade in a peaceful world. It must also be remembered that France looked upon the world from the point of view of a third-rate maritime Power. Facing her as a rival was the winner of the European war, the only first-class naval Power in the world, and the only great colonial Power. France must

---

[1] Hyde de Neuville to Richelieu, October 3, 1816. Hyde de Neuville, *Mémoires et souvenirs*, II, 263. Jefferson to Gallatin, April 11, 1816. Gallatin, *Writings*, I, 692.

extend her interests in the face of English competition. She must therefore avoid friction, work for as much freedom of trade as possible, and do all she could to lessen the commercial dominance of that Power. "To balance the commercial influence of England," must be the constant care of French diplomats, wrote the French minister to the United States.[2]

This necessity grew all the more pressing as it became obvious that English merchants were bending their energies to obtain the one great undeveloped market in the West for themselves. South America must remain free and open to all, if the French were to develop an overseas trade, for France could not dream of keeping such areas open by force. Diplomacy alone would insure to France support against England and would enable her to combat the intrigues of the English in many parts of the world.[3] Furthermore, it was plain that the virtual economic war which was raging in Europe as a result of the efforts of the Continental states to protect themselves from the competitive power of England was to make the fight for foreign trade more bitter, more dangerous, and more vital.[4]

These moral and commercial elements were clearly reflected in the political factors in America's relations with France. The key to French foreign policy was England. She had defeated France in a series of wars which had lasted over a hundred years and had gathered the fruits of victory to herself. The war which ended in 1815 merely

---

[2] Hyde de Neuville to Richelieu, January 14, 1819. Hyde de Neuville, *Mémoires et souvenirs*, II, 388.

[3] The reports of Hyde de Neuville are an excellent reflection of French apprehensions.

[4] See an article on this rivalry in Europe, in the *National Intelligencer*, November 5, 1816.

capped the climax. Up to that time, France had disputed English sway in the world by force of arms; after 1815 she was no longer a challenger, but a defeated foe whose one hope was to lessen the power of her conqueror to injure her.

Hostile sentiment is often mentioned as an important force in international affairs. When it is the result of history and of basic interests, as was true in Anglo-American relations, its influence cannot be overestimated. But it is also axiomatic that mere difference of political or social theory will not keep two nations apart when their interests dictate a contrary course. French policy toward America after 1815 is an excellent example of the application of this proposition. The foe of France was England. England was a naval Power, a colonial Power, and a great commercial nation. How could an isolated France cope with such a rival? Realists that they were, French statesmen saw only one answer to this question: France must find a friend who was an enemy of England and who was in a position to compete with her on the sea and in foreign lands. That that friend was the United States seemed obvious to the French, and Americans must always remember that the fundamental principle of French policy toward the United States was this concept of America's rôle in world politics. This policy had two very important implications. On the one hand, France must do all she could to prevent too close a *rapprochement* between England and America, and especially must she avoid frightening the United States into the arms of England. To oppose the United States too much would spell ruin in the form of an *entente* between the two sea Powers. On the other hand, France must pursue a generally conciliatory policy toward America. If they differed, she could argue and explain, but she could not threaten. Let us consider the evidence which supports this view of the French position.

The French minister to the United States, Hyde de Neuville, was explicit in his statements. In one of his first reports to his superior, the Duke of Richelieu, he wrote:

> I speak here as a man who gauges the future and who, without entertaining toward the English nation those vulgar prejudices against which one must seek to be on guard, knows very well that events can arrive which, by separating our interests from those of that Power, will make us desirous of finding beyond the ocean a counterweight to her maritime ambition. The Americans are our friends and, so to speak, our natural allies.[5]

He repeated this analysis on various occasions and warned the French foreign office of the danger of English commercial competition and political influence in America.[6] He was supported in his arguments by the writings of the publicist, the Abbé de Pradt. This avowed royalist and partisan of the Bourbons asserted in one of his works that the independent naval Powers of America, combined with France, would be the only means of challenging the maritime power of England.[7] Royalist that he was, De Pradt was enough of a practical Frenchman to see the handwriting on the wall and to refuse to allow even his beloved theory of absolutism to dim his vision.

---

[5] Hyde de Neuville to Richelieu, October 3, 1816. Hyde de Neuville, *Mémoires et souvenirs*, II, 265. The notion of "natural allies" was to play a part in drawing America into a European war a century later.

[6] Hyde de Neuville to Richelieu, January 14, 1819. *Ibid.*, II, 388.

[7] De Pradt, *Des Colonies et de l'Amérique*, quoted in *The Quarterly Review*, XVII (1817), 544; in *Niles' Weekly Register*, XXIII, 169, November 16, 1822; and in the *National Intelligencer*, November 10[?], 1822.

Richelieu saw the problem in the same light as did his minister in Washington. In an interview he told Hyde de Neuville that France should do everything in her power to maintain her ancient ties with the United States and to prevent too sharp a distinction between the interests of the Old World and the New.[8] It was assumed that America was part of the world system and that, as long as she had friends in Europe, France would benefit from her amity. In short, French policy as presented to the Americans was to be one of cordiality and ostensible friendship, in spite of the differences which separated the two countries. Hyde de Neuville did more to guide Franco-American relations and to interpret French policy at this time than anyone else,[9] so it will not be amiss to let him explain his own idea of French policy.

As for us, what must we do in the midst of so many opposing interests? We must prove to this government that we wish to live in peace with it and to tighten our bonds of friendship and commerce, that we have no mental reservations, that our policy is frank and loyal, that we do not intend to meddle in its internal administration, but that we wish to be respected by those who call themselves our friends and that we will never submit to insults at the hands of agents of a government with which we maintain relations of esteem and friendship.[10]

Americans recognized almost at once the position of France in world affairs. Adams wrote, when he was minister to England, that consideration should always be taken of the fact that Continental Powers such as France wished

---

[8] Hyde de Neuville to Richelieu, December 11, 1817. Hyde de Neuville, *Mémoires et souvenirs*, II, 331.

[9] See White, *American Opinion of France*, Chap. II.

[10] Hyde de Neuville to Richelieu, October 3, 1816. Hyde de Neuville, *Mémoires et souvenirs*, II, 266.

to keep the United States separated from England."[11] Jefferson touched the heart of the matter even more closely. He observed to Gallatin that, though the ministers of Louis were ultraroyalists who had no love for the form of government of the United States, "the pride and pressure of England is more present to their feelings, and they must be sensible that, having a common enemy, an intimate connection with us must be of value to them."[12]

Many examples of the effect of the position of France on her policy and of the knowledge which the United States had of that relationship might be cited, but two will suffice to illustrate the point. After the invasion of Florida by Jackson, relations between the United States and Spain became strained. France immediately did what she could to prevent war. The part played by Hyde de Neuville in obtaining a settlement is well known and needs no elaboration here. It was made clear to Gallatin that France wanted peace, that she preferred American seizure of the Floridas to English occupation of them, and that, "provided an accommodation takes place, the terms are a matter of indifference to . . . [her]."[13] War, he reported to Adams, would seriously affect the friendly attitude of France, but even hostilities would not cause her to aid Spain against the United States.[14] The reason for French policy was plain to American diplomats. She might sympathize with Spain and deplore the action of

---

[11] J. Q. Adams to Monroe, September 5, 1815. J. Q. Adams, *Writings*, V, 370.

[12] Jefferson to Gallatin, April 11, 1816. Gallatin, *Writings*, I, 692.

[13] Gallatin to Forsyth, July 9, 1819. *Ibid.*, II, 110.

[14] Gallatin to J. Q. Adams, October 26, 1819. *Ibid.*, II, 125. The same view was expressed in a memorandum submitted to Monroe, March 20, 1820. J. Q. Adams, *Writings*, VII, 2.

the United States, but "The government of France sees that in the event of a rupture between the United States and Spain the natural progress of things will necessarily lead to an alliance or at least a very dangerous concert of measures between the United States and Great Britain."[15] Her hands were tied by the force of her own interests, and the American government was aware of that fact.

This apprehension on the part of France was a reason for the frank explanation of policy which was made to Gallatin in 1818. The minister of foreign affairs told the American that France was supporting the idea of joint mediation in the Spanish-American question solely because she feared "that if something was not done in common, the whole subject would fall exclusively in the hands of Great Britain." Hauterive went further and referred to the great importance which France attached to the position of the United States and to her connection with the European state system. In the past America had played a part in the affairs of Europe; it was to be hoped that she would continue to do so.

Their [the Americans'] point of contact was the sea, and there they had been eminently useful to the general cause of social order and of civilization, by maintaining alone and preserving the maritime rights at the time they were crushed or abandoned everywhere else. He would see us with great regret raising in some degree the standard of America against Europe, and thereby enabling our only rival to excite a general jealousy against us.[16]

---

[15] Erving to J. Q. Adams, October 22, 1818. White, *American Opinion of France*, 51.

[16] The account of this important interview is in a letter from Gallatin to J. Q. Adams, November 5, 1818. Gallatin, *Writings*, II, 78.

Thus the position of France was made plain to the Americans—she had practically asked for their support against England. To become an element in a new Balance of Power was not agreeable to American policy, but knowledge of the attitude of France was of the utmost value in the game of diplomacy. France could be placed in a very unpleasant position if necessary, and the American government was aware of it.

However, French and American ideas clashed in a number of ways, and it will be useful to notice the more important points of friction. At the beginning of this period America and France stood at opposite poles in their attitude toward South America. America sympathized with the cause of the revolutionists and believed that independence and republican government were to be the inevitable result. France, just as naturally, disapproved the revolts and regarded monarchy as the only stable political institution on earth. Only in commercial outlook did the views of the two Powers coincide to any great degree. The germ of change, however, was contained in the realism of the French statesmen's view. Hyde de Neuville, for example, was a royalist who believed in the institutions of the old régime, but he admitted that Vergennes, another realist, was correct when he said of revolution in the New World, "Ce n'est pas une colonie qu'on émancipe, c'est un Empire qu'on fonde."[17]

The first stage in the development of French policy toward South America was that in which the natural inclinations of the government prevailed. It desired to see the colonies reconciled to Spain under the leadership of

[17] Hyde de Neuville, *Mémoires et souvenirs*, II, 206.

Ferdinand.[18] Such leaders as Richelieu admitted that mod-
ifications of the old system might be arranged, but the
submission of the colonies to Spain would remain the
basis of the settlement.[19] This policy soon met with obstacles which led to its abandonment. It became more and
more apparent that it was a poor weapon with which to
combat English influence. The specter of English commercial dominance which haunted Hyde de Neuville
would take on reality if the affairs of South America were
forced to a crisis. "The commercial despotism of England
must be opposed not by war . . . but by a steady and concerted pacific opposition," declared the French minister.[20]

The firm opposition of the United States to this policy
was clear from the first. Gallatin repeatedly told Richelieu that all arrangements between the colonies and the
mother country would be unstable unless they were made
upon the basis of liberal principles and independence.
Adams instructed him to let the duke "understand . . .
that . . . [the United States] can neither accede to nor approve of any interference to restore any part of the Spanish supremacy in any of the South American provinces";[21]
and the secretary himself told the French minister at
Washington that approval would be given only to a plan
upon which *all* the parties concerned could agree.[22] The

---

[18] Rush to J. Q. Adams, March 21, 1818. Manning, ed., *Diplomatic Correspondence*, III, 1440.

[19] Gallatin to J. Q. Adams, January 17, 1818. *Ibid.*, II, 1374. Richelieu to Hyde de Neuville, July 29, 1817. Hyde de Neuville, *Mémoires et souvenirs*, II, 325.

[20] J. Q. Adams, *Memoirs*, IV, 200.

[21] Gallatin to J. Q. Adams, January 17, 1818. Manning, ed., *Diplomatic Correspondence*, II, 1374. J. Q. Adams to Gallatin, May 19, 1818. J. Q. Adams, *Writings*, VI, 318.

[22] J. Q. Adams, *Memoirs*, IV, 161.

reiterated declarations of the position of the United States had their effect.[23] The proposed mediation of 1818 failed principally because of the stubbornness of Spain and the policy of England, and after its failure France seems to have realized that the combined opposition of England, Spain, the United States, and the colonies constituted an insuperable obstacle to reconciliation. It was reported that

... The disposition to afford assistance to Spain in her colonial difficulties still continues; but the manner in which it can be made effectual (other than by a direct and open participation in arms, which the present state of France, and indeed, of all Europe, forbids) has not yet been discovered.[24]

In 1819 France was by no means reconciled to the emancipation of South America. Spain was hopelessly reactionary and was blamed for pursuing a course which would surely end in ruin; but France was still far from the position of the United States.[25] In this uncertain frame of mind, France paused. She favored such measures as would please Spain,[26] yet refused to aid Spain directly in her schemes for reconquering South America.[27] France was clearly opposed to the recognition of South American independence,[28] though her minister to the United States admitted "that the course of events would assume their own character, in spite of anything that could be done by the allies."[29]

---

[23] Gallatin to J. Q. Adams, January 4, 1819. Gallatin, *Writings*, II, 92.
[24] Sheldon to J. Q. Adams, October 20, 1818. Manning, ed., *Diplomatic Correspondence*, II, 1385.
[25] Gallatin to J. Q. Adams, August 10, 1818. Gallatin, *Writings*, II, 70.
[26] Gallatin to J. Q. Adams, November 5, 1818. *Ibid.*, II, 75.
[27] Gallatin to J. Q. Adams, February 19, 1819. Manning, ed., *Diplomatic Correspondence*, II, 1394.
[28] Gallatin to J. Q. Adams, November 5, 1818. Gallatin, *Writings*, II, 75.
[29] J. Q. Adams, *Memoirs*, IV, 170.

The second phase of French policy toward South America grew naturally out of the failure of the first. Support of Spain had always been somewhat dangerous to France, for success would have reinstated the Spanish colonial system, while failure in any active attempt to restore that dominion would have given England great advantages.[30] Either eventuality would have injured the chances of French commercial expansion in South America. French statesmen therefore turned to a plan which had been in their minds for years—that of establishing independent monarchies in South America.[31] Such a scheme obviously had much to recommend it to a shrewd French government. These monarchies would preserve the institutions which seemed so essential, would avoid plunging South America into the "anarchy" of republicanism, and would be closely united to Europe by bonds of interest, of sentiment, and of commerce.[32] It was believed that there would be no objection on the part of the United States to such a project and that the interests of both Europe and South America would be served by it.

In 1819 and 1820 France appears to have gone far in feeling out South American governments and in furthering the plan for monarchies on that continent,[33] but noth-

[30] Erving to J. Q. Adams, January 10, 1818. Manning, ed., *Diplomatic Correspondence,* III, 1957.

[31] As early as 1817 Richelieu avowed his support of this plan but feared that the opposition of Spain would prevent its execution. By 1819 her wishes were no longer a factor in French policy. Richelieu to Hyde de Neuville, July 29, 1817. Hyde de Neuville, *Mémoires et souvenirs,* II, 325.

[32] See the explanation of this plan which Richelieu made to Gallatin. Gallatin to J. Q. Adams, August 10, 1818. Gallatin, *Writings,* II, 70.

[33] The extent of these negotiations and indications of what the United States knew of their progress may be learned from the dispatches of American agents in South America. For example, see Prevost to J. Q. Adams, March 9, 20, 1820. Manning, ed., *Diplomatic Correspondence,* I, 541, 545.

ing definite was accomplished. A variety of circumstances ended this attempt of the French government to compromise the issue in a way that would benefit France. It was evident, first, that the United States was in no mood to support the plan. Gallatin told the French officials immediately that he doubted very much if monarchies would be regarded as securing the independence of South America,[34] and it became plain as time went on that the United States would take an even stronger stand.[35] The opposition of England to French influence in South America was another obstacle to success, and the burst of unfavorable comment which accompanied the revelation of the intrigue to the English must have convinced France of its hopelessness.[36] However, the project never became the subject of official diplomatic representations between the Powers. The fall of the government of Puerreydon in Buenos Aires in 1820 resulted in the exposure of all the details of the affair, and the overthrow of the semiliberal government in France and the problems presented by internal disturbance and European revolution diverted French energies.[37]

---

[34] Gallatin to J. Q. Adams, August 10, 1818. Gallatin, *Writings*, II, 70.

[35] The United States was not sure that real independence would result from this arrangement, but Adams revealed the deeper reason when he wrote: "It is impossible that *any* great American interests should be served by importing a petty Prince from Europe to make him a king in America. . . . The special right that we have to object to them is, that they are always connected with systems of subserviency to *European* interests—to projects of political and commercial *preferences*. . . ." J. Q. Adams to Rodney, May 17, 1823. J. Q. Adams, *Writings*, VII, 431. See below, pp. 219 ff., for the genesis of this attitude.

[36] On English opposition to French monarchies in America see Prevost to J. Q. Adams, March 20, 1820. Manning, ed., *Diplomatic Correspondence*, I, 545; Rush to J. Q. Adams, July 20, 1820. *Ibid.*, III, 1463; and Rush, *Memoranda*, Second series, 326.

[37] The attitude of the United States did not pass the stage of watchful-

Thus the third phase of French policy was reached, in which the government, occupied with other matters, acquiesced in a state of affairs which it was powerless to alter. It will be recalled that France opposed the recognition of South America in 1818 and that Gallatin feared its effect on Franco-American relations.[38] By 1822, in spite of the fact that the government of Richelieu had been succeeded by an extremely conservative régime, the recognition of South America was "not unfavorably received." Gallatin asserted that the Continental Powers were indifferent and that the French ministers had not even mentioned the subject to him. The only reaction appeared to be a remark by Monsieur,[39] "who always expresses himself in a very friendly way towards the United States," that this action caused him a little concern because of the moral effect which it might have on Europe.[40] Fair-minded conservatives had already reached the conclusion expressed earlier by the Austrian ambassador to England: that recognition was natural for the United States and

. . . that whatever differences of opinion might exist as to the principle of the struggle going on in Spanish America, nothing seemed more certain to all observers out of Spain, than that it must end, sooner or later, in the separation of the colonies from the parent state.[41]

---

ness. See J. Q. Adams to Forbes, July 5, 1820. Manning, ed., *Diplomatic Correspondence*, I, 130; Richardson, comp., *Messages and Papers of the Presidents*, II, 642. For a complete survey see the recently published monograph by Mario Belgrano, *La Francia y la monarquía in la Plata, 1818–1820* (Buenos Aires, 1933).

[38] Gallatin to J. Q. Adams, November 5, 1818. Gallatin, *Writings*, II, 75.
[39] Monsieur was the Count of Artois, later Charles X.
[40] Gallatin to J. Q. Adams, April 26, 1822. Gallatin, *Writings*, II, 240.
[41] Rush, *Memoranda*, Second series, 92.

The facts of the situation were gradually overcoming the theories. England was drifting away from the Continental Powers; the United States was championing the principle of the new states; and France could not challenge all three while Europe blazed with revolution.

A second point of friction between France and the United States was commercial intercourse. Trade between the countries had been thrown into disorder by the disturbances of the Revolutionary era and was entirely without regulation. As the years passed, discriminations and reprisals created a state of economic war which was most unpleasant and unprofitable. The long tradition of the Napoleonic period was thus continued with the result that until 1820 official relations grew worse. France showed little inclination to effect a settlement, and the United States was equally stubborn in demanding equality of treatment. Affairs reached a crisis in 1819–1820 when each party levied heavy retaliatory duties on the shipping of the other. The outlook was not a pleasant one, and gloomy predictions were made for the future.[42] France had already begun to offer competition to America in southern areas, and bitter rivalry seemed likely.[43]

Men in both countries, however, had long realized the need for a commercial treaty. Hyde de Neuville regarded it as a necessity for the protection of French commerce and as a means of combatting English influence in America,[44] and Adams and Gallatin repeatedly urged the French government to act.[45] It was not until the Americans had

---

[42] J. Q. Adams, *Memoirs*, IV, 497.
[43] *Niles' Weekly Register*, XVIII, 286, June 17, 1820.
[44] Hyde de Neuville, *Mémoires et souvenirs*, II, 315.
[45] J. Q. Adams, *Memoirs*, IV, 497.

become convinced that France was determined not to agree with them on any of the points at issue that a solution appeared to be possible.[46] Adams wrote despairingly at the end of 1821: ". . . there is evidence nearly conclusive of a disposition inveterately hostile to this country in the French government, and I am convinced it is approaching a crisis."[47] The growing preoccupation of France with European affairs, which influenced her policy toward South America, made her realize at last the need for a settlement with America. The cleavage between the two countries presented a dangerous situation of which England might take advantage. It was obvious that England would soon separate herself completely from the Continental Powers, and it did not behoove France to antagonize America. There is evidence that Russia, as well, became alarmed at the way the two nations were drifting apart and that she used her influence to bring about a settlement.[48]

Upon the return of Hyde de Neuville to the United States in 1821, the negotiation moved more quickly, and on June 24, 1822, a treaty was signed which provided for the reduction of discriminating duties, for fixed tonnage standards, and for the return of deserters.[49] It was not a perfect agreement, but its importance lay in the fact of its existence. Somehow, after twenty-two years of commercial hostilities, France and the United States had signed a treaty which removed the more aggravating points of ir-

---

[46] J. Q. Adams, *Memoirs,* V, 424.

[47] *Ibid.,* V, 426.

[48] Gallatin to J. Q. Adams, October 5, 1821. See *ibid.,* V, 425, for letter and comment.

[49] Malloy, ed., *Treaties, Conventions* . . . , I:2, 343. This was the first commercial treaty with France since 1800.

ritation. It was evidence, at least, of a lack of open antagonism; and, at a critical moment in world history, it gave new life to the traditional American belief that France was a friendly Power. The *National Intelligencer* commented upon the value of the direct trade with France, but emphasized the fact that

> There is another light in which we regard this treaty with great pleasure. It re-establishes relations of perfect amity with France, our old friend and ally, which have been somewhat disturbed by the recent collisions of the commercial regulations of the two countries. . . .[50]

French opinion agreed that this was the real significance of the treaty, and the foreign minister himself declared in the Chamber of Deputies that he was completely satisfied with an agreement "which completely reëstablishes relations of good understanding between two peoples who ought equally to love and esteem each other and who are already united by so many bonds."[51] While all the differences between France and the United States were not composed by the treaty, an air of cordiality was created which could not fail to affect their relations.

Though neither French political theory in South America nor French commercial policy in North America had been pushed to the breaking point, other elements in Franco-American relations caused considerable ill feeling. The long-standing claims of Americans against France,[52] the delicate problems caused by American seizure of

---

[50] Leading editorial in the *National Intelligencer*, June 29, 1822. Some papers felt that the treaty favored France, but the general opinion commended it.

[51] Chateaubriand speaking on July 24, 1822, quoted in Hyde de Neuville, *Mémoires et souvenirs*, II, 505.

[52] J. Q. Adams, *Memoirs*, IV, 497.

French slavers on the high seas,[53] and other high-handed acts of American naval officers did little to promote a friendly spirit. Indeed, Gallatin repeatedly warned Adams that the captures of French ships were ruining the American case for claims against France, and on one occasion bluntly told his chief that

. . . unless the military and naval officers of the United States are kept within proper bounds, our reputation of being the supporters of the principles of the law of nations will be lessened, and our friendly relations with other countries will often be inconveniently affected.[54]

By the end of 1822, therefore, while relations between the United States and France were ostensibly good and were in reality better than they had been for years, there was a ground swell of hostility which might easily rise to the proportions of a storm.

Events in the spring of 1823 put French policy toward America squarely to the test. In 1822 the United States could not be certain what French plans were with regard to the New World; by the middle of 1823 she was as sure of the position of France as it was possible to be. The close of the Congress of Verona and the announcement of French plans for the invasion of Spain coincided in point of time with a most complicated state of affairs within France herself. Wild expressions of nationalism and of French preëminence were made,[55] but the internal situation was not encouraging, and more than one observer in America

[53] J. Q. Adams, *Memoirs*, V, 415.
[54] Gallatin to J. Q. Adams, November 16, 1821. Gallatin, *Writings*, II, 215.
[55] See the statement of Villèle about South America, Temperley, *The Foreign Policy of Canning*, 108, and the speech of Louis XVIII to the Chamber of Deputies, January 28, 1823, *British and Foreign State Papers*, X, 758.

considered the war in Spain as an expedient to prevent revolt at home and to gain prestige for an inglorious ruler.[56]
Adams was reluctant to believe this explanation, but
Charles Ingersoll told the secretary that, in the opinion of
Joseph Bonaparte, the Bourbons were compelled to "go
to war with free principles or fall by them, and they had
better do so now while they can have the aid of the holy
alliance than hereafter when it may be dissolved or indisposed."[57] While Adams, Poinsett, and others may have dis-
counted this theory, they cannot have escaped the feeling
that France was not so powerful as appearances indicated.
It was also patent that England was now in complete disagreement with the policies of the Continental Powers,
and that she would oppose the extension of their principles. France was not a free agent in 1823, notwithstanding
the superficial aspect of her military glories.

While the French expedition into Spain was being prepared, the future of the island of Cuba and the possible
interference of another Power in its affairs aroused England and the United States. Temperley has rightly remarked that "suspicion was everywhere," and that neither
government trusted the other.[58] In this atmosphere much
could happen. Adams knew that France and England had
agents in Cuba to observe the course of events,[59] and he

[56] *Niles' Weekly Register*, XXIV, 17, March 15, 1823.
[57] Ingersoll's diary, February 14, 1823. Meigs, *Life of Charles Jared Ingersoll*, 121. Ingersoll was a member of Congress from Pennsylvania.
Joseph Bonaparte, the former king of Naples and of Spain, had lived in
the United States since the collapse of the Napoleonic régime.
[58] Temperley, "The Later American Policy of George Canning," *The
American Historical Review*, XI (1906), 789.
[59] J. Q. Adams to Forsyth, December 17, 1822. Moore, ed., *Digest of
International Law*, VI, 379. Also J. Q. Adams to Randall, special agent in
Cuba, April 29, 1823. *Ibid.*, VI, 284.

realized also that no European Power desired to see England in possession of the island.[60] Therefore, when Stratford Canning, under instructions from the foreign office, made a specific disavowal of any English intentions against Cuba,[61] the apprehensions of Americans turned toward France. The disclaimers of the English were not entirely trusted,[62] but it was felt that there was now reason to dread French action more than that of England.[63] A variation of this belief was the fear that if England did move, it would be to block the French.[64]

There is every reason to believe that the rumors about the possible plans of the French at this time came from English sources. They appear *after* Stratford Canning had made his disavowal to Adams, and the tenor of the Englishman's instructions make it highly probable that he did not fail to mention the "designs" of the French. It should be noted further that, in the spring of 1823, English papers taunted Americans for being suspicious of England without taking into account the possibility that the French might be intriguing in Cuba.[65] Gallatin's reports in the early spring contained nothing alarming, but revealed on the contrary that there was no disposition on the part of France to commit "infractions of our neutral

---

[60] Rush, *Memoranda*, Second series, 116.

[61] See letters of G. Canning to S. Canning, October 11, December 7, 1822, *in* Southern History Association, *Publications*, XI (1907), 1.

[62] See Ingersoll's diary, February 17, 1823. Meigs, *Life of Charles Jared Ingersoll*, 129. J. Q. Adams to Nelson, April 28, 1823. J. Q. Adams, *Writings*, VII, 377. Also see above, n. 58.

[63] Ingersoll's diary, February 14, 1823. Meigs, *Life of Charles Jared Ingersoll*, 121.

[64] See above, n. 62.

[65] *National Intelligencer*, May 24, 1823. This newspaper did not take the warnings of its English contemporaries very seriously.

rights," or in any way to antagonize the United States.[66] The emergence of the Cuban problem at this time, therefore, was the result of the exaggerated fears of George Canning, a fact of which more than one American was suspicious.

By June, however, the United States was sure of the position of France and was no longer in a mood to be frightened by the threat of French or allied (the two were synonymous) interference in the New World. George Canning was to find this out later in the year, much to his discomfiture. He cried "wolf" in January, 1823, and succeeded in disturbing the equilibrium of the Americans; when he repeated the performance in August, the results were very different. What information had the Americans gained in the meantime?

In the first place, the status of Anglo-French relations had become clear and definite. Adams was informed in March of the futile attempt of England to mediate between France and Spain.[67] The offer of England was rejected, but her policy was made plain and her opposition to French action in Spain was manifested. France was to receive no support from England, though neutrality was promised.[68] Canning was not so mild in declaring

[66] Gallatin to J. Q. Adams, February 28, 1823. Gallatin, *Writings*, II, 267.

[67] The correspondence between England and France was read to Adams by S. Canning. J. Q. Adams, *Memoirs*, VI, 138. It included three letters: (1) Wellington to Montmorency, December 16, 1822; (2) Montmorency to Wellington, December 26, 1822; and (3) G. Canning to Vicomte de Marcellus, French chargé d'affaires in London, January 10, 1823, all printed in *British and Foreign State Papers*, X, 17–19.

[68] It was clear even at this time (prior to March 31, 1823) that England might be neutral in Continental affairs, but that on the sea she would "not permit the French marine, by a new family compact, to erect itself once more in formidable array . . . and form the rallying point of a maritime confederation against the British empire." The *Constitutionel*

the policy of England in extra-European affairs. He told France in the most direct fashion that war would result from threatening moves in the direction of the western world. In his famous dispatch of March 31 to the English ambassador at Paris, he reviewed the recent course of Anglo-French negotiations concerning Spain, warned France to leave Portugal alone, and concluded thus:

... Disclaiming in the most solemn manner any intention of appropriating to Himself the smallest portion of the late Spanish Possessions in America, His Majesty is satisfied that no attempt will be made by France to bring under Her Dominion any of those Possessions, either by Conquest or by Cession, from Spain.[69]

· This was rather strong language for diplomacy, but Canning was also determined to let the world know of the stand which England had taken. Five days after Ambassador Stuart had presented this dispatch to the French government, Canning laid it before Parliament together with all the correspondence relating to the Congress of Verona and to Spanish affairs. This unprecedented haste was followed two weeks later by a specific and unqualified threat of war if France did not heed the English warning. In a speech before the House of Commons, he declared:

... In that despatch our neutrality is qualified with certain specified conditions. To those conditions France has given her consent. When we say in that despatch, we are "satisfied" that those conditions will be observed, is it not obvious that we use a language of courtesy, which is always most becomingly employed between independent powers? Who does not know that, in diplomatic correspondence, under that suavity of ex-

[Paris], March 13, 1823, in *Niles' Weekly Register*, XXIV, 113, April 26, 1823.

[69] G. Canning to C. Stuart, March 31, 1823. *British and Foreign State Papers*, X, 69.

pression is implied an "or," which imports another alternative?[70]

The threat was unmistakable. It should be observed that Canning stated plainly that France had "consented" to the conditions imposed by England. Previously, France had refused to accept English mediation in the affairs of Spain on the ground that vital interests were at stake. But when England now declared her policy toward South America, France did not protest. This distinction was illuminating and revealed French aims and policies. The challenge had been thrown down; France did not accept it.

Americans soon became cognizant of these developments and were quick to note their implications. All the correspondence which Canning laid before Parliament on April 14 was published in America at the end of May,[71] and the declarations which he made in his speeches were communicated as well. As a result, Adams's mind was set at rest about French activities in the New World, for on June 19 he told Stratford Canning:

With regard to South America and the islands of Cuba and Porto Rico, I said it appeared, from the published diplomatic

---

[70] G. Canning on negotiations relative to Spain, House of Commons, April 28, 1823. G. Canning, *Speeches*, V, 129. He meant what he said, for Henry Wellesley testifies that Canning told him that, had the cabinet supported him, "we should have gone to war rather than have allowed . . . [the French expedition into Spain] to proceed." Wellesley, *Diary and Correspondence*, 96. Cabinet support would have been easier to obtain had France interfered in the New World. In fact, Wellesley's testimony leads to the conclusion that Canning had the support of the cabinet in making this threat on April 28. If lack of cabinet support restrained him from threatening war in case France invaded Spain, must it not be assumed that *this* threat could not have been made without cabinet approval?

[71] Abstracts of all the documents were printed in the *National Intelligencer* of May 31 and June 4, 1823, but the dispatch of March 31 was printed *in full*.

papers and from Mr. G. Canning's speeches in Parliament, that France, at least, was to make no conquests in this hemisphere.

He said he believed the expressions were, "the late Spanish colonies."

I said, that taking all the documents together, they included also Cuba and Porto Rico.[72]

It was plain to the administration that, whatever might be the difficulties to be faced in the future, French interference in America was eliminated. No French government could turn from a revolutionary, war-torn Europe to tilt at windmills in the New World if that meant naval war with England.

The warning from England was undoubtedly enough by itself to reveal the position of France and to quiet American nerves; but, on the return of Gallatin to the United States in June, Adams received a positive assurance of French policy which complemented the negative inferences which had been drawn from the earlier information. Gallatin reported that in May in a conversation with Chateaubriand, the chauvinist minister of foreign affairs, he had recalled the policy of the United States in the past and had outlined its course for the future.

I did not leave Mr. de Chateaubriand [he wrote] without adverting to the affairs of Spain. That our sympathies were entirely on her side, and that we considered the war made on her by France as unjust, I did not pretend to conceal; but I added that the United States would undoubtedly preserve their neutrality, provided it was respected, and avoid every interference with the politics of Europe. Even in the questions connected with South America they had not interfered, and, although their wishes were not doubtful, they had neither excited nor assisted the Spanish colonies. But I had every

---

[72] J. Q. Adams, *Memoirs*, VI, 154.

reason to believe that, on the other hand, they would not suffer others to interfere against the emancipation of America. If France was successful in her attack on Spain, and afterwards attempted either to take possession of some of her colonies or to assist her in reducing them under their former yoke, I was of opinion that the United States would oppose every undertaking of this kind, and it might force them into an alliance with Great Britain.[73]

Again a foreign minister had threatened the French with war and with the one coalition that France wished most to prevent.[74] The force of this threat of war and an Anglo-American alliance cannot be overestimated, and it illustrates once again the ability of American diplomats.

Chateaubriand's reply to this plain statement was equally direct and to the point. "Mr. de Chateaubriand [continued Gallatin] answered in the most explicit manner that France would not make any attempt whatever of that kind or in any manner interfere in the American questions." If words mean anything, and if those of the most able member of the American diplomatic service can be trusted, France made here a complete and unequivocal renunciation of designs on America. She may have harbored secret hopes, and Chateaubriand may have lied; but there is no indication that Gallatin and Adams so judged the value of this statement. With knowledge of England's recent action in mind, this assurance from the highest French source carried conviction and set at rest

[73] Gallatin to J. Q. Adams, New York, June 24, 1823. Gallatin, *Writings*, II, 271.

[74] Gallatin himself regarded this as a threat of war. In 1826 he wrote: "You will see by to-day's papers that Chateaubriand, in his speech to the House of Peers, said 'that England could not take Cuba without making war on the United States, and that she knew it. *This I had told him when he was Minister, and included France in the declaration* [italics mine]." Gallatin to Clay, December 30, 1826. *Ibid.*, II, 353.

the apprehensions which had been aroused at the beginning of the year.

French policy toward America did not have the characteristics of hostility. At no time after 1815 did France let differences with America result in a definite break. Faithful to their traditions and ideals and to the interests of France, the directors of French foreign policy did not display undue eagerness to agree with their transatlantic friend; but not once did they fail to give America satisfactory proofs of good will before irremediable damage had been done. They did not agree with America on political theory, on commercial principles, or on the future of South America; yet in 1822–1823 they acquiesced in her recognition of the independence of the southern continent, they ratified the first commercial treaty between the two states in twenty-two years, and they gave a guaranty that France would not "in any manner interfere in the American questions." These are facts of history; they could not fail to have an important effect on the state of mind of the American government and people. They were strong evidence of the unwillingness of France to antagonize the United States. When a new crisis arose later in the year, they were to play their part in the formation of American foreign policy.

CHAPTER V

Russia, Europe, and the New World

THE POSITION of Russia in the European state system after 1815 was very different from that of France. Victorious in the war against Napoleon, Russia was the leading military Power on the European Continent and, by virtue of her armed force, was an important factor in diplomacy. The personal ability and influence of Tsar Alexander gave to this diplomatic position something akin to pre-eminence. Americans in general recognized this fact, and one Republican newspaper remarked upon Russian influence as follows: "... every power will first enquire what part Russia is likely to take. Her position is, therefore, superior in consequence to any power of the old world."[1] Years later another shrewd observer pointed out that the power of Russia in Europe was so great that every other state feared her dominance as much as revolution itself.[2]

Russia was strong while France was weak, but the ambitions of both alike limited their freedom of action. That Russia would expand in the Near East was regarded by Americans as a foregone conclusion. It was clear, observed the *National Intelligencer,* that the old plans of Russia for aggrandizement in the direction of India and Constantinople would be taken up again;[3] and Henry Clay expressed the conviction that

... Paris is transferred to St. Petersburg. ... Russia—that

[1] *The Aurora* [Philadelphia], in the *National Intelligencer,* November 29, 1817.
[2] Poinsett on the Greek revolution. *Annals of Congress,* 18 Cong., 1 sess., House, January 20, 1824.
[3] *National Intelligencer,* December 6, 1817.

huge land animal—awing by the dread of her vast power all continental Europe, is seeking to encompass the Porte; and . . . is anxious to lave her enormous sides in the more genial waters of the Mediterranean. . . .[4]

The power of Russia was clear to all, and her ambitions were equally plain; but there were two obstacles in her path to success. The spirit of revolution, against which Alexander had crusaded, and the jealous watchfulness of England were to prevent active measures on her part.

From the first, American papers noted the signs of Anglo-Russian rivalry in the Near East. In 1817 Niles reported that the apprehensions of England were being aroused by the relations of Russia with Persia,[5] and declared that the only explanation of Turkish policy toward Russia was that it had the support of England.[6] *The Aurora* agreed that conflict between England and Russia was extremely probable if Russian moves in the direction of India continued.[7] The outbreak of the Greek revolution increased the tension between the two Great Powers, and it also complicated the problem by involving it in the question of legitimacy. Would Russia support the Greeks in order to absorb Turkey, or would she disavow this revolution as she had those in western Europe? It is unnecessary to review the many details of the Russian situation which Americans watched with interest. They recognized that Russia was becoming more and more involved in an extremely delicate situation in the Near East

---

[4] Clay on the emancipation of South America, March 24, 1818. Clay, *Works*, VI, 157.

[5] *Niles' Weekly Register*, XIII, 46, September 13, 1817.

[6] *Ibid.*, XIII, 97, October 11, 1817.

[7] *The Aurora* [Philadelphia], in the *National Intelligencer*, November 29, 1817.

in which her ideals and her interests clashed, that she was incurring the enmity of England to a marked degree, and that her power in the extra-European field was being diminished accordingly.

As early as 1817 the hope was expressed that war between England and Russia would come soon, with the "complete emancipation of Spanish America, as its natural consequence."[8] Somewhat later, Adams realized that England was using her influence against Russia in the Near East, and told Stratford Canning that for England to succeed in her object without humiliating the Tsar would be very difficult.[9] Indeed, it was clear that only the most powerful forces prevented a conflagration. Everything was at cross-purposes, and the Near Eastern situation in 1822–1823 gives an excellent example of the effect of the chaotic political, social, and economic conditions of Europe upon international relations. "There are ten fold the Materials [wrote LaFayette] which at an other period would Have precipitated Russia Upon Turkey, and all Christian potentates Upon each other."[10] But nothing happened. Americans hoped that England and Russia would fight it out and that both would be crippled. Such a result would obviously benefit the United States.[11] In any event, it was argued, conditions in the Near East made England apprehensive of Russian sea power, and she might therefore be relied upon to check the eastern empire on the sea.[12] England, stated one correspondent, "will

---

[8] *Niles' Weekly Register*, XIII, 98, October 11, 1817.

[9] J. Q. Adams, *Memoirs*, V, 499.

[10] LaFayette to Jefferson, June 1, 1822. Chinard, ed., *Letters of LaFayette and Jefferson*, 410.

[11] *Niles' Weekly Register*, XXII, 244, June 15, 1822.

[12] *Ibid.*, XXI, 67, September 29, 1821.

never suffer Russia to become a maritime power, and to encircle Europe with her ships. . . . [She] will never permit her to acquire colonies in America, in Asia, or in the Mediterranean sea."[13] Anglo-Russian rivalry would engage the energies of England and would seriously restrict the power of Russia outside the Continent.

The effect of the conflicting interests of Russia and England on the diplomatic position of the United States was considerable. Russia and the United States were weak sea Powers; and the resulting fear and hatred of England did much to unite them. They both desired to lessen the danger from English maritime supremacy, and, though they stood for exactly opposite political ideals, their common interest furnished a basis for friendly relations. From the time of the Armed Neutrality of the North in the days of Catherine the Great, the operation of this force may be observed. As American minister to Russia, Adams had been informed in so many words that the United States was an important element in Russia's diplomatic system. Count Romanzoff told him that it was the aim of Russia

. . . to encourage and strengthen and multiply the commercial powers which might be rivals of England to form a balance to her overbearing power. Russia herself had not the advantages for it. She could not hope to be a great naval or maritime power, nature had in a great measure denied her the means. She ought then to support and favor those who had them. The propriety of extending this spirit to the U.S. had become more obvious and strong by the decay and disappearance of the old commercial states.[14]

---

[13] The *Constitutionel* [Paris], in *Niles' Weekly Register*, XXIV, 113, April 26, 1823.

[14] Statement of Count Romanzoff to J. Q. Adams, June 9, 1811. Thomas, *Russo-American Relations, 1815–1867*, 144, n.

Similar expressions by American diplomats are to be found, and it is not an exaggeration to infer that hostility to England made friendship with Russia a principle of American foreign policy. One of the agents of the United States in South America declared:

> . . . it is perhaps the better policy of the United States to cultivate the particular friendship of Russia, thereby to counterpoise, the maritime pretensions of England, as it has been conceived, that the policy of the two nations ought to be the same in that respect. . . .[15]

As with French policy, interest soon overcame political differences. Russians who hated republicanism and Americans who damned autocracy agreed that, in the international field, Russia and America had much in common. One of the most outspoken Republicans in America commented upon the rumor of a treaty between the United States and Russia as follows:

> We are pleased with these reports; they are such as we hope may be realized. It is every way the interest of the United States to be on the best terms with Russia; and to the interest of Russia, also, to have a liberal intercourse with the United States.[16]

Four years later, Niles became even more direct and stated: ". . . it is the interest of Russia to encourage the growth of the American navy in order to present a barrier to a complete naval ascendency of Great Britain."[17] Supporters of absolutism in Russia made it equally plain that their country desired close and friendly relations with America. Nesselrode instructed his minister at Washing-

---

[15] Worthington to Tagle, secretary of state of the United Provinces, October 30, 1817. Manning, ed., *Diplomatic Correspondence*, I, 359.

[16] Leading editorial in *Niles' Weekly Register*, XI, 17, September 7, 1815.

[17] *Ibid.*, XVII, 181, November 20, 1819.

ton to impress upon the United States the fact that isolation from Europe would only weaken the diplomatic power of America in world affairs.[18] Thus men in both countries expressed a willingness to forget differences in political theory for the sake of their maritime interests. The growing tension in the Near East made Russia more and more eager to balance English power, and the American press was quick to notice English comments upon a rumored Russian-American *entente*. If England disliked harmony between America and Russia, the value of an understanding was obvious.[19]

Russian diplomacy was to be directed toward drawing America into the orbit of European politics so that a Balance of Power might be created once more. The implications of this major premise affected Russian policy in the same way that they influenced French diplomacy. Russia must avoid undue rivalry with the United States, and she must work constantly against English influence in America. France chose negative means to effect this—she sought to *prevent* things from happening and made as few concessions to republican America as possible. Russia, however, took active steps to bring the United States into the European system of alliances.

Two distinct episodes in Russian-American relations after 1815 cast Russia in the rôle of bidder for the moral

---

[18] Nesselrode to Polética, November 21, 1818. Russia, *Correspondence*, XVIII, 315. In order to avoid confusion it should be observed that both Nesselrode and Capodistrias acted as minister of foreign affairs. Nesselrode headed the Russian foreign office; Capodistrias held the title of "Minister of Foreign Affairs near the Person of the Tsar." Both wrote instructions to Russian diplomats abroad. Nesselrode dealt with the technical aspect of diplomacy, and Capodistrias presented the aims of the Tsar's policies.

[19] *Niles' Weekly Register,* XI, 48, September 14, 1816.

and political support of the United States. Repeated attempts were made from 1816 to 1820 to gain American adherence to the treaty of the Holy Alliance. The universal acceptance of this treaty for the improvement of international morality was one of the dearest ambitions of the Tsar. Capodistrias, minister of foreign affairs, made overtures to the American representative at St. Petersburg in order to ascertain the views of the United States and emphasized the pleasure which the Tsar would feel in obtaining American support.[20] This move, although harmless in appearance, would have made the United States a party to a general European concert in which Russia was the guiding spirit and of which England was not a member. These proposals came to naught as America declined to act,[21] but a few years later Russia reopened the question and urged most strongly the value of American approval of the Holy Alliance. Despite the growing tendency of the Tsar to become reactionary, a process which was completed by 1820, the support of the republican state *par excellence* was desired. Polética gave Adams a Russian cabinet memoir which explained in detail the purposes of the alliance and defended it from the criticisms of its enemies. "It defends the system [wrote Adams] . . . and holds it forth as a righteous and pure-hearted league of powerful sovereigns for the maintenance of justice, of good understanding, and of peace between them and all the world."[22]

The purity of the Holy Alliance might commend it to the United States, but the Tsar urged other reasons which were less speculative and more practical. As a party to this

---

[20] Harris to Monroe, January 16, 1816. Cresson, *The Holy Alliance*, 49.
[21] J. Q. Adams, *Memoirs*, IV, 394.   [22] *Ibid.*, V, 141.

compact, America could rely upon the influence of powerful friends in Europe which isolation denied to her.

... it was intimated [by Russia] that if any question should
arise between the United States and other governments of
Europe, the Emperor Alexander, desirous of using his influence in their favor, would have a substantial motive and justification for interposing, if he could regard them as *his allies,*
which as parties to the Holy Alliance he [*sic;* they?] would be.[23]

In plain language, Russia desired an alliance with the
United States, an *entente* so close that the two countries
would stand together in international controversies. Russia would support the United States in its difficulties with
Spain, with England, or with France; America, in turn,
would be an "ally" of Russia against—England. It should
not be forgotten that by 1820 England was the only western European Power which had *not* signed the treaty of
the Holy Alliance and that she had practically withdrawn
from the concert of Europe. It was beginning to look suspiciously as if Europe, united in aims and purposes, were
facing two detached naval Powers which formed no part of
the general system. Anglo-Russian rivalry was becoming
acute, and Russia needed all the support that she could
get. A large part of her carrying trade was in American
hands, and, in the event of war with England, Russia
would be dependent upon the American merchant marine for necessary supplies.

The United States again declined to accede to the proposals of the Tsar. She approved the principles and motives of the compact, but the political implications of the
plan did not appeal to the government. Adams's rejec-

---

[23] J. Q. Adams to Middleton, July 5, 1820. J. Q. Adams, *Writings,* VII, 49.

tion of the Russian offer was a masterpiece of tact and diplomacy. He flattered the Tsar by praising most cordially the aims of the alliance and by declaring the resolution of the United States to live up to them in every way. He did not believe the calumnies which hostile critics had directed against the pact;

... But independent of the prejudices which have been excited against this instrument in the public opinion, which time and an experience of its good effects will gradually wear away, it may be observed that for the repose of Europe as well as of America, the European and American political systems should be kept as separate and distinct from each other as possible. . . .[24]

Suave as was the tone of this message, the reply was definite and clear. Russia could not take exception to it with a very good grace, and she did not press her plan further.

As it became apparent that the United States did not intend to agree to a political alliance, Russia took a step which was even more innocuous in form than was the proposal concerning the Holy Alliance, but its real purpose was obvious to Adams. One of the trusted ministers of the Tsar suggested to Middleton, the American minister to Russia, that a commercial treaty would be acceptable. Frankly, the American was told, the position of Russia was so precarious that she needed the support of the United States, possibly in the form of aid from the American squadron in the Mediterranean.

Why do you not . . . [asked the Russian] propose a Commercial Treaty. Your predecessor have [*sic*] done so without success but it was English influence which prevented it. Matters are about to change. . . . His Majesty is much disappointed

<hr>

[24] J. Q. Adams to Middleton, July 5, 1820. J. Q. Adams, *Writings*, VII, 50.

with his position. Austria and perhaps England too hath formed an alliance with the Porte.[25]

Again a European Power had bid for the aid of the United States, and again the knowledge strengthened her diplomatic position. If Russia so desired American assistance that she would take such a step, the United States could be sure that no issues would be forced to a crisis.

Since Adams and Monroe agreed that political entanglements with Russia were undesirable, this plan was checked at once, as the earlier one had been. It is extremely interesting, however, to analyze the first reactions of the two men to Middleton's report. Monroe was as opposed to political connections with Europe as was Adams. Given the facts, he was just as definite in his decisions as his secretary of state. But there is proof in this instance of a very important quality of Monroe's mind. He did not grasp at once the ramifications of European diplomacy. He read Middleton's dispatch and accepted the proposal at its face value. Here was a chance to make a commercial arrangement which might benefit the United States and which would injure England, and Monroe asked Adams if he did not think that Middleton should be "instructed to propose and negotiate a commercial treaty with Russia."[26] Adams, on the contrary, saw in the proposal nothing but an inducement to draw America into a Russian alliance. The European-trained diplomat in Adams nowhere finds expression so clearly as in his explanation of the reasons for refusing the treaty.

Now, the object of this [overture] was apparent, to bring us

[25] Middleton to J. Q. Adams, September 11, 1821. Thomas, *Russo-American Relations, 1815–1867*, 157, n.

[26] J. Q. Adams, *Memoirs*, V, 429.

into a *political* connection with the Emperor. Our squadron
in the Mediterranean was its object. A commercial treaty was
the lure. But we were supposed to be anxiously desirous for
such a treaty. Our true policy was to be always willing and
ready to treat of commerce with Russia, and rather desiring
it; because that desire would always be received as a mark of
esteem and respect; but we can really obtain nothing from
Russia of any importance in a commercial treaty. She has no
discriminating duties, no colonial monopolies to remove. All
the trade between us is carried on in our vessels. She imports
from us sugar, coffee, and raw cotton without heavy duties;
and all we could possibly obtain would be a trifling reduction
of them. For everything thus obtained an equivalent would
be exacted, and that would now evidently be political. I knew
the Emperor Alexander had a rooted personal aversion to
commercial treaties, considering them, as they really were,
uncongenial to the policy of Russia. He had always refused to
renew the old commercial treaty with Great Britain, and
always hitherto declined a treaty with us. If he had now
changed his mind, we should soon discover that for any advantage he might be disposed to yield he would claim for
equivalent more than it would be worth.[27]

Monroe saw the point which Adams had made and agreed
emphatically that such connections should be avoided. It
is interesting and revealing, however, to compare the suggestion of Monroe with the keen analysis of Adams. Even
if allowance is made for some measure of self-esteem in
Adams's account, the truth of the facts is hardly open to
question. Indeed, as it was a minor episode compared
with later crises, it may be considered as an accurate reflection of the minds of the two men.

In the general relations between Russia and the United
States there was exhibited an air of cordiality which cannot be disregarded as an element in the determination of

[27] J. Q. Adams, *Memoirs*, V, 430.

policies. Russian ministers avowed principles which were opposite to those of America,[28] and Adams never hesitated to defend her views; but irritation and harshness seem never to have marred their contacts. On various occasions, special evidences of diplomatic courtesy were given by Adams to Polética.[29] So marked did this atmosphere of good feeling become that one South American diplomat told his North American associate that the United States had the reputation of showing too much deference to the views of the Russian government.[30]

The actions of the Russian government did much to create this attitude on the part of the United States. The acceptance of the American explanation of the Kosloff affair had proved that Russia did not intend to stand too exactly upon the technical forms of diplomatic usage.[31] The difficulties between the United States and Spain over Florida presented an opportunity for Russia to offer friendly advice. She did so in such a delicate manner that even Adams could find no fault with her interest in American affairs. It was intimated to the government that Russia desired a peaceful solution above all else;[32] and, as a result, Adams recommended caution and forbearance in

[28] J. Q. Adams, *Memoirs*, V, 156.

[29] Adams gave Polética a copy of the treaty with Spain before it had been published. "... I have shown him [wrote Adams] an unusual mark of confidence, with a view to its effect upon himself, but still more upon the Emperor." *Ibid.*, IV, 376.

[30] Minute of a conference between Forbes and Rivadavia, August 5, 1821. Manning, ed., *Diplomatic Correspondence*, I, 577.

[31] This affair involved the arrest of the Russian consul general at Philadelphia on a criminal charge. The Russian minister, Dashkov, broke off relations, but was repudiated by his government.

[32] The policy of Russia is defined in the instructions of Nesselrode to Polética of November 21, 1818, and November 27, 1819. Russia, *Correspondence*, XVIII, 315, 321.

Spanish problems as the best course for America. Russia clearly stood for conciliation and supported the United States after the signing of the Florida treaty. In 1820 Adams stated the position of Russia in these terms:

... it appears that the Russian government takes an earnest interest in the late transactions between the United States and Spain; that they have a full knowledge of the facts relating to the negotiation of the Florida treaty, and have manifested unequivocally the opinion that Spain was bound in good faith to ratify it. ....[33]

The support of Russia in the Florida question was a valuable aid to diplomacy, as it was felt that England was working against the settlement.[34] On other occasions as well, there were indications that Russian influence was at work to prevent clashes between the United States and Europe. Gallatin reported that the hand of Russia was visible in the commercial negotiations with France and that the Russian ambassador even suggested to the French ministers that they hold discussions with Gallatin on certain points.[35] Finally, the arbitral award rendered by the Tsar in 1822, under the first article of the treaty of Ghent, produced a feeling of satisfaction in the United States and reawakened the popular admiration for Alexander which recent events in Europe had diminished.[36] These incidents are merely indications of the disposition of Russia, but, taken together and interpreted in the light of pre-

[33] Paper submitted to the President, March 20, 1820. J. Q. Adams, *Writings*, VII, 2.

[34] See below, pp. 160–162.

[35] Gallatin to J. Q. Adams, October 5, 1821. J. Q. Adams, *Writings*, V, 425.

[36] Ellisen to Nesselrode, December 13, 1822. Russia, *Correspondence*, XVIII, 537. The award ordered England to indemnify the United States for slaves carried away at the end of the war of 1812.

vious overtures, they show a drift of Russian policy which is unmistakable. The impression which Americans gained was not one of hostility on the part of the European country. This was especially convincing since there was no reason to doubt the sincerity of Russian friendship.

There were matters of policy, however, which produced disagreement and conflicting views. Had either Russia or the United States so desired, very difficult situations might have been created which could have had most unpleasant aspects. The question of the independence of South America was one of these issues. It was observed immediately that the inclinations of the Tsar were on the side of Spain and that he might interpose in her favor.[87] A declaration of this view was made to Adams about the time of the Congress of Aix-la-Chapelle. Russia desired a form of government for the colonies which, under Spanish control, would give some scope to their national interests and would thus compromise the conflict between them and the mother country. Above all, the use of force was to be avoided.[88] The Tsar feared that any war which might break out would, "from the existing state of Europe, the smothered flames of passions everywhere burning under the embers . . . terminate no otherwise than by a general war." Thus the policy of Russia was to be one of peaceful mediation between the colonies and Spain.

Russia did *not* favor the independence of South America and she hoped to save the substance of the old colonial arrangement, even if the forms had to be surrendered.

---

[87] W. Pinkney to J. Q. Adams, September 25, 1817. Manning, ed., *Diplomatic Correspondence*, III, 1851.

[88] Capodistrias to Polética, April 30, 1818. Russia, *Correspondence*, XVIII, 310. This dispatch was read to Adams in 1819. See his *Memoirs*, IV, 446.

When the question of the recognition of South America by the United States came up for discussion, Russia made it plain that she disapproved such a step. Polética was instructed to work against it,[39] and the American minister to Russia was informed that Russia "would view in an unfavorable light the acknowledgment of the independence of the colonies, at this time, by the United States. . . ."[40]

The failure of the proposed mediation at Aix-la-Chapelle and the declared policy of the United States tended to lessen Russia's active interest in pushing her program. When Pinkney was minister at St. Petersburg, he had assured the Russians that Americans had no doubt of the final outcome of the struggle.[41] The United States expected to be consulted on all matters which pertained to the South American colonies, and Adams made it clear that no settlement would be acceptable which did not include independence.[42] The stubbornness of Spain, in refusing all compromise, played into the hands of the United States and confounded the plans of the Tsar. Without agreement among the Continental Powers and particularly without the support of Spain and England, nothing could be done.[43] Alexander, in the opinion of America, had no inclination to support a thankless cause for the sake of mere theory and would be forced to confine him-

---

[39] Nesselrode to Polética, November 21, 1818. Russia, *Correspondence,* XVIII, 315.

[40] Campbell to J. Q. Adams, February 18, 1819. Cresson, *The Holy Alliance,* 90.

[41] W. Pinkney to J. Q. Adams, September 25, 1817. Manning, ed., *Diplomatic Correspondence,* III, 1851.

[42] A good statement of this policy as presented to the European Powers is in J. Q. Adams to Rush, May 20, 1818. J. Q. Adams, *Writings,* VI, 324.

[43] Crawford to Gallatin, May 1, 1818. Gallatin, *Writings,* II, 61.

self to the use of influence." Gallatin emphasized the fact that international rivalries would block effective action and that Russia, while favoring any measure which would be agreeable to Spain, was being very careful not to commit herself too far.[45]

Good illustrations of the care which Russia took to reassure the United States that she intended nothing hostile with reference to South America are the statements which Polética made to Adams in 1819. The sale of Russian ships to-Spain had aroused considerable comment. Although the American press was inclined to scoff at the whole transaction as a sharp bargain on the part of Russia,[46] the incident was somewhat suspicious since it coincided with Spanish preparations for an expedition to South America. The Russian minister accordingly told the secretary of state that Russia had no special alliance or connection with Spain, that the sale of the ships was merely a routine affair, and that the Tsar had no intention of siding with Spain in her quarrel with the colonies.[47]

The failure of the mediation of 1818 left Russia no alternative but acquiescence in the inevitable. A moderate attitude was urged upon the Americans,[48] but the schemes advanced by France for separate monarchies in America seem to have found little favor in Russian eyes. The Russian ambassador at Paris characterized the idea as "chimerical" and blamed the failure to reach a settlement on

---

[44] Campbell to J. Q. Adams, December 22, 1818. Manning, ed., *Diplomatic Correspondence*, III, 1859.

[45] Gallatin to J. Q. Adams, November 5, 1818. Gallatin, *Writings*, II, 75.

[46] See *Niles' Weekly Register*, XIII, 297, January 3, 1818, and XIV, 116, April 11, 1818.

[47] J. Q. Adams, *Memoirs*, IV, 381.

[48] Polética to Nesselrode, November 18, 1819. Russia, *Correspondence*, XVIII, 318.

the "folly" of Spain.[49] South American monarchists did make overtures to the Russians, as well as to the French and English, but without results.[50] The American minister to Russia reported to Adams at this time that Russia was disgusted with the attitude of Spain and would take no further steps of any kind.

> The struggle in South America for Independence [he wrote], will, there is now reason to believe, be allowed to progress without interruption from this quarter. The conduct of old Spain, has not, it is presumed, been such as to induce, on the part of the Emperor, a disposition to interpose in her favor. The events there appear to be viewed with a less lively interest than formerly.[51]

Although Russia retained her belief in the monarchical theory of government, she recognized the realities of the situation. Polética expressed this view when he told Adams that he was "perfectly convinced that Spain never would recover the dominion of those provinces; but he was equally confident that in seven years from this time they would have no regular Government."[52] Russia was becoming more and more involved in European problems, and Alexander and his advisers understood her interests too well to jeopardize them by crusades on behalf of a principle.

This gradual development explains the generally conciliatory reaction of Russia to American recognition of the southern republics in 1822. Earlier, such a move would have been displeasing to the Tsar; when it did come, he

---

[49] Gallatin to J. Q. Adams, August 10, 1818. Gallatin, *Writings*, II, 70. It was Pozzo di Borgo who "complained bitterly of the folly of Spain."

[50] Forsyth to J. Q. Adams, June 29, 1820. Manning, ed., *Diplomatic Correspondence*, III, 1995.

[51] Campbell to J. Q. Adams, May 3, 1819. *Ibid.*, III, 1862.

[52] J. Q. Adams, *Memoirs*, IV, 442.

was not in a position to show his irritation. Gallatin noted the favorable reception of Monroe's message. Russia had other objects to occupy her attention, he wrote, and as a Continental Power was "indifferent about it."[53] Middleton's experience was even more encouraging. Anxious to ascertain the views of Russia, he discussed the move with one of the Tsar's ministers and explained the reasonableness of the action of the United States.

... The reply of the Minister [he continued] was made in a tone which impressed me with the belief that he in some degree assented to the justness of my observations. His manner & language taken together encouraged me to think that the policy we had pursued in relation to the So. American question had as yet in no degree impaired our good standing with the Emperor.[54]

A few days after obtaining this favorable intimation, Middleton was delighted to receive a testimonial of the good will and friendship of the Tsar. A copy of the reply of the Russian foreign office to the protest of the Spanish court was given to the American minister.[55] This document was noncommittal to the point of ignoring altogether the Spanish criticisms of the United States. It contained nothing but flowery assurances of the sympathy which the Tsar felt for the aims of Spain. The tone of the reply, as well as the fact that a copy was transmitted at once to the American, gave strong proof of the fact that the Tsar would not oppose the United States or even criticize her action.

---

[53] Gallatin to J. Q. Adams, April 26, 1822. Gallatin, *Writings*, II, 240.

[54] Middleton to J. Q. Adams, July 20, 1822. Manning, ed., *Diplomatic Correspondence*, III, 1866.

[55] Russian foreign office to the Spanish ambassador to Russia, the Chevalier d'Argaiz, June 13, 1822. Enclosure in Middleton to J. Q. Adams, July 20, 1822. *Ibid.*, III, 1867.

Two letters of instruction to Baron Tuyll, the successor to Polética as minister to the United States, confirm the impressions of Middleton. These documents pointed out that Russia naturally viewed the question differently from the United States and that a peaceful settlement between the parties involved was still considered desirable. It would please Russia if restraint could be exercised by the United States, as had been done in the Florida affair. Tuyll was directed to shape his conduct along the lines which had been laid down by Polética—on a basis of realism and conciliation.

We do not pretend to arrest the march of the future; the enfranchisement of South America is probable, it is imminent perhaps; but, I repeat, that was one more reason in the eyes of the Emperor for desiring that his minister may urge the government of the United States to follow an inoffensive course with regard to Spain, and as in a very similar situation the intervention of Mr. Polética produced the happiest results we are justified in placing the same hopes in your efforts.[56]

Thus America had nothing to fear from Russian policy toward the republics of the south. Russia would not intervene in any way or support Spain in her projects. She would not alienate the United States over an affair of no immediate importance to her, but she would counsel peace and the avoidance of conflict.[57]

Russian activities in the Pacific also caused contentions to arise between the two Powers. Prior to the publication

---

[56] Nesselrode to Tuyll, July 13, December 14, 1822. Russia, *Correspondence*, XVIII, 335, 538. The passage quoted is on p. 540.

[57] The separation of England from the Continental Powers after 1820 made this imperative. Gallatin observed that the Russian ambassador at Paris "fears that the part taken by Great Britain in the Spanish affairs may have a tendency to unite us with her." Gallatin to J. Q. Adams, June 24, 1823. Gallatin, *Writings*, II, 270.

of the famous ukase of 1821, Americans had shown interest, but not concern, in the expansion of Russia to the east. Reports circulated from time to time that Russia had acquired one of the Sandwich Islands or California, but these failed to arouse more than passing comment. One Republican paper calmly remarked that, if these rumors were true, "We shall shortly find that nation, with their resources and active government, in every part of the world."[58]The general impression seems to have been that these events were so far away that they did not touch the United States. To be sure, a few papers warned Americans of the danger of Russian expansion and aggrandizement in western North America, but the occasional appeals which they made form the exception to the general rule.[59]

Certain men who were very much interested in the West did advocate the establishment of a line of forts to the Pacific and the founding of permanent settlements in Oregon;[60] nevertheless, the prevailing attitude was one of indifference. Niles wrote in 1821 that a naval expedition to the Northwest Coast was unlikely, "for our commerce, except the whale fishery, which we have not heard of being disturbed, is not worth the cost of the expedition, and chiefly consists, so it is reported, of illicit transactions between the powers at war."[61] This view was reflected in offi-

---

[58] *Niles' Weekly Register*, XII, 299, July 5, 1817.

[59] See the articles from the *Enquirer* [St. Louis], and the *Herald* [Alexandria], *ibid.*, XVI, 361, July 24, 1819, and XVII, 157, November 6, 1819.

[60] Men like T. H. Benton and W. D. Robertson were enthusiastic in furthering this idea. See the article from the *Press* [Lynchburg], in the *National Intelligencer*, October 1, 1816; and a memorial by Robertson in both the *National Intelligencer* and *Niles' Weekly Register*, XX, 21, March 10, 1821.

[61] *Niles' Weekly Register*, XX, 63, March 24, 1821.

cial declarations of policy toward Russia. Adams did not feel that Russia was actively engaged in creating a powerful navy or a great merchant marine—the only agents which could seriously injure the United States.

... With the neglect of the navy [he wrote to Campbell], that of navigation and commercial shipping naturally follows; and without these, however the establishment of distant colonies may be attempted they can never flourish. It may be proper to observe attentively the movements of Russia with regard to their settlements on the north western coast; but they can never form a subject of serious difference, or jarring interest between that Empire and the United States.[62]

There was little popular concern, therefore, over the condition of the far-away Pacific Coast and no official apprehension that difficulties would arise as a result of Russian interests in that area.[63]

The publication in the United States of the Russian ukase of 1821 altered the situation considerably. Interest in the Northwest Coast was reawakened, and discussion resulted. At first, the popular reaction was slight. Polética reported that neither the newspapers nor official circles at Washington attached any importance to the news.[64] The *National Intelligencer* printed the terms of the Russian prohibition with the sole comment that they "may be of

---

[62] J. Q. Adams to Campbell, June 28, 1818. J. Q. Adams, *Writings*, VI, 372.

[63] It would be interesting to ascertain what effect the idea that the limits of American expansion had been reached had on the popular attitude toward the Pacific Coast. It was at this time that the belief became prevalent that the "Great American Desert" had put an end to westward expansion. Long's famous report to Calhoun on this subject was dated January 20, 1821, and was published in book form in 1823. See E. James, *Long's Expeditions*, II, 361. Monroe appears to have held this view in 1824. See J. Q. Adams, *Memoirs*, VI, 250.

[64] Polética to Nesselrode, December 20, 1821. Russia, *Correspondence*, XVIII, 333.

importance to our mercantile readers, and particularly to those interested in that trade."[65] Later in the year, *The North American Review* declared that the extreme claims of Russia were "extravagant and unfounded" and challenged the extent of the exclusion. It admitted that the immediate object was a monopoly of the fur trade but added that little trust could be placed in Russian diplomacy. In any event, attempts to enforce the ukase strictly would cause trouble.[66] In his comment on the article in the *Review,* however, Niles expressed no more concern than to remark that "we believe this trade will be thought too valuable to be quietly relinquished."[67]

Even in Congress, there was no outburst of sentiment against Russia. Either the Russian claim was ridiculous, or, if it was seriously intended, its execution could be prevented. When the occupation of the Columbia River was urged upon the House as a means of blocking the encroachments of Russia, Tracy of New York laughed the suggestion to scorn.

. . . he believed no gentleman could entertain a serious apprehension that the Emperor of Russia had ever thought of enforcing these pretensions. He believed they were the abstract speculations of a diplomatist, who had no object in presenting them but to amuse his master by his ingenuity, and to show his own adroitness in defending fanciful titles to wild and unoccupied territory. To suppose that the Russian Emperor ever contemplated exercising exclusive sovereignty over the wide ocean between the American coast and Asia, was to suppose him a madman. . . .[68]

---

[65] *National Intelligencer,* February 12, 1822. Same article reprinted in *Niles' Weekly Register,* XXI, 389, February 16, 1822.

[66] *The North American Review,* XV (1822), 370.

[67] *Niles' Weekly Register,* XXIII, 157, November 9, 1822.

[68] *Annals of Congress,* 17 Cong., 2 sess., House, January 13, 1823.

Even those who regarded the claim as a definite policy declared that it would never be put into effect.

... we can encounter him. Yes, sir, on that very sea which he calls his own. On that very shore which he claims, he there shall meet our ocean-warriors; and, notwithstanding the hopes and wishes and anticipations of our trans-Atlantic kindred, the dominion of "the bearded men with green jackets" would soon be terminated on the Western coast of America.[69]

American public opinion *did* become aroused, however, over reports that Russian cruisers had so far interfered with commerce in the Pacific Ocean as to warn an American trading vessel off the coast. It was the fur trade with the Indians in which Americans were interested, not territorial settlements, and it was not until the *trade* was threatened that feeling developed against Russian action. So heated did the protests become, that the Russian minister was alarmed and took steps to reassure the Americans. The newspapers were giving a false impression of the situation, and Tuyll pleaded with Adams for some official statement to calm the public mind.[70] The Tsar was very desirous, he said, to "stand fair in public opinion." However successful the diplomatic solution of the question might be, the emperor would regret exceedingly the creation in America of a spirit unfriendly to Russia.[71] Accordingly, Adams prepared an editorial for insertion in the *National Intelligencer* which revealed the favorable state of Russian-American negotiations on the

---

[69] Baylies on the Columbia River. *Annals of Congress*, 17 Cong., 2 sess., House, January 24, 1823.

[70] See reports of conversations with Adams in letters from Tuyll to Nesselrode, May 10, 1823. Russia, *Correspondence*, XVIII, 542, 545.

[71] J. Q. Adams, *Memoirs*, VI, 151.

subject of the ukase. This editorial, which was widely re-printed, produced its effect as further evidence that Russia and the United States did not desire to irritate each other. The public could not follow the intricate workings of diplomacy, but it could understand official news that the United States minister at St. Petersburg

. . . will be furnished with powers and instructions to confer with the Russian cabinet for the adjustment, to the satisfaction of all parties, of their conflicting claims in relation to the north-west coast of America: and from the well known moderation and regard to justice of the emperor Alexander, no less than from the friendly dispositions towards the United States, so long and so constantly manifested by him, there is reason to expect that this adjustment will be accomplished in a manner satisfactory to him, and, at the same time, consistent with all the rights of this nation. . . ."[72]

Long before the general public became concerned over the Russian ukase the government of the United States had lodged a stiff protest against its claims. Monopoly and exclusion in the commercial field were not to be tolerated by a nation which had long been jealous of its maritime rights. The territorial extent of the Russian claim did not conflict with American rights, but the commercial provisions did. After demanding explanations from Polética and receiving only a routine answer, Adams declared that the rights which Americans had long enjoyed north of the fifty-first parallel could not be surrendered and that "the President is persuaded that the citizens of this Union will remain unmolested in the prosecution of their lawful commerce, and that no effect will be given to an inter-

---

[72] *National Intelligencer*, June 30, 1823. Also reprinted in *Niles' Weekly Register*, XXIV, 281, July 5, 1823.

diction manifestly incompatible with their rights."[73] The new instructions to the American minister to Russia, in which the secretary of state warned Russia that the United States would never accept the principle upon which the ukase was based, completed the remonstrance. It was regretted that Russia seemed to be following the age-old policy of England on the seas.

... It will be deeply lamented by the President [ran the dispatch] not only as an example of encroachment upon the freedom of the seas by a power which we have relied upon as among the most strenuous vindicators of their liberty, but as countenancing and even outstripping the doctrines of those who are led by the possession of predominant power upon that element to seek apologies for the abuse of it in the practice of other nations more interested in the support of the common rights of all. . . ."[74]

The results of these representations were immediate and must have done much to calm the fears of the United States. Middleton reported to Adams in August, 1822, that the whole affair had the aspects of a tempest in a teapot and that the ukase did not represent a well-considered policy of the Russian government. There was even taint of fraud on the part of the powerful Russian-American Fur Company in obtaining the issuance of the ukase.

For some time past [reported Middleton] I began to perceive that the provisions of the ukase would not be persisted in. It appears to have been signed by the Emperor without sufficient examination, and may be fairly considered as having been surreptitiously obtained. There can be little doubt,

---

[73] Adams's three letters to Polética which constitute the official protest of the American government are dated February 25, March 30, and April 24, 1822. J. Q. Adams, *Writings*, VII, 212, 214, 245.

[74] J. Q. Adams to Middleton, May 13, 1822. Alaskan Boundary Tribunal, *Proceedings*, II, 39.

therefore, that with a little patience and management it will be molded into a less objectionable shape. . . ."[75]

Middleton was also told directly by Capodistrias that the decree would not be enforced since "The Emperor has already had the good sense to see that the affair should not be pursued too far." In accordance with this determination, Baron Tuyll was instructed to inform the American government that its protests had induced Russia to suspend the operation of the ukase and to enter into negotiations for a treaty settlement of the problem.[76]

The details of this negotiation do not concern us, and they have been ably discussed elsewhere.[77] It should be noticed, however, that the conciliatory disposition which was manifested on both sides, entirely removed all ill feeling between the countries so that little apprehension was felt that a solution would not be reached.[78] The United States accepted the explanations of the Tsar at their face value and exhibited no undue haste to sign an agreement.[79] Therefore, when it was suggested by Russia that the entire negotiation be transferred to St. Petersburg, the United States readily acceded and gave Middleton full powers to reach a settlement.[80] By the summer of 1823 this

[75] Middleton to J. Q. Adams, August 8, 1822. Alaskan Boundary Tribunal, *Proceedings*, II, 42.

[76] Nesselrode to Tuyll, July 13, 1822. Russia, *Correspondence*, XVIII, 335.

[77] Notably by Hildt and Thomas in their detailed accounts of Russian-American relations during this period.

[78] See the tone of the cabinet discussions on the policy to be followed by the United States. J. Q. Adams, *Memoirs*, VI, 100, and 157.

[79] Tuyll to Nesselrode, June 12, 1823. Russia, *Correspondence*, XVIII, 547.

[80] Care must be taken to distinguish between what Adams told Tuyll personally and the policy of the United States. For example, on July 17, 1823, he told Tuyll that "we should contest the right of Russia to *any*

latest difference between the United States and Russia was practically settled, and the negotiation had proceeded in such a way that hostility had been reduced to a minimum. The United States had declared her policy clearly, and had even threatened Russia,[81] but the Tsar had shown no disposition to challenge her assertions.

In spite of the wide differences in the political theory and ideals of the two nations, a steady undercurrent of sympathy and good understanding can be detected in the course of their relations after 1815. As isolated, weak naval Powers they had mutual fears of England and mutual desires for freedom of the seas. Like France, Russia assumed that the United States was a member of the European state system, and she exerted considerable effort to obtain American friendship. By attempting to draw the United States into treaty relations with herself, by using her good offices in the interests of the United States, and by exhibiting an extremely conciliatory attitude in matters upon which the countries disagreed, Russia succeeded in keeping her contacts with America on a friendly plane. She prevented the dissemination of the feeling that she

---

territorial establishment on this continent." *Memoirs,* VI, 163. On July 22, 1823, he instructed Middleton as follows: "You are authorized to propose an article of the same import [as that of Article III of the Anglo-American Convention of October 20, 1818] for a term of ten years from the signature of a joint convention between the United States, Great Britain, and Russia." J. Q. Adams to Middleton, July 22, 1823. Alaskan Boundary Tribunal, *Proceedings,* II, 50. A similar overstatement of American claims is to be found in Adams's arguments with Stratford Canning in 1821. See below, pp. 238–239.

[81] As when Gallatin told the Russian ambassador at Paris that it was "contrary to sound policy . . . to attempt to extend settlements in that remote quarter without any real national advantage and without the means of protecting them in case of a rupture with any maritime power." Gallatin to J. Q. Adams, June 24, 1823. Gallatin, *Writings,* II, 272.

was hostile, and she did much to create the impression that she was the sympathetic friend of the United States.

It was no more the purpose of American diplomats to become involved in the European Balance of Power on the side of Russia than on the side of France, but it was a distinct advantage to know that it was plainly to the interest of both these countries *not* to antagonize the United States to the point of hostility. This knowledge freed American diplomacy from many limitations, made it more able to protect the interests of the United States, and encouraged a clear enunciation of the foreign policy of the American nation. Why should the American government not make plain to all the world the principles for which it stood, if it knew in advance that neither Russia nor France would challenge them in an unfriendly way? There is no doubt that the position of Russia and of France with relation to the United States, as the years from 1815 to 1823 revealed them, had a definite bearing on the American reaction to the events of the summer and fall of 1823.

CHAPTER VI

The Aims and Purposes of England

ENGLAND'S RELATIONS with the United States were outlined to the view of Americans against a background of
hostility, whose steady development after 1815 has already
been traced. Their interpretation of events was conditioned by it, and their estimates of English policy were
colored accordingly.

There was little in the course of Anglo-American relations following the war of 1812 which could counteract
the bad effect of this spiritual antagonism. In the liquida-
tion of the problems which the treaty of Ghent had left
unsettled, irritating and provoking legalistic arguments
dominated diplomacy.[1] The disarmament of the Great
Lakes and the determination of the boundary to the
Rocky Mountains hardly offset the influence of trade wars,
controversies over the fisheries, the difficulties of the
Northeast boundary settlement, and unsettled claims. In
the course of the nineteenth century it became clear that
peaceful and fairly satisfactory agreements were to be
reached upon all these problems, but this was far from
obvious in the years 1815–1823.

In the wider field of world politics, there was much to
cause Americans to regard England with suspicion and
alarm. The tremendous consolidation and extension of
her naval power throughout the world appeared to constitute a definite threat to other commercial nations.[2] There

---

[1] For a short account of these affairs see Latané, *A History of American
Foreign Policy* (Garden City, 1927), 157–168.
[2] *The Chronicle* [Boston], in the *National Intelligencer*, October 3, 1816.

was not the least doubt that England was the leading Power in world affairs. "Great Britain [declared the *Franklin Gazette*] by her immense wealth, her vast marine, her military posts and possessions, which encircle the globe, has a preponderance in the affairs of the world which all the armies of Russia cannot countervail."[3] To this naval and commercial dominance was added another resource whose importance was beginning to be recognized. In the realm of finance, England stood alone. Her wealth made her the banker of the other states, and their economic difficulties led them to turn often to the English for loans.[4] That these transactions were not without political significance was noted from time to time by the American press. In 1821 it was stated that

England, as the common centre of commerce in Europe, must necessarily have a powerful control over the circulating medium of the continent. Russia, Austria and Prussia have drawn vast funds from her for the pay and support of their armies, and are greatly indebted to her. The finances of each of these states are exceedingly deranged. . . .[5]

Consequently, it was felt that the influence of England on the Continent and throughout the world must of necessity increase. Financial, commercial, and naval power made it easier for England to injure her rivals, and the very fact of its existence disturbed the American outlook.

In this state of nervous apprehension, individuals, the press, and even officials of the government in the United States saw the unfriendly influence of England every-

---

[3] *Franklin Gazette* [Philadelphia], in the *National Intelligencer*, September 11, 1822.

[4] *National Intelligencer*, March 15, 1817, and *Niles' Weekly Register*, XVII, 169, November 13, 1819.

[5] *Niles' Weekly Register*, XX, 74, March 31, 1821.

where. The repeated attempts of the English to injure the United States by intrigue were recalled. From the time of Blount's conspiracy to the Hartford Convention, asserted *The Aurora,* England had been trying to disrupt the Union, and Americans must therefore be ready "to guard against the insidious progress of her arts," by every means at their command.[6] The fact that an English pamphleteer, whose writings were well known in America, argued quite seriously in 1819 that the separation of the West from the remainder of the Union was still highly probable did little to allay the fears of Americans.[7]

The definitely expressed interest of England in the American navy was ominous. The rather absurd controversy over the alleged under-rating of American naval vessels, which occupied the attention of Parliament and the Anglo-American press, was only the symptom of the concern which each felt over the naval power of the other.[8] Again the English confirmed American apprehensions by making it plain to all that they looked upon the United States as their chief rival on the seas and that they intended to be able to defeat her decisively in a naval war.[9] England not only appeared to be preparing for a naval conflict with America, but also seemed to be using her influence and policy to injure American trade.[10] The trade

[6] *The Aurora* [Philadelphia], in the *National Intelligencer,* March 28, 1815.

[7] Rattenbury, "Remarks . . . ," *The Pamphleteer,* XV (1819), 267–269.

[8] *Niles' Weekly Register,* XIII, 193, November 22, 1817, and XIV, 319, July 4, 1818.

[9] See *ibid.,* XVI, 398, August 7, 1819, where several debates in the House of Lords are reported. It was argued that England must build large frigates of the class of those of the United States in order to be able to meet America on equal terms.

[10] *Ibid.,* IX, 64, September 23, 1815. Many Englishmen regarded with

war between the two countries over West Indian commerce, which continued throughout this period, did much to arouse hostile sentiment in the United States and to alienate those classes which had previously been friendly to England.

Rivalry was not confined to commerce between the United States and England. They were also competing for the carrying trade of the world, particularly for that of South America, and, in the course of this conflict, suspicions of English diplomacy reached a high pitch. The more emotional Americans saw evidence of a deliberate attempt of the English to cripple their commercial power and thereby reduce their naval strength.[11] In diplomatic correspondence an equally watchful attitude may be detected. On many occasions, Adams declared that there was a necessity for guarding against the attempts of England "to secure advantages or preferences to . . . [herself, which would be] burdensome to us."[12]

In many ways it seemed evident that there was little hope of friendship from England. The old, old game was to be played again, and it was believed that trust in England would only injure the United States. Thomas Ritchie, for example, was firmly convinced that "as long

alarm the increasing commercial importance of the United States. It was felt that only a vigorous, aggressive, and far-sighted colonial policy on a large scale would prevent the United States from assuming permanent dominance over commerce and the carrying trade in the New World. See *The Colonial Policy of Great Britain* for an Englishman's view of the relations existing between the two countries, and the prospect for the future. The policy there suggested for England's adoption must indeed have alarmed Americans.

[11] *Niles' Weekly Register*, XIV, 406, August 8, 1818.

[12] For example, in instructions to Rodney, May 17, 1823. J. Q. Adams, *Writings*, VII, 435. Monroe expressed the same view in a letter to Jackson, June 2, 1817. Jackson, *Correspondence*, II, 296.

as America preserved a name amongst the nations of the earth, she would be opposed by a foe, haughty and cruel, and more faithless than Carthage."[13] Let it be repeated that suspicion and fear conditioned all American interpretations of English policy during these years. Monroe had revealed very clearly this state of mind when he wrote a rather interesting letter to John Quincy Adams, who was then minister at London.

Before entering into any communications with the British government, relating to the part Great-Britain will take towards the Spanish provinces in South-America, . . . you will satisfy yourself that the British government puts a just value on the existing relations between the United-States and Great-Britain, and will not convert the communication which is a proof of amity, and intended to be confidential, into an instrument for promoting hostility between Spain and the United-States. Your communication, in any view, had therefore better be informal, and apparently proceeding from yourself only.[14]

This was the frame of mind in which American diplomats approached discussions with the English. Throughout this period, popular hatred of England increased steadily. Would the knowledge which American statesmen and the public received about English policy increase or lessen this sentiment?

Americans viewed with interest the relations of England with the Continental Powers and the developments of her policy with reference to the New World. It is quite unnecessary to trace the process by which England gradu-

---

[13] Ambler, *Thomas Ritchie,* 61. Ritchie was one of the leading Republican journalists in the United States. He was editor of the influential *Enquirer* of Richmond.

[14] Monroe to J. Q. Adams, December 10, 1815. Manning, ed., *Diplomatic Correspondence,* I, 18.

ally withdrew from the concert of Europe. The divergent opinions of England and the Continental states on the purpose of the confederation of Europe were given prominence in the American press;[15] the opposition of liberal leaders to the reactionary measures of the despots was noted;[16] and the growing disinclination of England to support her European associates was recorded.[17] In 1818, at Aix-la-Chapelle, she blocked Russian attempts to make the concert of Europe effective and to mediate in the affairs of Spain and South America;[18] in 1821 she refused to take any part in the suppression of revolution in Italy;[19] in 1822 she tried to prevent war between France and Spain; and in 1823, having failed to avert the invasion of the peninsula, she boldly threatened the French with war if they extended their operations beyond the Continent.[20]

The public and the officials of the American government were convinced by 1823 that England was completely separated from the Holy Alliance. In that year, Adams told the English minister that the alliance

... was virtually dissolved so far as Great Britain was a party to it. I did not mean to say I thought it dissolved as to the Continental powers. I wished I could think it was. But Great

---

[15] Important circulars such as Castlereagh's on Naples, January 19, 1821, were printed in full in *Niles' Weekly Register* and in the *National Intelligencer*. Papers laid before Parliament and statements made in debates in that body were also given publicity. Cf. *Niles' Weekly Register*, XXIV, 137, May 3, 1823.

[16] *Ibid.*, XIII, 344, January 17, 1818; XX, 65, March 31, 1821; and XX, 95, April 7, 1821.

[17] *National Intelligencer*, May 10, 1821.

[18] J. Q. Adams to Sumter, August 27, 1818. Manning, ed., *Diplomatic Correspondence*, I, 79. J. Q. Adams to Anderson, May 27, 1823. J. Q. Adams, *Writings*, VII, 441.

[19] See comment on her action, *National Intelligencer*, May 10, 1821.

[20] See above, pp. 107–108.

Britain had separated herself from the counsels and measures of the alliance. . . ."[21]

Concerted action by England and the European states was obviously impossible. Again England was playing a lone hand in world politics and was pursuing her interests in her own way. On the one hand, this encouraged Americans, for it ensured English opposition to Continental ambitions in the New World; but, on the other hand, her divorce from the internal affairs of Europe left her more free to act abroad. While they welcomed English isolation, Americans also feared its effect on their own interests.

It was plain that England was not following a liberal, democratic, or enlightened policy. The middle course which she adopted as a result of the many crosscurrents in her national life was liberal compared with that of the Holy Alliance, but conservative in comparison with the ideas which filled the western hemisphere. Nor may it be forgotten that England's national interests motivated all her actions. It was this phase of her policy that touched the United States and the New World most closely, and its effect did not reassure them. Let us review the aspects of English policy which Americans watched with especial interest during these years.[22]

The gulf between the sentiment of the English people and that of their government toward the cause of the South

---

[21] J. Q. Adams, *Memoirs*, VI, 152.

[22] So much has been written on the European side of English policy that it would be the most useless sort of duplication to repeat any of that story. Writers have failed to emphasize, however, the way in which English policy toward South America and toward the United States appeared to contemporary Americans. It is unnecessary to minimize the importance of the European, liberal phase of English policy, but it is quite essential to observe that there is another side to the problem which in the long run had even more influence on the formation of American policy.

Americans was plain. The general feeling in England was decidedly in favor of the emancipation of the Spanish colonies, Adams reported in 1816, but "A different and directly opposite sentiment is entertained by the the government. Their disposition is decided against the South Americans, but by a political obliquity not without example, it is not so unequivocally in favor of the mother country."[23] This two-faced policy aroused the suspicion among Americans that only the force of a strong public opinion prevented the English government from taking steps which would favor Spain and which might give England exclusive privileges in the restored colonies.[24] It was not sincere sympathy which determined the policy of England, but interests which ran counter to the inclinations of the governing group. As a result of this situation, England could not be trusted to adopt a straightforward, consistent course of action with regard to South America and the United States. She would hedge at every opportunity and would favor both sides as long as possible. One of the shrewdest American diplomats that ever lived confessed his inability to predict England's actions.

It would be more important [wrote Gallatin], but it is more difficult to ascertain the real views of Great Britain. That she has not interfered to prevent the ratification of our treaty appears to be more than probable; but her situation impels her to seek at almost any risk markets for her manufactures and employment for her seamen. Her conduct seems to prove that, though under peculiar restraints from previous engagements, she wishes the emancipation of the Spanish colonies,

[23] J. Q. Adams to Monroe, January 22, 1816. J. Q. Adams, *Writings*, V, 487.

[24] Rush to J. Q. Adams, March 21, 1818. Manning, ed., *Diplomatic Correspondence*, III, 1440. J. Q. Adams to Campbell, June 3, 1819. *Ibid.*, I, 107. *Niles' Weekly Register*, XV, 155, October 31, 1818.

without which she can never obtain a free trade with them. I cannot, therefore, help thinking that she would see a war without regret take place between us and Spain, of which she would hope to reap the fruits without expense, without risk, and without altering her relations with that country or with the other European powers.[25]

This analysis only confirmed the earlier conclusions of Adams and LaFayette that the aggrandizement of English trade and commerce and the restoration of colonial monopoly in favor of English interests were the aims of English policy in the New World.[26] American agents in South America and the press in the United States saw in the English attitude toward mediation in 1818 not altruism but interest. Worthington warned Adams that only extreme care would prevent England from getting a "footing here [South America] too firm to be displaced, and our countrymen will lose all the glory and profit to be derived from this great contest . . . ;"[27] and the *National Advocate* declared that the whole project for mediation was an English plot to keep the colonies in a state of technical subjection to Spain while England obtained a commercial monopoly.[28]

Americans saw that the concern which Englishmen did exhibit for South America was based principally on the prospect of commercial gain. Even war between Spain and Portugal, or between Spain and the United States, would not be displeasing to them, remarked the *National In-*

---

[25] Gallatin to J. Q. Adams, October 26, 1819. Gallatin, *Writings*, II, 126.

[26] J. Q. Adams to Monroe, September 30, 1815. J. Q. Adams, *Writings*, V, 395. LaFayette to Jefferson, December 10, 1817. Chinard, ed., *Letters of LaFayette and Jefferson*, 391.

[27] Worthington to J. Q. Adams, January 15, 1818. Manning, ed., *Diplomatic Correspondence*, I, 372.

[28] *National Advocate*, in the *National Intelligencer*, February 12, 1818.

telligencer, since the result would be the enlargement of the markets for English manufactures.[29] It was affirmed time and again in Congress that it was the "interest" of England to see the colonies emancipated, but with almost equal frequency the fear of English "monopoly" was expressed.[30] Clay thought that interest and tradition had more force than honor in shaping England's policy.

. . . Excluded almost as she is from the Continent, the commerce of America, South and North, is worth to her more than the commerce of the residue of the world. . . . Looking to the present moment only, and merely to the interests of commerce, England is concerned more than even this country, in the success of the cause of independence in Spanish America. The reduction of the Spanish power in America has been the constant and favorite aim of her policy for two centuries. . . .[31]

Robertson of Louisiana agreed with Clay that the independence of the southern continent was the common desire of all commercial countries.[32] The commerce of South America was daily becoming an essential part of the economic life of England, declared Niles,[33] and a correspondent of his paper argued that the immense profits which England derived from her trade with South America contributed to "her colossal power and political influence over the world."[34] The English papers themselves did not conceal their indifference to anything but the profits to be gained. "Let them fight it out, and let us hope for that

[29] *National Intelligencer,* May 12, 1817.

[30] A good illustration of the juxtaposition of these ideas is in a speech by Smith of Maryland. *Annals of Congress,* 14 Cong., 1 sess., House, January 24, 1817.

[31] Speech on the emancipation of South America. *Works,* VI, 159.

[32] *Annals of Congress,* 15 Cong., 1 sess., House, March 26, 1818.

[33] *Niles' Weekly Register,* XVII, 93, October 9, 1819.

[34] *Ibid.,* X, 93, April 6, 1816.

happy result which . . . *will extend the compass of British Commerce*,' was the wish of the leading commercial journal in London.[35] The Tory press did not approve of the cause of the South Americans but had, nevertheless, a keen eye for the possibilities of profit to England. It is hardly an exaggeration to say that *The Quarterly Review* was voicing one of the eternal principles of English policy toward belligerents when it said, "Whatever may be the issue of the contest . . . advantages must accrue to British commerce. . . ."[36]

The English, it is true, denied having any monopolistic designs on South American commerce,[37] and Adams did feel that the ambiguous position of the English government would alienate the southerners themselves;[38] but English activities in South America did not amuse Americans. Her aid to the revolutionists was notorious. She posed as the ally of Spain, but permitted her citizens to help the South Americans without hindrance from their government.[39] So treacherous did Forsyth of Georgia believe England's policy to be that he charged her with lending money to Spain with one hand and sending arms to the revolutionists with the other.[40] Rush reported that men who were otherwise closely associated with the gov-

---

[35] *Bell's Weekly Messenger*, in the *National Intelligencer*, October 18, 1817.

[36] *The Quarterly Review*, XVII (1817), 560.

[37] Rush to J. Q. Adams, April 20, 1818. Manning, ed., *Diplomatic Correspondence*, III, 1442.

[38] J. Q. Adams, *Memoirs*, VI, 25.

[39] See reports in *Niles' Weekly Register*, IX, 34, September 16, 1815, and XIII, 181, November 15, 1817. Also Rush to J. Q. Adams, October 5, 1819. Manning, ed., *Diplomatic Correspondence*, III, 1458.

[40] Forsyth on South American independence. *Annals of Congress*, 15 Çong., 1 sess., House, March 25, 1818.

ernment were active in the support of private expeditions to aid the patriots, and the financial backing which these enterprises received indicated that powerful groups were in sympathy with their aims.⁴¹ In fact, there were many indications that England was pouring money into South America both to aid the revolution and to create a financial control which would give her command of the economic life of the continent. Rush stated that Rothschild's name was being linked to the financing of expeditions to aid the patriots,⁴² and Niles declared that a highly respectable banking firm had advanced one hundred thousand pounds to aid a venture from Ireland.⁴³ All these reports, true or false as they might be, created a firm conviction in America that England was "playing a deep game" in which the only rule was her own self-interest. She had never been a very scrupulous opponent in the commercial field, and Americans had every reason to believe that she would now employ any means in order to gain her ends.

Reports from South America told of the ways in which England was maintaining friendship with both parties to the struggle. Vessels which were the property of American shippers had been seized by royalists for the offense of trading with the patriots, while English "vessels so situated and equally in the power of the Spanish authorities, were not molested."⁴⁴ On other occasions, the royalists were reported to have opened ports under their control to English ships, while they continued to exclude those of other

---

⁴¹ Rush to J. Q. Adams, October 5, 1819. Manning, ed., *Diplomatic Correspondence,* III, 1458.

⁴² Rush to J. Q. Adams, July 21, 1819. *Ibid.,* III, 1456. The sum mentioned in connection with Rothschild's name was £500,000.

⁴³ *Niles' Weekly Register,* XVI, 191, May 8, 1819.

⁴⁴ *Ibid.,* XIV, 96, April 4, 1818.

nations.[45] Many such items emphasizing the connection between English influence and Spanish policy are to be found in the current press.

As the power of Spain in the New World declined, England's attachment to the old institutions took another form. There is not a great deal of evidence on this point, but unquestionably England supported the idea of independent monarchies in America as a basis for solving the problem. As early as 1817, one London paper proposed that a Spanish prince be sent to South America under the joint guaranty of England and the allied Powers.[46] A few years later, the American minister to Spain wrote to his chief that agents of the South American provinces were intriguing in London for the establishment of monarchies in the former colonies, and that members of the English royal family were mentioned as candidates for the new thrones.[47] This plan was too extreme to succeed, but Forsyth continued to encounter hints and rumors of the anti-republican bias of the English government. In 1822 he was assured by the Russian chargé d'affaires at Madrid that, at the beginning of the year, England had expressed the wish that the Infante Don Francisco be sent to Mexico.[48] Even after the news of the American recognition of the South American republics had reached him the American minister wrote as if the plan had not yet been abandoned. The wording of his dispatch even confirms

[45] *Niles' Weekly Register*, XVI, 286, June 19, 1819.

[46] *The Courier* [London], *ibid.*, XIII, 158, November 1, 1817.

[47] Forsyth to J. Q. Adams, June 29, 1820. Manning, ed., *Diplomatic Correspondence*, III, 1995. Russia and the German states were approached with suggestions "that of their families and that of G. B. should be selected princes for Spanish America. . . ."

[48] Forsyth to J. Q. Adams, May 20, 1822. *Ibid.*, III, 2014.

the conclusion that monarchies in the New World formed a part of the designs of England.

> . . . I have seen I think several indications lately of a strong desire on the part of England to acquire influence with this Govt. Is this with a view to the affairs of Europe or of America? As it regards America and especially Mexico, I should be sorry to see them successful in acquiring it. I know not what changes may have been made by recent events in the policy of England, but her old plan to erect Mexico into an independent Govt. with one of the Spanish Infantes at its head, is in my view, one of the worst modes of settling the affairs of that country that could well be devised, both for the happiness of Mexico and the interests of the United States. The Mexicans are said to adhere to this plan. . . .[49]

Although the plan for monarchies in America was chiefly a Continental and French conception, it is worth noticing that English policy was tarred with the same brush. For selfish reasons, England might check the extension of French or Spanish influence which would result from the establishment of such régimes under their auspices, but that was no guaranty that she might not attempt the same thing for her own benefit. That she had the naval power to give effect to her ideas had a part, no doubt, in creating the apprehensions expressed by Forsyth in his dispatches to Adams.[50]

England was also working to extend her commercial in-

[49] Forsyth to J. Q. Adams, July 18, 1822. Manning, ed., *Diplomatic Correspondence*, III, 2022.

[50] The representatives of the South American states probably did a great deal to create the impression in the United States that England had hostile designs on the New World. See account of an interview between Torres of Colombia and Adams in which the South American told the secretary that his government was "above all, jealous and fearful of Great Britain. . . . Great Britain had designs upon them which must produce a war." J. Q. Adams, *Memoirs*, V, 115.

fluence among the patriots. Open violation of her neutrality laws was countenanced for a long time. Diplomatic and press reports viewed with interest the close economic relations which were being fostered between England and the revolutionary states. English investments in land and in business enterprises in Buenos Aires provoked the comment from Niles that South American freedom was doomed.[51] Poinsett, whom Adams considered one of the ablest observers ever sent to South America,[52] reported that Buenos Aires was entirely English in its sympathies.

Their principal resources since the commencement of their revolution have been derived from the commerce of Great Britain, and the manufactures of that country have become necessary to the people. The great benefits derived from that trade will never be sacrificed to their gratitude to us, for having been the first nation to acknowledge their Independence. And they will never willingly adopt any measures, which might give umbrage to Great Britain.[53]

A year later an American agent in South America likened English policy there to that which she had pursued in India and remarked that English domination was increasing on the southern continent.[54] The new governments of South America needed money, and many of the loans made to them were floated in England.[55] England appeared to be gaining a control over the destinies of South America which would injure the commercial interests of the

---

[51] *Niles' Weekly Register*, XII, 319, July 12, 1817.

[52] J. Q. Adams, *Memoirs*, IV, 388.

[53] Poinsett to J. Q. Adams, November 4, 1818. Manning, ed., *Diplomatic Correspondence*, I, 441.

[54] Worthington to J. Q. Adams, March 7, 1819. *Ibid.*, I, 519.

[55] See reports of Forbes to J. Q. Adams, August 21, 1822, and April 30, 1823. *Ibid.*, I, 609, 620. There was mention of a loan "to the extent of four Millions of Dollars."

United States. If the former colonies should remain independent, England stood ready to dominate their economic life; if they returned to any form of Spanish rule, she could claim special privileges from the royalists, whose cause she had befriended.

The persistent refusal of the English government to recognize the revolted colonies gave weight to the charge made by many Americans that she could not be trusted. Recent research has revealed the motives which restrained Castlereagh and Canning from taking this step.[56] At the time, Americans knew less about the secrets of the foreign office than they do now, but England's reluctance to accord recognition, together with other indications of her policy, caused great distrust. Rush and Adams knew in 1818 that England had no intention of favoring recognition, even by the United States. Adams averred that she so disliked the idea that if the United States should suggest a concerted measure, "she would at once decline . . . and make it an engine to injure us with the other European powers."[57] As the years passed, England maintained her attitude of refusal until she was caught in the mesh of her own complicated policy. By 1822 the English ministry had nearly reached the limits of its ability to ride two horses at once. Gallatin wrote to Adams that, as a result of the force of events, American recognition of the southern republics was welcomed in England and that she would "be glad of a pretence to do the same thing substantially, though probably not in the same fair and decisive way."[58]

---

[56] Temperley, *The Foreign Policy of Canning*, 113.

[57] J. Q. Adams, *Memoirs*, IV, 92, May 13, 1818. Also see Rush, *Memoranda*, Second series, 14.

[58] Gallatin to J. Q. Adams, April 26, 1822. Gallatin, *Writings*, II, 240.

The European connections of the English government, however, continued to prevent it from taking action, in spite of the rising tide of public opinion in the country.[59] England had drifted away from the concert of Europe, but she had not yet presumed to defy it completely. There was still much to be gained from a position at the council table of the Great Powers. As Rush declared,

... To motives so powerful for fully acknowledging the independence of South America, her ministers have nothing to oppose but their connexions with the European Alliance, and their obligations to old Spain. . . . In the meantime, British interests are suffering, and will probably continue more or less to suffer, as long as the full recognition is delayed.[60]

No reliance whatever could be placed upon England's policy. She had broken with the Holy Alliance, but, if she still had such a vital interest in the *Continental* policy of nonrecognition that she allowed her trade to suffer, there was no assurance that she would soon embark upon a program which would benefit the New World.

If Americans had reason to doubt the sincerity of England's South American policy, they had even more cause for distrusting completely her attitude toward Florida and Cuba. The most distressing impression became current concerning English designs upon these areas; and, although England professed innocence of sinister motives, she never set the Americans at ease about her policy in the Caribbean area. Cuba and Florida are vital to the life of the United States, and it is a fundamental principle of

[59] Rush to J. Q. Adams, June 10, 1822. Manning, ed., *Diplomatic Correspondence*, III, 1467. See also *Niles' Weekly Register*, XXII, 221, June 1, 1822.

[60] Rush to J. Q. Adams, July 24, 1822. Manning, ed., *Diplomatic Correspondence*, III, 1471.

American foreign policy that their fate is of the utmost importance to the safety of the Union. Accordingly, the press and the government exhibited considerable interest in the reports which circulated freely with reference to Cuba and Florida from 1815 to 1823. Hardly had the war of 1812 ended, when it was reported that the Floridas had been ceded to England and that there was danger of an extension of English authority in the direction of New Orleans.[61] These rumors continued, and Niles regarded it as a "certainty" that the transfer had been made and that the United States might henceforth consider the Floridas as a base whence English-directed Indian raids would ravage the southern frontier.[62] The *National Intelligencer* sketched the dangers which English possession of the Floridas would hold for the political, social, and economic institutions of the South and concluded that the cession would "put it in their power to quarrel with us, upon very plausible pretenses, whenever they desire."[63]

These rumors filled the press. They also disturbed the peace of mind of American diplomats, and in 1816 interesting proof of this anxiety occurred. In December, 1815, and again the following February, Monroe directed Adams to ascertain if possible the real policy of England and to investigate reports that she was supporting Spain against the United States in the discussions about the Floridas.[64] As a result, Adams broached to Castlereagh the

---

[61] Articles in the *National Intelligencer*, March 4, 17, 1815.

[62] *Niles' Weekly Register*, IX, 214, November 25, 1815.

[63] *National Intelligencer*, February 13, 1816.

[64] The first instruction was dated December 10, 1815. Manning, ed., *Diplomatic Correspondence*, I, 17. The fact that Monroe repeated his request without waiting for an answer indicates the degree of his concern. The second instruction, February 2, 1816, *ibid.*, I, 21.

rumored cession of Florida. The explanation given to the American minister was the first of a series of equivocal statements of English policy which effectually prevented Americans from feeling sure of England. Adams quoted Castlereagh as follows:

As to that (said Lord Castlereagh with a little apparent emotion) I can set you at ease at once. There is not and never has been the slightest foundation for it whatever. It never has been mentioned. . . . No! If it is supposed that we have any little trickish policy of thrusting ourselves in there between you and Spain, we are very much misunderstood indeed. You shall find nothing little or shabby in our policy. We have no desire to add an inch of ground to our territories in any part of the world. We have as much as we want or wish to manage. There is not a spot of ground on the globe that I would annex to our territories, if it were offered to us tomorrow. . . . Do you only observe the same moderation. If we shall find you hereafter pursuing a system of encroachment upon your neighbors, what we might do *defensively* is another consideration.[65]

The qualification contained in the last two sentences and the threat which it implies were typical. England repeatedly made the most thoroughgoing disavowals of hostile designs, only to spoil their effect by provisos which left Americans with a definitely uncomfortable sensation. In an atmosphere of suspicion and apprehension, such limitations upon the completeness of English statements only heightened the prevailing uncertainty.

Despite Castlereagh's emotional assurances, rumors of English plots upon the Floridas continued. South American agents in the United States and in England constantly reminded Americans that the unseen factor in the prob-

---

[65] J. Q. Adams to Monroe, February 8, 1816. J. Q. Adams, *Writings*, V, 502.

lem of the Floridas was the determination of England to prevent the United States from occupying them.[66] The Republican press in America declared "on good authority" that England had an option on the Floridas if Spain did decide to sell them.[67] Even after the signing of the treaty of 1819, it was repeatedly stated that Spain's delay in ratifying it was caused by the fact that she no longer possessed the Floridas.[68] These reports circulated until Spain finally did act favorably on the treaty after two years' delay. Their persistence over a long period of time is proof of the suspicion with which Americans viewed English policy; the lack of any absolute denial of them by England intensified that feeling.[69]

After the signing of the treaty in which Spain ceded the Floridas, the impression quickly gained ground in the United States that England was opposing its ratification. The undoubted fact that the press in England raged at the "unparalleled rapacity" of the United States,[70] and that pamphlets were written which argued that England must oppose the cession by every means at her command,[71] gave a sinister aspect to Spain's delay in ratifying the treaty. English opposition was the cause of the reluctance

[66] *National Intelligencer*, April 4, 1816. Rush to Monroe, May 20, 1818. Rush, *Recollections*, 223.

[67] *Democratic Press* [Philadelphia], in *Niles' Weekly Register*, XIII, 181, November 15, 1817.

[68] *The Herald* [Norfolk], *ibid.*, XVII, 194, November 27, 1819.

[69] The invasion of Florida and seizure of Pensacola by Jackson in 1818 released Castlereagh from his pledge to Adams. It was valid only as long as the United States did not pursue a system of encroachment upon its neighbors.

[70] Rush, *Memoranda*, Second series, 58.

[71] See such works as Rattenbury's "Remarks on the Cession of the Floridas . . . ," *The Pamphleteer*, XV (1819), 264.

of the Spanish government to act quickly, Niles declared;[72] and the Richmond *Enquirer* emphatically stated: "Great Britain will try to defeat it [the treaty] by all the the secret machinations in her power."[73] The *National Intelligencer* was forced to admit that this might be true; and, toward the end of 1819, Niles surveyed a series of reports from Europe and concluded that there was "no doubt but that England, the declaration of her ministers in parliament to the contrary notwithstanding, has interfered to prevent the ratification of the treaty by Ferdinand. . . ."[74] Thus the leading newspapers in the United States expressed almost identical views on this important question.

Reports from the American ministers in Europe did not remove the basic distrust of English policy which was reflected in the Florida affair. Forsyth wrote from Spain that the transfer of Florida was offensive to England.[75] Gallatin, however, declared in more favorable fashion that the outcry in the English press did not entirely reflect the views of the government and that probably England would acquiesce in the transfer.[76] Rumor of English intrigue against the ratification of the treaty was also rife in diplomatic circles in London, according to Rush, and he mentioned the fact to Castlereagh on at least two occasions.[77] Each time the foreign secretary declared that England had done nothing to prevent the ratification, but at

[72] *Niles' Weekly Register,* XVI, 225, May 29, 1819, and XVI, 385, August 7, 1819.
[73] *The Enquirer* [Richmond], in the *National Intelligencer,* August 25, 1819.
[74] *Niles' Weekly Register,* XVII, 115, October 23, 1819.
[75] Forsyth to J. Q. Adams, August 22, 1819. Manning, ed., *Diplomatic Correspondence,* III, 1986.
[76] Gallatin to Forsyth, July 9, 1819. Gallatin, *Writings,* II, 109.
[77] Rush, *Memoranda,* Second series, 149, July 16, 1819.

the second interview he made a statement of the same sort as the one which he had made to Adams in 1816. In spite of the assurances which Castlereagh had given to Rush in July, the American raised the question again in August (a fact which proves that his mind was not at rest) and drew from the Englishman this explanation:

"I will say more," he continued. "As far as we have given expression to any opinion or wish to Spain, it has been the other way; *it has been that the treaty may be ratified.*"

*   *   *   *   *   *

"Let me deal candidly," he proceeded. "It can little be supposed, were it an open question, that we would not prefer that Spain should own the Floridas, to their falling into your hands. She is weak; you are strong; but the treaty has been made, and we prefer its ratification to the possibility of any serious disturbance to the pacific relations between the United States and Spain. These we are sincerely desirous to see maintained, from the propitious influence it will continue to shed upon the general repose of the world."[78]

In plain English, the foreign secretary had declared that England did not like the transfer; that she would have opposed it were it still an open question (and from this it must be inferred that she *did* oppose it while it was an open question—that is, before February 22, 1819); but that, since the treaty was now a *fait accompli*, she preferred its ratification to war. In short, she would not fight to maintain Spain in possession of the Floridas, but she had no sympathy with the interests of the United States which dictated the annexation as a strategic necessity. It was not friendship for the United States, but the fact that English interests would gain more by peace than by war, that determined England's attitude. Again there was no defi-

---

[78] Rush, *Memoranda*, Second series, 179, August 26, 1819.

nite assurance that her policy would favor the United States, and again the declaration left behind an undercurrent of uncertainty.

The cession of the Floridas to the United States and the removal of that threat to its security quite naturally focused American attention upon Cuba. Concern over its future was not a new feeling for thoughtful people in the United States, but the growing importance of the West and of the commerce of the Gulf area gave to Cuba and Florida in 1819 the same significance that the mouth of the Mississippi had had twenty-five years earlier. Just as New Orleans in the hands of a hostile Power was a menace to the economic life of the West then, so Florida and Cuba might now threaten the security of America's ocean commerce. Spain was relaxing her grip on her transatlantic possessions in 1815, and there was no indication that she could hold them indefinitely. Americans had had fears that Florida might have been ceded to England. Those fears were ended by the ratification of the Florida treaty by Spain, but similar apprehensions were now directed toward Cuba and the alleged plots of England to acquire it.

Prior to 1819, reports circulated occasionally that Spain had transferred Cuba to England in payment of claims.[79] These rumors increased, and in 1819 the *National Intelligencer* commented editorially upon one statement of this kind and declared that, while there was hope that it was not true, "such an event is not impossible."[80] The importance of the problem could not be overestimated, said the *Intelligencer*, and the United States should be prepared

[79] *Niles' Weekly Register*, XIII, 174, November 8, 1817, and XIV, 189, May 9, 1818.

[80] *National Intelligencer*, May 4, 1819.

to acquire Cuba, rather than allow England to get it. In the hands of a strong naval Power, it would be,

... from its locality, a source of continual collision, a provocative to hostilities, which would be little less provoked, by the system of colonial exclusion which Great Britain might be expected to establish in regard to that, as to her other colonies.

This statement sums up very well the reasons for American interest in Cuba. It was important strategically, but it was also a valuable customer. American ships carried the major portion of Cuban commerce and the United States sold more to Cuba than to all the other European West Indian colonies combined.[81] Therefore, Americans would suffer a heavy loss if England should extend her exclusive colonial system to the island. Once more one is reminded that Americans regarded England as the greatest commercial monopolist and that to them she stood for the "European system" in commerce as well as in politics.

The cession of the Floridas to the United States caused an immediate and violent demand in the English press for the acquisition of Cuba to check the growing dominance of the United States in the Gulf of Mexico. The hostile influence which English journals had in the United

---

[81] An indication of the dominance of the United States in the Cuban trade and of its importance is contained in the following figures for the year 1821, which are typical of the postwar period. Of the total shipping which entered Cuban ports in that year, 655 vessels were American, 385 were Spanish, 128 were English, and 72 were French. *Niles' Weekly Register*, XXII, 71, March 30, 1822. America's exports to Cuba were valued at $6,584,589 as compared with a value of $6,126,296 for the trade to all the other West Indian colonies combined. Her imports from Cuba amounted to $4,540,680, so that there was a balance in her favor of more than $2,000,000, an item of considerable importance in international payments. *Ibid.*, XXII, 75. See also J. Q. Adams, *Memoirs*, IV, 205, "The trade to the Havanna alone was now almost the only resource we had for procuring specie, and if it should be cut off it would greatly increase the embarrassments of our circulating medium."

States makes it easy to imagine the effect of this paragraph from *The Quarterly Review:*

Why does not England, *as part of the indemnity* due to her from Spain, transfer to her own sceptre the sovereignty of Cuba; seeing that the Havanna commands the passage from the gulf of Mexico? Why does she not take possession of Panama on the south, and Darien on the north, and join the Waters of the Atlantic with those of the Pacific ocean, in order to resuscitate her drooping commerce? Or is it her intention still to slumber on until she is awakened from the stupefaction of her dreams by the final fall of Spanish America, and of her own North American provinces, beneath the ever-widening power of the United States?[82]

The textbook for all English writers appeared in the form of a pamphlet by J. Freeman Rattenbury entitled, "Remarks on the Cession of the Floridas to the United States of America, and on the Necessity of Acquiring the Island of Cuba by Great Britain." In this work, which aroused considerable interest and comment in the United States,[83] Rattenbury emphasized the need for England to check the United States by blocking the ratification of the Florida treaty, or, if that were not possible, by the acquisition of Cuba. He reviewed the importance to England of the control of the Straits of Florida, and argued in blunt language that England should gain possession of Cuba at all hazards—by fair means or foul. This was no time for a passive policy, he wrote.

It is our bounden duty, it is our imperative policy to antici-

---

[82] *The Quarterly Review,* XXI (1819), 20.

[83] See an article with extracts from Rattenbury's work in the *National Advocate,* reprinted with some very pithy comment in *Niles' Weekly Register,* XVII, 353, January 22, 1820. Rattenbury was merely echoing in a new form earlier appeals to England to check the growth of the United States. See *The Colonial Policy of Great Britain,* 120.

pate the rivalship of the United States, and by erecting a power capable of contending with them, in their own hemisphere, prevent the destruction of our commerce, . . . for . . . hereafter the contest for the empire-of the sea will be between England and the North American Union, a warfare suited to the prejudices of their people, and the character of their country.

Spain will doubtless reluctantly consent to the alienation of . . . Cuba from her sovereignty, but I trust that the Ministers of Great Britain will not permit that nation to withhold from us a possession rendered necessary to the protection of our commerce, by the weakness which has induced her to cede to the demands and menaces of the United States, the important position of the Floridas. If ever there existed a necessity for departing from the ordinary courtesy and delicacy of nations—if ever self-defence justifies coercion, surely the present is the moment; and the apologists for the seizure of the Danish fleet at Copenhagen, cannot want an excuse for this equally necessary violence.[84]

This plain statement of the policy which England was urged to pursue was bitterly denounced in the American press, and the support which it received from the London newspapers did much to disquiet Americans. *The Times*, for example, declared that American possession of the Floridas was a foregone conclusion which brought with it "an invincible necessity for the acquisition of Cuba by the British crown. . . . The two transactions are necessary parts of the same whole, and must be, if possible, put out of hand together [all italics]." Niles accepted this as proof

[84] Rattenbury, "Remarks . . . ," *The Pamphleteer*, XV (1819), 278–279. Rattenbury knew whereof he spoke. His pamphlet is strangely in accord with the later secret deliberations of the English government. Compare these statements with (1) Cabinet memorandum of November 15, 1822, and (2) Memoranda on Cuba presented to Canning by Colonel Evans, April 9, 1823, both in Stapleton, ed., *Some Official Correspondence of George Canning*, I, 48, 116.

that England wanted only a pretext for the seizure of Cuba. "She will obtain it—if she can. She regards the United States as her great rival in manufactures and commerce, and will do all [that] in her lies to hinder our progress to the power she fears."[85] This violent outburst of English sentiment, which was also the subject of speeches in Parliament and of reports from American diplomats abroad, confirmed the earlier suspicions of Americans that English policy in the areas which bordered upon the United States was not friendly.[86] The *National Intelligencer* stated that it would not be surprising to find that England had demanded Cuba if the Florida treaty should be ratified,[87] and both Niles and Ritchie counseled the United States not to seize the Floridas but to pursue a peaceful policy in order to deprive England of any pretext for carrying out her alleged Cuban policy.[88]

Adams and Rush alike expressed distrust of the aims of England at this time, and Hyde de Neuville probably added to their apprehensions by his perennial fears of English influence. In any event, the affair served to continue in force the idea of English opposition to the United States.[89] Three years before, Castlereagh had made an omi-

---

[85] *The Times* [London] in *Niles' Weekly Register*, XVII, 305–306, January 8, 1820. The editorial accompanying this report makes the whole typical of the news which filled the pages of Niles' journal in 1819 and 1820.

[86] See report of statements in Parliament in *Niles' Weekly Register*, XVI, 381, July 31, 1819; and a report from the American chargé d'affaires at Brussels, A. H. Everett, to J. Q. Adams, August 8, 1819. Manning, ed., *Diplomatic Correspondence*, III, 1711.

[87] Leading editorial in the *National Intelligencer*, October 23, 1819.

[88] *Niles' Weekly Register*, XVIII, 46, March 18, 1820; and a summary of editorials in *The Enquirer* of October 26, 29, December 16, 1819, and May 9, 1820, in Ambler, *Thomas Ritchie*, 71.

[89] J. Q. Adams, *Writings*, VI, 377, and *Memoirs*, IV, 367, where he writes, "Yet there has been some mysterious negotiation between Spain and Eng-

nous remark about what England might do *"defensively"* if the United States should encroach upon her neighbors, and his noncommittal attitude in 1819 did not lessen the force of his warning.[90]

The liberal revolution in Spain in 1820 and the popular enthusiasm in England for the new constitutional government seem to have quieted the clamor for a seizure of Cuba. England realized that a serious defeat for the party of the Cortes would threaten the existence of the new government. By 1822, however, the hopeless condition of the Spanish cause in South America and the financial straits in which the home government struggled reawakened American concern for the future of the remaining Spanish colonies.[91] In Congress this fear found expression in the debates upon the recognition of South America.

. . . What, sir, is more reasonable [asked one Congressman] than to suppose that Spain, finding herself about to lose all her American territories, will seek to turn to some account those that remain to her, by selling them to some purchaser who will be able to retain them? . . . Now, suppose Spain should cede Cuba to England. . . .[92]

This is a typical statement of the American view at this time. A transfer was likely, and it would be made to Eng-

---

land about Cuba, the secret of which is not unfolded." Perkins has ascertained that this negotiation concerned the slave trade. That defends England from plotting to take Cuba, but it is not clear how John Quincy Adams benefited from the results of this research.

[90] When Rush related that the cession of Cuba to England had apparently been admitted publicly by a high Spanish official, Castlereagh "replied that the Duke of San Carlos probably knew as little of it as he did." This illuminating remark meant exactly nothing. Rush, *Memoranda,* Second series, 108.

[91] Although Cuba was the colony that was most discussed, it was generally understood that Porto Rico shared its destinies.

[92] Garnett of Virginia on recognition of South America. *Annals of Congress,* 17 Cong., 1 sess., House, April 10, 1822.

land. The fact should be emphasized that, until February, 1823, England was the only nation which was regarded as a possible recipient of Cuba. Adams, indeed, expressed the view that, if the Cubans clung too closely to Spain, they incurred the danger of being transferred to England, no matter who ruled Spain. The cession might be made,

... first, by the present revolutionary government of Spain, to purchase support against the Holy Alliance; and, secondly, by Ferdinand, to purchase the aid of Great Britain to consummate a counter-revolution in his favor. ....[93]

The fear that the United States might in the near future find her old rival facing her across the Straits of Florida was increased by a variety of circumstances. First, she was almost powerless to prevent it by war. If Anglo-American rivalry should result in naval hostilities, Cuba would be seized and England would dominate the Caribbean. Diplomacy and watchfulness alone could protect the United States. Second, the suspicions which England undoubtedly felt about the aims of the United States made the problem a very delicate one.[94] Castlereagh might have been telling the truth when he declared that he did not want another foot of territory, but the fear that the United States was about to seize Cuba might easily lead England to take it as a defensive measure. Such things are not unknown in world politics. The fact that England had a large fleet cruising in the West Indies for the ostensible purpose of hunting pirates was another disturbing element in the situation. There *were* pirates around Cuba, and the island itself was their base. The United States, as well as England, was engaged in suppressing them; but

[93] J. Q. Adams, *Memoirs*, VI, 72.
[94] *Ibid.*, VI, 71, 105.

the fact remained that England could seize Cuba on a moment's notice and be firmly entrenched in Havana before the government of the United States knew what had happened. The movements of the English fleet in the West Indies kept the Americans in a constant state of excitement and suspense which increased the atmosphere of suspicion that surrounded the Cuban problem.[95]

Finally, the reports which Forsyth sent from Spain in the winter of 1822–1823 were not reassuring. English influence there and the ambitions which she was known to harbor made the situation very critical.

. . . The Squadron sent to Havana by the British [he wrote], the pressure upon Spain at this moment when she has so much reason to dread the determination of the European Sovereigns, by Great Britain, all combine to shew the necessity of watchfulness on our part as to the designs of that Power and the probability of their accomplishment afforded by the present condition and attitude of this Country.[96]

Besides her European aims, England desired to obtain Cuba, the Isthmus of Darien, and Montevideo, declared Forsyth. He would not "affirm positively" that England had a "fixed determination" to obtain those objects, but his impressions were strong that she had. There was evidence that Spain realized her difficult position and that she feared the outcome. Forsyth concluded one of his dispatches with these words: "What will be the result will depend much upon the Congress of Verona. If Spain is pressed by an armed force or by the Continued use of the means of corruption, she must make great sacrifices. . . ."

[95] See *Niles' Weekly Register*, XXIII, 164, November 16, 1822, and the *National Intelligencer*, February 13, April 3, 1823.

[96] Forsyth to J. Q. Adams, November 20, 1822. Manning, ed., *Diplomatic Correspondence*, III, 2025.

The later dispatches of the American minister and the reports which found their way into the press only served to confirm this prediction and to reinforce the idea that the affairs of Cuba were about to reach a crisis.[97]

It will be both interesting and worth while to review the steps which the American government took to safeguard its position and to avoid being caught unawares by a sudden development of English policy. The United States maintained a considerable naval force in the West Indies to hunt pirates and to protect American commerce.[98] It did no harm to remind the English that the American navy also had an interest in maintaining order in that area. Toward the close of 1822, Congress took a significant step. A resolution was introduced, debated, and passed which called upon the secretary of the navy to furnish information about the condition of Key West. It was argued at length that that outpost should be fortified at once as a precautionary measure. Among the supporters of the project was Trimble of Ohio, a man who was unafraid of the Powers of the Continent. His argument was direct and typical.

. . . Let any one look at this point, in its relation to Florida and to Cuba, and he would be satisfied that the United States ought to expend two millions of dollars, at least, if necessary, in fortifying it, not to guard against pirates, but for the more important purpose of defending the commerce of the United States against the island of Cuba, if that island should ever fall into the hands of a Power hostile to the United States. . . .[99]

[97] Forsyth to J. Q. Adams, January 10, 1823. Manning, ed., *Diplomatic Correspondence*, III, 2030. *Niles' Weekly Register*, XXIII, 305, January 18, 1823.

[98] J. Q. Adams, *Memoirs*, VI, 10.

[99] *Annals of Congress*, 17 Cong., 2 sess., House, December 20, 1822.

The real necessity for fortifying this post was to lessen the danger of English occupation of Cuba.

The reply of Secretary Thompson is full of interest.[100] He reported that an investigation of Key West as a possible naval station had *already* been made and that possession of the island had been taken. In other words, the government had not waited for the House resolution but had acted on its own initiative. Thompson added that the post could be fortified and that it should be made formidable as soon as possible. In the meantime, a guard of marines was to be sent to the post to establish a naval depot. He concluded his report as follows:

... These are some of the obvious benefits of this position in time of peace; but its advantages in time of war with any European Power having West India possessions, are still more important, both as it respects the protection of our own commerce, and the annoyance of our enemy. An enemy, with a superior naval force, occupying this position, could completely intercept the whole trade between those parts of our country lying north and east of it and those to the west, and seal up all our ports within the Gulf of Mexico.

These measures, which were clearly aimed against the possible aggressions of England, coincided with a mild warning to the Spanish government. The United States could not take more definite steps on the basis of mere suspicions, but it would be diplomatically correct for her minister to Spain to make cautious inquiries and "to communicate to the Spanish government in a manner adapted to the delicacy of the case the sentiments of this Government, which are favorable to the continuance of Cuba in

---

[100] S. Thompson to the House, December 29, 1822. *American State Papers: Naval Affairs*, I, 871.

its connection with Spain."[101] The American minister was instructed accordingly, and there was then nothing further for the United States to do but to await developments and to observe the situation with extreme care.

Rumors continued, however, and reports of the possibilities of revolution in the island disturbed American statesmen. Charles Ingersoll concluded, after a talk with Poinsett,[102] that, in such a circumstance, the United States would probably be forced to take the island. "The Western States are all anxiety for it [he wrote]—to them Cuba in British hands would be intolerable."[103] The prevalence of this fear of *English* possession of Cuba is undeniable.

It was at this critical time that Stratford Canning made his disavowal of any sinister English designs on Cuba.[104] Adams was inclined to accept the English minister's statement and to suspect the French for the first time. But other men of consequence responded to the disavowal with a threat, so deep was their suspicion of England. Ingersoll wrote: "Clay says that Canning told him . . . that England has no views on Cuba. Clay told him distinctly that we would fight for it should they attempt the possession, which sentiment I find more general than I supposed." He then added the interesting sentence: "Mr. Baylies of Massachusetts a federalist is for it as he said this afternoon."[105] If even Federalists were ready to fight Eng-

---

[101] J. Q. Adams to Forsyth, December 17, 1822. Moore, ed., *Digest of International Law*, VI, 379.

[102] Poinsett had recently returned from a trip of investigation to Mexico and Cuba.

[103] Ingersoll's diary, February 7, 1823. Meigs, *Life of Charles Jared Ingersoll*, 113.

[104] See above, p. 105.

[105] Ingersoll's diary, February 17, 1823. Meigs, *Life of Charles Jared Ingersoll*, 129.

land, the conviction that vital American interests were threatened must have been very general and very real. *The Enquirer* went further and stated that, though England might not want the island herself, "if Great Britain did intend temporarily to occupy Cuba to keep France from getting it and to save it to Spain, then we should occupy it temporarily to keep it from falling to Great Britain permanently."[106] Again the uncertain factor was what England might do *defensively*—even if it could be assumed that she would not pursue an active policy on her own account.

Less than a month after Canning's statement to Adams, its good effect seems to have disappeared completely, for the secretary reported cabinet conferences in March which centered entirely about the subject of Cuba and England. The fear of French aggression was absent. The whole problem of Cuba was discussed pro and con, and Adams summarized well the currents of thought involved when he wrote: "Cabinet meeting. . . . Consistency with what we have done to be observed. Fears of what England may do. Prospects of Spain. Danger of treachery."[107] In this atmosphere, with war about to break out between France and Spain, and with the press reporting the most alarming developments, the government of the United States sought to formulate a policy which would adequately meet all contingencies.[108]

---

[106] *The Enquirer* [Richmond], February 13, 1823. Editorial quoted in Ambler, *Thomas Ritchie*, 83.

[107] J. Q. Adams, *Memoirs*, VI, 137.

[108] See *Niles' Weekly Register*, XXIV, 72, April 5, 1823, and XXIV, 113, April 26, 1823. In the latter issue it was reported: "The British minister has stated that orders had been given *to the British troops to take possession of Cuba, by force, if pacific means would not do, and that Spain had consented to the arrangement,* for the ostensible purpose of suppressing

Consistency characterized the steps which the government decided to take. A secret agent was sent to Cuba to observe conditions, to keep the government informed of developments there, and to remind the Cubans that "the first wish of the Government was for the continuance of Cuba in its political connection with Spain, and that it would be altogether averse to the transfer of the island to any other power."[109] Having warned the Cubans, Adams wrote a masterly letter of instructions to Hugh Nelson, the new American minister to Spain, in which he analyzed the situation in the clearest terms. The admonition which had been given to Spain in December was mild; this remonstrance minced no words.[110]

The secretary of state reviewed the relations of the United States and Europe, pointed out America's interest in all naval wars, and emphasized her particular concern with the existing war between France and Spain. The fate of Cuba and Porto Rico was involved in its outcome, he wrote; and, while the future of the islands would not normally disturb the United States, their importance to her welfare made it necessary to consider the problem now. Adams did not let his republicanism obscure his view of the realities of the European scene. He recognized the fact that France would probably restore the old régime in Spain and he realistically directed Nelson's attention to the crux of the matter—Cuba. He did not know whether France and her allies contemplated the subjugation of

piracy." This was substantially true and was publicly confirmed by George Canning in Parliament, April 14, 1823. See below, p. 180.

[109] J. Q. Adams to Randall, April 29, 1823. Moore, ed., *Digest of International Law*, VI, 385.

[110] The text from which the following summary and extracts are taken is dated April 28, 1823. J. Q. Adams, *Writings*, VII, 369.

the colonies, but the condition of Cuba was of immediate concern. A French attack on the island in the course of a war with Spain was unlikely because of the "probable incompetency of the French maritime force to effect the conquest, and the probability that its accomplishment would be resisted by Great Britain." Revolution in Cuba was more imminent, but Cuba could not stand alone.

... They must rely [continued Adams] for the support of protection upon some force from without; and as, in the event of the overthrow of the Spanish constitution, that support can no longer be expected from Spain, their only alternative of dependence must be upon Great Britain, or upon the United States.

Omission of France as a possible protector is significant.

The position of England, moreover, made her interference in the affairs of the island probable. The motives for such a step were powerful, guaranties against it were lacking, and the recent actions of the English government were not reassuring. It is necessary to quote this passage from the instructions to Nelson at length, for the wording employed is important.

The motives of Great Britain for desiring the possession of Cuba are so obvious, especially since the independence of Mexico, and the annexation of the Floridas to our Union; the internal condition of the island since the recent Spanish revolution, and the possibility of its continued dependence upon Spain, have been so precarious; the want of protection there; the power of affording it possessed by Great Britain, and the necessities of Spain to secure, by some equivalent, the support of Great Britain for herself; have formed a remarkable concurrence of predispositions to the transfer of Cuba; and during the last two years rumors have been multiplied, that it was already consummated. We have been confidentially told by indirect communication from the French government, that more than two years since Great Britain was negotiating with Spain for the cession of Cuba; and so eager in the pursuit as to have offered Gibraltar, and more, for it in exchange. There is reason to believe that, in this respect, the French government was misinformed; but neither is entire reliance to be placed on the declaration lately made by the present British Secretary for Foreign Affairs to the French government, and which, with precautions indicating distrust, has been also confidentially communicated to us; namely, that Great Britain would hold it disgraceful to avail herself of the distressed situation of Spain, to obtain possession of any portion of her American colonies. The object of this declaration, and of the communication of it here, undoubtedly was to induce the belief that Great Britain entertained no purpose of obtaining the possession of Cuba: but these assurances were given with reference to a state of peace, then still existing, and which it was the intention and the hope of Great Britain to preserve. The condition of all the parties to them has since changed; and however indisposed the British government might be, ungenerously to avail themselves of the distress of Spain, to extort from her any remnant of her former possessions, they did not forbear to take advantage of it, by orders of reprisals [in the West Indies]. . . .

The war between France and Spain changes so totally the circumstances under which the declaration above-mentioned of Mr. Canning was made, that it may, at its very outset, produce events, under which the possession of Cuba may be obtained by Great Britain without even raising a reproach of intended deception against the British government for making it . . . and in the event either of a threatened attack upon the island by France, or of attempts on the part of the islanders to assume their independence, a resort to the temporary occupation of the Havana by British forces may be among the probable expedients, through which it may be obtained, by concert between Britain and Spain herself. It is not necessary to point out the numerous contingencies by which the transition from a temporary and fiduciary occupation to a permanent and proprietary possession may be effected.

This summary of England's position in the spring of 1823 is very important to any understanding of the American attitude toward English policy. Even with the knowledge that France was making war on Spain, the American government feared *English* interference in the New World and hardly entertained the possibility of Continental action. Even the assurances received from England were suspected, for they were not so unqualified that they remained in force after war had broken out in Europe.

As a result of this view of affairs, the United States was resolved, concluded the secretary of state, to warn Spain against transfer of the island to England. The diplomatic form of the warning does not detract from its bluntness.

You will not conceal from the Spanish government the repugnance of the United States to the transfer of the island of Cuba by Spain to any other power. The deep interest which would to them be involved in the event gives them the right of objecting against it; and as the people of the island itself are known to be averse to it, the right of Spain herself to make the cession, at least upon the principles on which the present Spanish constitution is founded, is more than questionable. . . . In casual conversation, and speaking as from your own impressions, you may suggest the hope, that if any question of transferring the island to any other power is, or shall be in agitation, it will not be withheld from your knowledge, or from ours; that the condition of Cuba cannot be changed without affecting in an eminent degree the welfare of this Union, and consequently the good understanding between us and Spain; that we should consider an attempt to transfer the island, against the will of its inhabitants, as subversive of their rights, no less than of our interests; and that, as it would give them the perfect right of resisting such transfer, by declaring their own independence, so if they should, under those circumstances, resort to that measure, the United States will be fully justified in supporting them to carry it into effect.

The logical culmination of the line of action which the United States had followed thus far had been reached. The policy of watchfulness and informal diplomatic representation could be carried no farther, for almost at this very time Gallatin made a similar declaration to Chateaubriand and received a clear reply which confirmed the American impressions of the French position. So far as the Continent was concerned, the United States could do no more. England remained the one state upon which reliance could not be placed.

Events which became known in America shortly after this dispatch to Nelson was written made the situation even more clear—and more ominous. About the first of May, Adams received a dispatch from the American chargé d'affaires at Madrid which revealed that, while there appeared to be no immediate danger of English action, most of the apprehensions of the American government were justified.[111] Appleton believed that the English had ceased their intrigues for the moment, but Spanish officials had told him that an English request for permission to land on the island of Cuba in the pursuit of pirates had been refused.[112] This information naturally caused no relief at Washington; nor was the Spaniard's concluding statement more soothing: "Mr. San Miguel acquiesced in

---

[111] Appleton to J. Q. Adams, March 20, 1823. Manning, ed., *Diplomatic Correspondence*, III, 2037.

[112] "Pirate hunting" in the West Indies at this time is analagous to the more recent English pastime of "chasing the wild tribes" on the northwest frontier of India.

my observations [about Cuba, concluded Appleton], and said that he felt no concern about the Island of Cuba. That were it threatened, he was sure it would be succour'd by the United States." Small comfort was to be derived from knowing that America was expected to defend Spanish possession of Cuba by war if England's actions should threaten the *status quo!*

Declarations made in Parliament by George Canning in April removed any lingering remnants of the American belief that earlier English assurances still had any force. First, Canning admitted on April 14 that orders had been

... given to the commander [of the West Indian squadron], in the event of the owners of pirate vessels continuing to find refuge on the shores of Cuba, that, after first communicating with the Spanish governor of the island, and asking his assistance—if assistance he could give—then, conjointly, *or, upon his refusal, separately* [italics mine], to effect a landing in Cuba, to root out the nest of marauders. . . .[113]

No invasion of Cuba took place, as the Spanish authorities did aid the English to capture the pirates; but this public statement by Canning not only confirmed some of the wildest rumors in the American press and thereby validated all reports which were not proved to be false, but it also showed plainly that England was ready to defend her interests by any means. She had threatened to fight the French if they intervened and she had declared her readiness to intervene on her own account if necessary. Second, on April 16, Canning was asked directly in the House of Commons whether or not England would occupy Cuba. If anything were needed to complete the picture of English policy which so alarmed Americans, it

---

[113] G. Canning, *Speeches,* V, 11.

was the minister's reply, that "considering the emergencies arising out of the state of war [in Europe] it was impossible to give a direct answer on this point."[114] When a naval Power of the rank of England in 1823 decides to consult her interests without reference to the feelings of other Powers, a very dangerous situation has been created.

The conclusion is inescapable that, in the years from 1815 to 1823, Americans gained the impression that England was as hostile to their interests as ever. She had not favored the cession of the Floridas, and there was considerable evidence that she had acquiesced in the ratification of the treaty only because she did not want to fight. She had pursued a suspicious course toward Cuba which seemed to continue her persistent attempts to block the expansion of the United States. Her declarations had been uniformly ambiguous and incomplete, and by June, 1823, every one she had ever made had lost its value as an assurance upon which the United States could rely. England would consult her interests. That was all that was definitely known about her future conduct.

These developments were set against a background of commercial rivalry, political hostility, and virulent social antagonism which was not duplicated in America's relations with any other state. To Americans, England stood for imperialism, aristocratic rule, commercial exclusion, and the denial of the rights of neutrals. Her "system" was practically as incompatible with theirs as that of the most reactionary Power in Europe, and the direction which her policy had taken more than offset the fact that she was a constitutional state. Old-régime monarchies that they

---

[114] The report of this declaration was printed in *Niles' Weekly Register* and in the *National Intelligencer* on the same day, May 24, 1823.

were, France and Russia had given the United States an impression of their intentions which was almost the exact opposite of the one which England had made so definite. It is with these concepts in mind that the events of the autumn of 1823 must be analyzed; but first let us consider those personal factors which had a great part in shaping the diplomacy of the United States.

CHAPTER VII

American Statesmen and World Politics

FOREIGN POLICY is determined, in the United States, by the national attitude toward foreign affairs modified by the experience, the knowledge, and the prejudices of the leaders of the country. It is appropriate, therefore, to examine the opinions of those individuals who exercised a direct influence on the formulation of American foreign policy. To some extent, this has been done in previous chapters, but, because the Monroe Doctrine was a personal, executive declaration rather than the result of popular, congressional action, it will round out this study to emphasize certain of its personal features. To a greater or to a lesser degree, these men reflected the popular attitude toward world conditions which has just been analyzed in detail. All were members of the administration or were very close to its councils, and there can be little doubt that the direction of American foreign policy in the fall of 1823 was their work.

Henry Clay revealed his conception of the European situation in 1818 in the debates on South America. Though he did not fear the interference of the Continental Powers, he did realize the key position which England held in world affairs. Her interest, he observed, would ensure the freedom of South America. But the former "war-hawk" was by no means a believer in the friendship of England.^c He urged the emancipation of South America as a means of opening new channels of trade which would relieve the

United States from the need for trading with English possessions in which exclusion was the rule.

> . . . The time will however come [he said], must come, when this country will not submit to a commerce with the British colonies, upon the terms which England alone prescribes. And, I repeat, when it arrives, Spanish America will afford us an ample substitute. . . .[1]

As a realistic statesman, he prayed for the separation of Mexico from Cuba, which, in the hands of one Power, constituted a serious threat to the safety of the United States. Later, when there seemed to be danger of English possession of Cuba, he made the blunt threat to Stratford Canning which has been mentioned above.

Clay rather consistently asserted his belief that America had nothing to fear from Europe. In 1820, after quoting statements by De Pradt on the internal condition of Europe, he reaffirmed this view.[2] He had not advocated a separate course of policy for the United States from fear of any Power or group of Powers, he declared in a speech at Lexington, but because he desired his country to be self-reliant and independent; "*his* desire had been to pursue a course exclusively American, uninfluenced by the policy of my lord Castlereagh, count Nesselrode, or any other of the great men of Europe. . . ."[3]

Clay's only lapse from this assurance of American immunity from European designs occurred in 1821. As was also true of many other Americans, the apparent power which Austria displayed in Naples shook his calm. Perhaps, he told one Kentucky audience, the United States will be exempt no longer from antirepublican crusades.

[1] Clay, *Works*, VI, 148.   [2] *Ibid.*, VI, 238.
[3] *Niles' Weekly Register*, XVIII, 327, July 1, 1820.

The "giddiness and intoxication of power" might cause the allies to take rash steps which only a republican coalition in the western hemisphere could check.'These doubts soon passed, however, as additional information from Europe revealed the precarious state of affairs on the Continent. Letters from LaFayette, of which a few are included in Clay's *Works,* had a part no doubt in restoring his confidence. The picture of intrigue and conflicting forces which LaFayette painted must have removed Clay's fears of the Continental Powers and revived his old suspicions of England.' By 1823 Clay had completely regained his composure. Whereas he had viewed the Austrian invasion of Italy with alarm, he had nothing but condemnation for the French invasion of Spain. He foresaw its success, but

... Whatever may be the issue [he declared at a public banquet in Philadelphia], we shall, at least, have the consolation of cherishing our own principles. . . . And, in all the changes of human affairs, let us cling, with a closer and fonder embrace, to our own excellent governments, and be thankful to the kindness of Providence, for having removed us far from the power and influence of a confederacy of kings, united to fasten forever the chains of the people. . . .'

Despite the quality of political trickery which made Adams distrust Clay, one may notice from even this brief sketch certain typically American aspects of his thought which were to be reflected in the foreign policy of the United States. His nationalism was clear. Self-conscious, independent, and aggressive, it had a distinct anti-English cast. Realism made it inevitable that Clay should perceive

---

' *Niles' Weekly Register,* XX, 301, July 7, 1821.

' See a letter from LaFayette to Clay, November 5, 1822. Clay, *Works,* IV, 67. LaFayette's influence in forming opinions concerning Europe among cultivated classes in America was considerable.

' *Niles' Weekly Register,* XXIV, 95, April 12, 1823.

the truth that, as far as the United States was concerned, England was the strong Power, France and Russia the weak ones. Like the general public and every other American leader, Clay's attention was directed to Cuba and the Caribbean as the area of most imminent danger to the safety of the United States.

Another westerner and nationalist who did much to influence the administration was Andrew Jackson. His close political relations with Calhoun, which reached their climax in 1823–1824, and his habit of corresponding with "Jim Monroe," brought Jackson's ideas to the immediate attention of the cabinet. From the time when he took command of the American forces in the Southwest, Jackson hammered away at the idea that fortifications were necessary for the safety of the United States. Florida and the lands near it were worthless, but they should be made strong lest they should "fall into the hands of an Enemy possessing a superiority on the Ocean."[7] In characteristic style, he argued with the chief executive for the defense measures which he thought necessary.

. . . *Then we will have peace,* for then we will be prepared for war. Every man with a gun in his hand, all urope combined, cannot hurt us, and all the world will be anxious to be upon friendly terms with us, because all the world will see, we wish peace with all, but are prepared for defence against all those who would wantonly infringe our national rights.[8]

This typical military view colored Jackson's outlook toward Europe. Economy measures in Congress, which threatened to curtail army funds, drew his sharpest criticisms. In its *"mania* for retrenchment," he told Monroe,

---

[7] Jackson to Monroe, March 4, 1817. Jackson, *Correspondence,* II, 278.
[8] Jackson to Monroe, March 18, 1817. *Ibid.,* II, 283.

Congress had "lost sight of the safety of our country at home, and its character abroad." Such action "at once invites invasion. . . ."[9] This dread of military weakness caused Jackson to entertain undue fears when he regarded the armed strength of Europe.

Jackson further influenced Monroe's administration by giving advice to the President upon the general aspects of foreign policy. "The General" did not pretend to have mastered the finer points of diplomacy, but he was sure that one method alone would bring success. In 1818 he laid down the fundamental principle that

. . . it is by bold strokes of policy accompanied with Justice towards other nations, that shews the world that altho we love peace, we will protect our citizens, and punish duplicity and perfidy, whenever attempted to be practised upon us by foreign governments, which draws forth the admiration of the world, and not a temporising policy, the latter allways leads to war, the former to admiration and respect.[10]

This was the tone which the government should adopt toward Europe in order to maintain its dignity and self-respect. Americans must either be free men or slaves, Jackson argued, on the score that vacillation is a greater disgrace than bondage.[11]

Only if a bold front were presented to Europe, would there be nothing to fear from the Holy Alliance; for "the moment it is discovered, that we hesitate to do ourselves Justice . . . , it will be construed, that our forbearance originates from a fear of the combined powers. . . ."[12] So Jackson argued, almost pleaded, with Monroe for a clear

[9] Jackson to Monroe, February 11, 1821. Jackson, *Correspondence*, III, 38.
[10] Jackson to Monroe, August 10, 1818. *Ibid.*, II, 387.
[11] Jackson to Livingston, January 7, 1820. *Ibid.*, III, 1.
[12] Jackson to Monroe, January 15, 1820. *Ibid.*, III, 7.

foreign policy. His military mind led him to feel uneasy about the future and to counsel action as the best means of averting catastrophe. In this way he joined forces with Monroe's secretary of state. While Adams did not share Jackson's apprehensions concerning the prospects of the United States, he agreed with Jackson's idea of the course which American diplomacy should take. Thus Jackson's influence played a great part in shaping foreign policy. His letters to Monroe supported Adams's arguments for a vigorous handling of problems and must have done much to convince Monroe of the soundness of his secretary's opinions on international affairs.

It is not surprising that in 1823 Jackson was quite alarmed at the ostensible power of the Holy Alliance. Less informed than Adams and Clay, less experienced in European affairs than the other members of the administration (if Calhoun be excepted), and having the weaknesses as well as the strength of a military man, Jackson reached the conclusion that French success in Spain would be followed by measures against the United States as the birthplace of civil liberty. Indeed, the whole western world would become the object of attack by the combined despots of Europe.[13] It is of interest to note that, though his estimate of conditions differed from those of the others, he arrived at the same conclusion. England must be watched, for her king and nobility were in sympathy with the autocrats and would support them as long as possible, and Cuba was the point of immediate danger. Though all the western hemisphere was threatened, according to Jackson, Cuba was the one place which "should not be per-

---

[13] His views are outlined in a letter to Calhoun, August, 1823 [*sic*]. Jackson, *Correspondence*, III, 202.

mitted to fall into the hands of any European power." It is ✓ curious how all Americans who considered the situation returned to Cuba and the power of England as the keys to the future. Directly or indirectly, and regardless of differing interpretations, these elements are mentioned. Why, if France restored absolutism in Spain and attempted to restore Spanish rule in the revolted colonies, *Cuba* should be endangered is not clear. What Jackson's interpretation does prove is that fear of England and consequent concern over the fate of Cuba were the currents of thought which were ever-present in his mind, as they were in the minds of so many of his countrymen. There is no doubt that Jackson feared the Holy Alliance in 1823, but that fear was based as much on the conviction that England would aid the Continental Powers as it was on French success in Spain.[14] "I have no confidence in England," he wrote soon after the Monroe Doctrine was pronounced, and this statement truly reveals his deepest feelings.[15]

Thus Jackson, whose influence on Monroe and Calhoun was considerable, expressed in his forthright way his ideas about America's position in the world. His nationalism was of the same type as that of Clay and Adams. He, too, counseled independent, assertive action. He constructed no systems as did Clay, and his dispatches did not possess Adams's clarity of statement, but he was no less the advocate of an *American* policy which would be unhampered by subservience to Europe. He instinctively realized that English sea power was a danger to the United

[14] Jackson to Major Lewis, December 7, 1823. New York Public Library, *Bulletin*, IV (1900), 193.

[15] Jackson to Captain J. Donelson, February 9, 1824. Jackson, *Correspondence*, III, 226.

States, but he did not evaluate the world situation so accurately as did Clay and Adams. His military background and training made him unusually fearful of the Holy Alliance. Since fear is the basis of all military thought in time of peace, Jackson's apprehensions are understandable.

The opinions of Thomas Jefferson are inevitably discussed in any work on the Monroe Doctrine because Monroe consulted him on the subject of a joint declaration with England. Few writers, however, do more than consider Jefferson's reply to Monroe's query, in spite of the difficulty of interpreting a man's opinions correctly on the basis of one or two letters.

Jefferson was one of the first Americans to grasp the fact that peace in Europe in 1815 removed the protection which the United States had long enjoyed. "We were safe ourselves from Bonaparte; because he had not the British fleets at his command [wrote Jefferson]—we were safe from the British fleets; because they had Bonaparte at their back. But . . . [now] we have uncommon reason to look to our own affairs."[16] No longer could the United States play one party off against the other and benefit as a result. The obvious policy for her to follow was one which would eliminate all possible conflict. In many letters now well known, he urged the desirability of excluding European and, particularly, English influence from the western hemisphere and of maintaining a restrained attitude toward Europe.[17] America's own interests and the problems closely concerning her would require all her

----

[16] Jefferson to Logan, October 15, 1815. *Niles' Weekly Register*, X, 189, May 18, 1816.

[17] One of the classic expressions of this view is in Jefferson's letter to Short, August 4, 1820. Jefferson, *Writings* (Mem. ed.), XV, 254.

energies. Jefferson realized the importance of Cuba to the Union and the danger which would result from its becoming politically or economically dependent on France or England. Expansionist that he was, he believed that the borderlands, Texas, Florida, and Cuba, were destined to become a part of the United States, and he urged upon Monroe a firm policy toward Spain as a means of gaining Texas. Firmness, but not war, would isolate Spain, would gain for America the support of France and Russia, and would eventually reward her with three of the richest provinces in the world.[18]

Jefferson strongly urged the merits of such a policy, for he was convinced that the United States would be left to its own devices if it avoided conflicts and unpleasant controversies. He regarded Europe as "covering at present [1820] a smothered fire, which may shortly burst forth and produce general conflagration."[19] The chief danger of war arose from the distressed internal condition of England, and moderation in conducting relations with Europe would avert even that peril. The successes of Austria in Italy and the prospect of a French invasion of Spain impressed him as being the prelude to general war. In March, 1823, he prophesied events in a way that revealed a sound grasp of the condition of Europe, though he erred in matters of detail.[20] In June he made some very interesting observations to Monroe which cannot have failed to influence the President. He condemned the principles

---

[18] Jefferson to Monroe, May 14, 1820. Jefferson, *Works* (P. L. Ford, ed.), XII, 160.

[19] Jefferson to De Tracy, December 26, 1820. *Ibid.*, XII, 183.

[20] Jefferson to Short, March 28, 1823. *Ibid.*, XII, 281. England, he wrote, "joins us . . . in a guarantee of the independence of Cuba, with the consent of Spain. . . ."

on which France had presumed to act and suggested that the United States owed itself "a bold and open declaration of . . . sympathies with the one party [Spain] and . . . detestation of the conduct of the other [France]."[21] He repeated his belief that European principles and those of America were mutually exclusive. "With Europe [he wrote] we have few occasions of collision, and these, with a little prudence and forbearance, may be generally accommodated. . . . And the foothold which the nations of Europe had in either America, is slipping from under them, so that we shall soon be rid of their neighborhood." In view of the fact that these lines were penned *after* France had invaded Spain, the absence of any fear of the Continental Powers is significant.

What was the one danger which Jefferson saw in prospect? It was English possession of Cuba. This "great calamity" should be avoided at all hazards, and he suggested a joint guaranty by England and the United States as a solution. If proof were needed that Jefferson regarded England as the only Power which threatened to take Cuba, it is contained in a second letter to Monroe written a few days after the one just discussed. A visit from a resident of the island had convinced him, he told the President, that the people of Cuba were averse to English rule. His previous suggestion had been based on the assumption that the Cubans would welcome English occupation. If they would oppose it, England would encounter such difficulties that the plan would be impossible to execute. Hence, Jefferson concluded, his proposal for a joint guaranty of the island should be withdrawn. An actual danger did

---

[21] Jefferson to Monroe, June 11, 1823. Jefferson, *Works* (P. L. Ford, ed.), XII, 292.

not exist.[22] Had Jefferson feared French action he would not have written this letter. It was England whom he suspected and feared, and, in his first letter to Monroe, he warned the President of her treachery. He believed none of her declarations and had no faith in her promises.

That England is playing false with Spain cannot be doubted. Her government is looking one way and rowing another.... The coquetry she is now playing off between her people and her allies is perfectly understood by the latter, and accordingly gives no apprehensions to France, to whom it is all explained. The diplomatic correspondence she is now displaying, these double papers fabricated merely for exhibition, in which she makes herself talk of morals and principle, as if her qualms of conscience would not permit her to go all lengths with her Holy Allies, are all to gull her own people. It is a theatrical farce, in which the five powers are the actors, England the Tartuffe, and her people the dupes.[23]

Is it any wonder that a man who so distrusted England feared the effects of her policy?

It is true that Jefferson was removed from public life and that his opinions were not based on a complete knowledge of the facts. He admitted this, but there was one source of information in which he had confidence. LaFayette and Jefferson were regular correspondents, and their published letters reveal the type of news which LaFayette included in his epistles.[24] The tenor of his observations is so similar to that of Jefferson's own statements to Monroe and others that the connection between them cannot be doubted. The designs of England, the conflicts of inter-

---

[22] Jefferson to Monroe, June 23, 1823. Jefferson, *Works* (P. L. Ford, ed.), XII, 296 ff. He wrote specifically, "I have thought it my duty to acknowledge my error on this occasion."

[23] Jefferson to Monroe, June 11, 1823. *Ibid.*, XII, 293.

[24] Chinard, ed., *Letters of LaFayette and Jefferson*. See letters to Jefferson on pp. 391, 405, 408, and 417.

ests among the European Powers, the internal weakness of such states as France, and the prevalence of the revolutionary spirit are often discussed. Jefferson must have derived much of his calmness toward the might of the Holy Alliance from his old friend, and unquestionably his suspicions of England were kept alive in the same way. These facts are important, for Jefferson's views carried great weight with Monroe.[25] Jefferson's attitude toward Europe and England, his pleas for a separate course of action (not because he feared Europe, but because he despised Continental ways and distrusted the motives of England), and his clear analyses of foreign affairs constitute an important link in the chain of thought which led to the Monroe Doctrine.

Though he was less given to the expression of his opinions than Jefferson, James Madison had similar views. He realized the equivocal position of England in world politics and suggested to Monroe that this might be utilized to the advantage of the United States.[26] Revolutions in Europe aroused his enthusiasm and he predicted that they would be ultimately successful, since the Great Powers were no longer strong. They "are. not now [1820!] sufficiently united among themselves, are controuled by the aspiring sentiments of their people, are without money of their own, and are no longer able to draw on the foreign fund which has hitherto supplied their belligerent necessities."[27] That he recognized the value of Cuba to the

---

[25] Besides consulting Jefferson on many occasions when political advice was wanted, Monroe often acted upon his suggestions. J. Q. Adams, *Memoirs*, V, 127.

[26] Madison to Monroe, October, 1818 [*sic*]. Madison, *Letters and Other Writings*, III, 110.

[27] Madison to LaFayette, November 25, 1820. *Ibid.*, III, 189.

United States is clear from his policy as President.[28] He had warned England that transfer of Spanish territory to a European Power would be regarded as an "unjust and unfriendly" act, and some writers have dignified his statements with the title, the "Madison Doctrine."

Madison's ideas paralleled those of Jefferson and at times anticipated them. In 1822 he tried to impress upon Monroe the value of a clear and definite declaration of the principles on which American policy was based. If the United States let Europeans know exactly where she stood and did it in such a way that there would appear to be no possible course but her own, difficulties would be avoided. As long as misunderstandings could arise, she would find herself in trouble.

... I cannot but think [he wrote to the President] it might be well to take away that pretext against us, by an Exposé, brought before the public in some due form, in which our conduct would be seen in its true light. An historical view of the early sentiments expressed here in favor of our neighbours, the successive steps openly taken, manifesting our sympathy with their cause, & our anticipation of its success, more especially our declarations of neutrality towards the contending parties as engaged in a civil, not an insurrectionary, war, would shew to the world that we never concealed the principles that governed us, nor the policy which terminated in the decisive step last taken [recognition]. . . .[29]

Thus he added his voice to those of Jackson, Adams, and Jefferson in support of boldness and a self-conscious national policy.

[28] Madison to W. Pinkney, October 30, 1810. Madison, *Writings*, VIII, 117. See also secretary of state to W. Pinkney, June 13, 1810, January 22, 1811. Manning, ed., *Diplomatic Correspondence*, I, 5, 9.

[29] Madison to Monroe, May 6, 1822. Madison, *Writings*, IX, 89.

It is also significant that the papers which George Canning laid before Parliament in April, 1823, concerning England's Spanish policy evoked from Madison statements of distrust. Jefferson had placed no confidence in England's sincerity; likewise, Madison wrote that he had perused these documents and that "notwithstanding the colourings given to its [the cabinet's] policy, the documents are not very promising." He recalled the ambiguous policy which England had followed toward Naples and was then pursuing in Spain and declared that he questioned the motives behind it.[80] The more intimate knowledge which Adams and Monroe had of the situation in Europe raised the value of the documents above that set upon them by Jefferson and Madison. Nevertheless, the attitude toward England which these elder statesmen exhibited undoubtedly had its effect upon the administration and certainly explains *their* reaction to the news of Canning's overtures to the United States in the fall.

When the views of William H. Crawford are examined, the curtain is drawn aside from a new aspect of the problem. Thus far we have been dealing with men outside the administration, men who advised it upon occasion but who did not take part in the making of decisions. Crawford, Calhoun, and Adams were the dominant figures in Monroe's cabinet. Two of these were active candidates for the Presidency, and the third, Calhoun, had definite ambitions in that direction. Crawford was Adams's perennial opponent on most issues, and it is probable that only his illness prevented a bitter clash of opinion in the fall of 1823. Though Crawford believed in independent and

---

[80] Madison to Rush, July 22, 1823. Madison, *Letters and Other Writings*, III, 329.

vigorous policies,[31] and though he often pointed out the danger of English domination in the Caribbean,[32] he is included in this chapter for another reason. His letters to Gallatin reveal antagonistic forces within the American cabinet and suggest that political ambitions sometimes affected diplomacy.

The political aspirations of Calhoun and Adams, he wrote in 1822, account for certain features of American policy. He deplored the harshness which characterized the notes of the state department and declared that had Adams possessed a free hand he would have wrecked the relations of the United States with every Power on earth.[33] This absence of moderation, as Crawford termed it, was a part of a scheme to exalt Adams over his rivals. In 1823 Crawford went so far as to tell Gallatin that the reason Adams had requested him to stay in France was because the secretary wished to keep the American minister out of the country for another year or two.[34] Crawford was unduly suspicious of Adams, but it is interesting to observe his conviction that the concern over Franco-American relations which administration circles displayed, was caused not by foreign but by domestic conditions.

The secretary of the treasury also said that Calhoun had espoused the cause of the military group and was supporting measures for fortifications and improved military organization. Calhoun's "intuitions" upon these subjects had stirred up friction between the President and Congress, but the desired result had been obtained, for the "Secretary of war is now, in the estimation of the public,

---

[31] J. Q. Adams, *Memoirs,* IV, 449.   [32] *Ibid.,* VI, 112.
[33] Crawford to Gallatin, May 13, 1822. Gallatin, *Writings,* II, 241.
[34] Crawford to Gallatin, May 26, 1823. *Ibid.,* II, 268.

lord of the ascendant."[35] Unquestionably the personal ambitions of the members of the administration colored their
outlook; and, when Calhoun, Adams, and Monroe discuss
foreign policy, it is easy to detect in their arguments the
influence of their personal ambitions and beliefs.

Because he was secretary of war and the political ally of
Jackson, the opinions of Calhoun are of interest. In 1823
he voiced fears of the Holy Alliance and thereby did much
to rivet upon the American mind a one-sided interpretation of Monroe's foreign policy. His estimates of the European situation had not always corresponded to those
which he revealed at this time. When the Florida treaty
was being negotiated, he wrote to Jackson that he agreed
entirely with the view that Florida was essential to the
peace and safety of the United States. A policy of moderation was advisable, he wrote, because war with Spain
would involve England against America. The Holy Alliance did not enter into the picture.

... We ought, it is true, never to resort to timid measures to
avoid war; but it appears to me, that a certain degree of caution (not from the fear of the Holy Alliance) ought ... to
mark our policy. A war with Spain, were it to continue with
her alone ... would be nothing, but such a war ... certainly
would in a few years be an English war. ... We want time;
time to grow, to perfect our fortifications, to enlarge our navy,
to replenish our Depots, and pay our debts. ... No one, who
has examined my political course, will, I am sure, think that
these opinions are influenced by timid council. ...[36]

Such were his views in 1818. The revolutions of 1820–1821
appeared to him to usher in a new era in which right
would prevail over force and in which feudalism and di-

[35] Crawford to Gallatin, May 13, 1822. Gallatin, *Writings*, II, 241.

[36] Calhoun to Jackson, September 8, 1818. Jackson, *Correspondence*, II,
393.

vine right would have no part. The failure of the Neapolitan revolt mortified him but caused him no alarm.[37]

Even for a time in 1823, he viewed the French invasion
of Spain with equanimity. He believed that the example
of the United States would be a powerful influence on
behalf of the patriots in Spain and prayed that it would
be "worthy of the great cause."[38] As late as August 7, he
was not apprehensive for America's safety. Spain would
probably be defeated because of the "moral discourage-
ment which she experiences from all of the European powers not excepting England,"[39] but there was no hint that
he feared the alliance. On August 24, however, he showed
signs of wavering and was soon making the wild predictions about the designs and power of the Holy Alliance
that so disturbed Monroe and amused Adams. Referring
again to the "good cause," he wrote on this date: "It may
be reserved for us to give it the ultimate triumph which
awaits it."[40] What caused this change of attitude? There is
the strongest evidence that Jackson's influence produced
it. Jackson's letter to Calhoun, which has already been
discussed, was written in August. In it Jackson predicted
that, if Spain were defeated, the United States would be
attacked.[41] Calhoun was close to Jackson, and he shared

[37] Calhoun to John Ewing Calhoun, May 6, May 13, 1821. Calhoun,
Correspondence, II, 187.

[38] Calhoun to Somerville, July 4, 1823. *Ibid.*, II, 209.

[39] Calhoun to James Edward Calhoun, August 7, 1823. *Ibid.*, II, 211.

[40] Calhoun to James Edward Calhoun, August 24, 1823. *Ibid.*, II, 213.

[41] This letter is undated but was written in reply to one of Calhoun's
dated July 31, 1823. Bassett, the late editor of Jackson's *Correspondence*,
says that it was written in August, and it is a safe deduction that Calhoun
received it about the middle of the month. For a detailed discussion of
this letter, which is to be found in Jackson, *Correspondence*, III, 202, see
pp. 188–189 above.

the views of the soldier on national defense.[42] His ready adoption of Jackson's ideas is the only possible reason for his sudden change of front in *August, 1823.*

Certainly, when Calhoun declares, as he did in June, 1824, that the Holy Alliance "In power and solidity . . . exceeds all other combinations against human happiness, and freedom which were ever formed," and condemns "those politicians" who crippled the army with their petty economy, no doubt remains that his views were formed in a subjective fashion.[43] No one who considered the state of affairs in the spring of 1824 could have found a sound basis for such conclusions. His military views, his connections with Jackson, and the increasingly pro-Jackson and anti-Adams character of his political position explain his extreme attitude in the fall of 1823.

Although his fears of Europe were exaggerated, Calhoun was as inclined to emphasize the power of England as were any of his colleagues. In 1819 he advocated coöperation with England in Spanish-American affairs, lest her power be used against the United States. It was important, he said, to work *with* her rather than to pursue an independent policy.[44] In 1820 he wrote to Jackson that England could not be trusted. Her Cuban policy alarmed him, for the importance of the island to the United States made it indeed the

. . . key stone of our Union . . . and the greatest calamity ought to be endured by us, rather than it should pass into the hands of England. That she desires it, and would seize it, if a fair

---

[42] See a letter from Calhoun to Poinsett, July 3, 1821. Calhoun, *Correspondence,* II, 190.

[43] Calhoun to General Dearborn, June 8, 1824. *Ibid.,* II, 218. He called it the "Armed Alliance."

[44] J. Q. Adams, *Memoirs,* IV, 205.

oppertunity presented itself, I cannot doubt; and that, such an event would endanger our union, is to me very manifest. These are my fixed opinions. . . ."[45]

These were, indeed, fixed opinions, and Calhoun reiterated them in 1822 and in 1823. He and Jefferson were agreed in 1822 that Cuba should be made a part of the United States in order to avert two dangers: "one, that the island should fall into the hands of Great Britain; the other, that it should be revolutionized by the negroes."[46] A year later, Calhoun again wrote to Jackson, in almost the very words of his first letter, that war in Europe would probably lead England to take Cuba and that America should therefore be prepared for the worst.[47]

It is evident from these facts that Calhoun's fears of the Holy Alliance were not based entirely upon his knowledge of affairs but upon his impressions as well, and that probably his concern about the future of Cuba and of English policy combined to make his judgment erratic. Like Jackson, he exaggerated the dangers from the armies of the Holy Alliance and jumped to conclusions to which a more reasoned and less instinctive process of thought would not have led.

A word or two on the views of James Monroe will complete this brief survey. Much ink has been spilt over Monroe's ability or lack of it, and a sectional controversy, as futile as it is ridiculous, has been precipitated. The question whether Monroe or Adams was responsible for the

---

[45] Calhoun to Jackson, January 23, 1820. Jackson, *Correspondence*, III, 12.

[46] J. Q. Adams, *Memoirs*, VI, 70.

[47] He wrote: "That England looks to that Island; and will be ready to seize on it, if a favourable opportunity offers, can hardly be doubted, and that such an event would be full of danger to this union, is not less clear." Calhoun to Jackson, March 30, 1823. Jackson, *Correspondence*, III, 193.

Monroe Doctrine has no place in this study.[48] Rather let us consider Monroe as the presiding member of the cabinet, as one of an able group of men discussing the affairs of the United States and formulating her policies. Monroe was as much a nationalist and self-conscious republican as any man in America. His career as a diplomat, as secretary of war, and as secretary of state is proof of that. Similarly, the charge of indecision which is often made against him cannot stand the test which his own administration provides. Let it not be forgotten that the bold strokes of policy which Adams and his associates carried out were made on Monroe's responsibility and that blame for their failure would most certainly have attached to him.

Monroe liked a definite policy as well as did Jackson, but his temperament and his position caused him to prefer caution to rashness. He considered the possibilities of a course of action before embarking upon it; and though he often sought advice, he followed it only when convinced of its soundness. In the Florida affair, for example, he was sure that forbearance and moderation had achieved more than boldness could have done. By proceeding slowly and without violence, he wrote Jackson, the United States had gained the support of France and Russia and had avoided antagonizing England. An opposite course might have alienated the Continental Powers and provoked a war with Spain and England.[49] This is just one illustration of Mon-

---

[48] Schouler, "The Authorship of the Monroe Doctrine," in American Historical Association, *Annual Report,* 1905, I; and MacCorkle, *The Personal Genesis of the Monroe Doctrine,* present the best examples of the literature on this momentous subject. Their defense of Monroe was evoked by the articles by W. C. Ford which gave all the credit to Adams.

[49] Monroe to Jackson, December 12, 1819. Jackson, *Correspondence,* II, 447.

roe's idea of foreign policy, but it is typical of his approach to important problems.

In the years from 1815 to 1823, he exhibited no fears of the Continental Powers and agreed that England's position and the status of Cuba and Porto Rico were of more significance to the United States. He discussed with Jefferson the means of averting a crisis, suggested the possibilities of a guaranty that would have tied England's hands, and finally admitted the impracticability of such an arrangement.[50] In his statements concerning the value of the island to the United States, however, he was as alert to American interests as Adams himself.

The situation of the world in June, 1823, appeared to Monroe to be critical but not threatening to the security of the United States. In a letter to Jefferson, he declared that the Bourbons had staked everything on their campaign in Spain; that England's aristocracy favored the Continental Powers and would play into their hands as long as the English people remained quiet; and that Russia was so occupied with the Eastern Question that she took little interest in remote developments in the New World. "Such is the state of Europe [he continued], & our relation to it is pretty much the same, as it was, in the commencement of the French revolution."[51] In 1789, it should be recalled, America was in no immediate danger unless the struggle developed into a naval war involving England. In 1823, had the United States been threatened by attack from the Continental Powers, Monroe would never have concluded his letter to Jefferson thus: "Can we, in

---

[50] Monroe to Jefferson, April 14, June 30, 1823. Monroe, *Writings*, VI, 304, 311.

[51] Monroe to Jefferson, June 2, 1823. *Ibid.*, VI, 309.

any form, take a bolder attitude in regard to it [war in Europe], in favor of liberty, than we did? Can we afford greater aid to that cause, by assuming any such attitude, than we do now by the form of our example?"

Monroe's recognition of the similarity of America's positions in 1789 and in 1823 and his suggestion that, as she had then declared her support of neutral rights and her determination to remain aloof from the turmoils of Europe, so she might now affirm her belief in republican principles, are illuminating. He was not the man to irritate an antagonist needlessly. Had the United States been in danger, his experience as secretary of war would have warned him to make preparations to meet it. His diplomacy had carried his administration through the Florida problem successfully, and it had brought about the recognition of South America in such a way that no crisis resulted. Surely he would not have suggested this additional step had he not been convinced that it would provoke no outburst of hostile sentiment in Europe. Monroe was a nationalist and a republican to the core, but he was no rash dreamer; and the real security of the United States is revealed by his proposal. The possibility of English interference in the New World was another problem which the failure of Spain would bring to the fore. Open support of republican ideals might avert this altogether.

Even this brief survey of the opinions of those who had the control of American foreign policy in their hands, and from whose number John Quincy Adams has been deliberately omitted, suggests interesting generalizations. All these men were firm believers in the value to the United States of a nationalistic spirit which would foster self-assurance and independence in relations with the rest of the world. As Republicans, they all believed in the political and social separation of the New World from the Old and in its development along new, free lines of thought. They were expansionists who believed in the destiny of the United States and who sought to protect it from the crippling influence of intrigue and collision with other Powers. By instinct and by experience they had no love for England. They had devoted their lives to the task of limiting her power to injure the United States, and their achievements in the first forty years of America's existence as a nation had left them convinced that the problem was not yet solved. Finally, all but two of them had had diplomatic experience in Europe, which had given them a grasp of world affairs which balanced their judgment and made them conscious of the realities of European politics.

This last consideration points to a very interesting distinction. The men who had served in Europe all tended to esteem the Continental Powers less and to fear England more. The longer their careers in Europe and the more thorough their knowledge, the more they realized the key position which England held. But Calhoun and Jackson, whose lives had been spent in the United States, were the two members of this group who became seriously alarmed at the idea of possible Continental interference in the western hemisphere. They distrusted England as did the others, but while their associates regarded the Holy Alliance as no menace at all or as a decidedly secondary element, Jackson and Calhoun saw in the combination of autocrats a real threat to the United States, a threat fully as dangerous as that of England. This should be kept in mind if we wish to understand the reaction of the leaders of the country to the events of the fall of 1823.

The foreign policy of the United States was in the hands of men who held these points of view. They were, in truth, representatives of the masses of the American people, and their attitudes corresponded very closely to those of the nation as a whole. The picture will not be complete, however, without a detailed discussion of John Quincy Adams, a man who dominated his fellows because he so thoroughly reflected their own hopes and fears, their own ideals and aspirations.

CHAPTER VIII

John Quincy Adams, the Nationalist

JOHN QUINCY ADAMS did more to give direction, unity, and leadership to American foreign policies from 1817 to 1825 than any other person in the United States. The prominent part which he played in one of the most exciting and momentous periods in America's relations with the rest of the world and the influence which he exerted on the administration, even when decisions were made which he opposed, entitle him to careful and thorough consideration in any study which has reference to this decade. Particularly will it be necessary to pivot the discussion of the critical year 1823 on his attitudes, beliefs, and ideas. It is not primarily for these reasons, however, that the rôle of the secretary of state is emphasized. While his management of the technical side of foreign relations was admirable, he is even more significant as the man who most accurately reflected in his ideology and actions that American nationalism which was so characteristic of the whole country during these years.

Though he was a scholar, a trained diplomat, and a man who, by family tradition and social rank, was destined to leadership in the political affairs of the United States, he was as thoroughly American as anyone then alive. He shared the faults as well as the good qualities of his countrymen, and, while he probably would have denied the fact, he was unusually responsive to the state of public opinion. Whether his position was that of the statesman who leads his fellows, or that of the politician who senses the thoughts of the people and expresses them in appealing fashion, is the concern of his biographer. We are interested, rather, in the correspondence between the feelings of the nation and the conduct of its secretary of state, for the two are so closely intertwined that they are at times inseparable, and each explains and complements the other.

Specific illustrations of this relationship cannot be understood unless some thought is first given to the man himself. His background is unusually important.[1] He was an Adams, and, as was true of all the members of his clan, personal characteristics played a dominant part in his public life. He was an independent man, a man who cannot be "grouped," no matter how great an effort is made. Independence of thought and action, regardless of the consequences, is a trait which repeatedly comes to the surface in the course of his career as secretary of state. Again and again, he formed a minority of one, pleading for a course of action which seemed right to him, but which was unacceptable to his colleagues.[2] He did not give up a position, once he had taken it. That he succeeded so often in convincing his associates of the merits of his views tended to confirm him in his ways, and occasional defeat only strengthened his opinion of the shallowness and lack of perception of the men around him.

---

[1] The sources of the information here presented are the well-known facts of Adams's life and his *Memoirs* and *Writings*. Of the biographies of Adams, mention may be made of that by Clark, *John Quincy Adams: "Old Man Eloquent,"* which presents a good picture of his life, although in some respects the account is distorted.

[2] Examples are legion, but mention must be made of his defense of Jackson in the cabinet (*Memoirs*, IV, 111–116), his opposition to the pro-Greek sympathies of his colleagues (*ibid.*, VI, 198), and his whole course of action in the cabinet discussions of November, 1823 (*ibid.*, VI, 177 ff.). Of course the example *par excellence* of this quality is Adams's refusal, while President, to remove a member of his own cabinet who was working for his political downfall.

This belief is not strange, for Adams was a clear-think-
ing man who saw through problems to the realities behind
them. The superficial appearance of a situation never misled him about the truth of things. He was thorough and
accurate, whether he was preparing a report on weights
and measures or a letter of instructions to a minister
abroad; and to this keenness of mind he added a realism
of view which gave to his conclusions a baldness and a cut-
ing quality that was often misunderstood by his more
emotional colleagues. Adams looked at the world around
him with a sense for the true nature of the forces with
which he had to deal. At a time when many Americans
had a tendency to rashness of judgment and looseness of
thought, Adams did not share these faults; and one impartial observer who knew him well could write, "I know
that he has dared to declare himself very strongly on many
occasions against indiscreet and purely speculative ideas."[3]
As a result of this trait, Adams's opinions carried unusual
weight at the time and have been singularly unaltered by
the passing years, whereas in the light of subsequent history many of the conclusions of his contemporaries appear to border on the ridiculous.[4]

Combined with his independence and level-headed
thinking was a self-confidence and assurance that was both
an advantage and a detriment. It made him intolerant of
opposition and stubborn in the defense of his own views.
It limited his ability to talk things over with his adversaries in the cabinet and in the realm of diplomacy, but it

---

[3] Hyde de Neuville to Richelieu, December 11, 1817. Hyde de Neuville,
Mémoires et souvenirs, II, 328.

[4] Compare Calhoun's views on the Holy Alliance in 1824 (above, p. 200)
with Adams's more reasoned observations in 1823. *Memoirs*, VI, 186.

also lent that drive to his policy which so often meant the difference between success and failure.[5] Indeed, he was so sure of himself that he usually preferred the bolder of two courses because it *was* the more vigorous.[6]

One of Adams's greatest faults, but one which also made him thoroughly American and sympathetic with the temper of the people, was his sensitiveness to criticism. This, too, was a family trait, but it reached its greatest development, perhaps, in the character of John Quincy. In the rough and tumble of political life, individuals must expect criticism, condemnation, and misinterpretation of motives which amounts to slander. Likewise nations must not be surprised if in the competition and rivalry of international affairs hard things are said and aspersions cast. It was the peculiar fate of John Quincy Adams to be at once a candidate for high office and the official representative of his country in foreign affairs. A man so sensitive to hostile criticism that he found it difficult to preserve his temper and sound judgment, became a leading figure in one of the most bitter personal political campaigns in American history, and probably at no time before or since

---

[5] Adams's own criticism of himself is pertinent and very revealing. To his wife he wrote the following comparison between himself and Clay: "They [Clay and J.Q.A.] are unquestionably the two members of the mission most under the influence of that irritability which we impute to Mr. Goulburn. . . . There is the same dogmatical, over-bearing manner, the same harshness of look and expression, and the same forgetfulness of the courtesies of society in both. An impartial person judging between them I think would say that one has the strongest, and the other the most cultivated understanding; that one has the most ardency, and the other the most experience of mankind; that one has a mind more gifted by nature, and the other a mind less cankered by prejudice." J. Q. Adams to Louisa C. Adams, December 16, 1814. J. Q. Adams, *Writings*, V, 239.

[6] J. Q. Adams, *Memoirs*, IV, 115.

his term as secretary of state has villification of the United States reached such a pitch of intensity.[7]

Only one aspect of this subject needs examination here: Adams's attitude toward the hostile press in the United States. It is typical, and will also throw light on the peculiar turn which his nationalism took. Smarting under the lash of a particularly keen criticism, Adams wrote:

... He [the editor] is, like all the editors of newspapers in this country who have any talent, an author to be let. There is not one of them whose friendship is worth buying, nor one whose enmity is not formidable. They are a sort of assassins who sit with loaded blunderbusses at the corner of streets and fire them off for hire or for sport at any passenger whom they select. They are principally foreigners. . . .[8]

Several points of interest may be detected in this passage. It was so difficult for Adams to regard his critics as sincere opponents of his policies that he always tended to look for some sinister motive as an explanation. Again, it was Adams's way to feel contempt for his foes as men not worthy of respect and esteem; and, lastly, we must notice the concluding phrase. There is the nationalist in Adams expressing itself. Characters so base cannot be American. The same charge was made on another occasion when Adams told his diary that *The Aurora* and the *Democratic Press* of Philadelphia were edited, the one by an Irishman who had been driven from India for sedition, the other by an Englishman who had been charged with treason. "They are both [he wrote] men of considerable talents

---

[7] In his biography of Adams, Mr. Clark seems to have been so much impressed by this quality of his subject that he allows it to give the tone to his whole work. It is arresting and important, to be sure, but it is only one phase of John Quincy's character.

[8] J. Q. Adams, *Memoirs*, V, 173.

and profligate principles, always for sale to the highest bidder, and always insupportable burdens, by their insatiable rapacity, to the parties they support."[9]

Two years later, in 1822, as the political campaign grew warm, the attacks of the pro-Crawford press increased; and Adams explained this support of Crawford as follows:

... Among the most powerful of his agents have been the editors of the leading newspapers. The National Intelligencer is secured to him by the belief of the editors that he will be the successful candidate, and by their dependence upon the printing of Congress; the Richmond Enquirer, because he is a Virginian and a slave-holder; ... the Democratic Press, of Philadelphia, because I transferred the printing of the laws from that paper to the Franklin Gazette; and several other presses in various parts of the Union upon principles alike selfish and sordid. ...[10]

Such a man was handicapped in politics and diplomacy, for, instead of disregarding partisan criticism, he always felt the urge to reply, to justify himself, his office, or his country in the eyes of the world. That he was no better and no worse in this respect than his countrymen only stamps him further as typically American.

The shafts of his enemies struck deeper and rankled more in Adams's soul because he loved public praise. He did not admit this even to his diary, but between the lines of his self-criticism it is not difficult to see that he was responsive to the plaudits of admirers. He often notes the possible popular reaction to a policy under discussion and remarks that his enemies may use it as a means of attacking him. The corollary of this feeling of apprehension of attack is love of praise, and often it seems that

---

[9] J. Q. Adams, *Memoirs*, V, 112.   [10] *Ibid.*, VI, 61.

Adams "protests too much" his strength in this respect, as when he writes of Calhoun that

. . . He is more sensitive to the transient manifestations of momentary public opinion, more afraid of the first impressions of the public opinion, than I am. . . . In such cases, I think the true policy is to let the hostile portion of the public journals extravagate to their heart's content; let them waste their strength and emit all their venom upon misapplications of law and perversions of fact; and when the victory is upon the balance, seize and turn their batteries against themselves.[11]

It is doubtful whether Adams was as calm and deliberate under fire as he paints himself, but there can be no question of the accuracy of the last observation. At all hazards, their batteries must be seized and turned against them.

One more trait which affected Adams's conduct was his ambition. Capable, conscientious, upright, and sincere, he felt that justice would place him in a position where his talents would be recognized. Intellectually, he *was* the superior of his fellows, and it was not conceit that made him conscious of this fact. He had two ambitions, one immediate and one of a more general nature. To succeed to the post his father had held would in a measure remove the cloud on the reputation of the elder Adams as the only President of the United States who had not been re-elected; it would also crown John Quincy's own political career. While he did not campaign as did Crawford, Adams none the less had his eye on the political situation at home and tried to avoid blunders while he was secretary of state. It would be unjust to say that he trimmed his policy to suit the popular will. Adams was far too honest for that, and he condemned it in others.[12] However, he did

[11] J. Q. Adams, *Memoirs*, V, 361.   [12] *Ibid.*, V, 109.

desire to encourage his friends in their endeavors to promote his candidacy and to convince the public of the
soundness of his views. He therefore resented being made
the scapegoat for the entire foreign policy of the administration, and he writhed at what he called the machinations of Crawford and other rivals.[13]

Perhaps it is unfair to take testimony on this point from
foreigners who had official relations with Adams, but the
coincidence of their opinions suggests that their estimates
are not far from the truth. Charles Bagot, minister from
England, testified to the political implications of Adams's
defense of Jackson,[14] and Polética, the Russian minister,
made the same criticism of a public speech by Adams two
years later.[15] Stratford Canning is probably a less reliable
witness than either his predecessor, Bagot, or Polética, but
his characterization of Adams is fair and unexaggerated.
In his memoirs Stratford Canning wrote of the secretary:

... He was more commanding than attractive in personal appearance, much above par in general ability, but having the
air of a scholar rather than a statesman, a very uneven temper,
a disposition at times well-meaning, a manner somewhat too

[13] J. Q. Adams, *Memoirs*, V, 109, and IV, 223, where he wrote: "In this
affair everything is insidious and factious. The call is made for the purpose of baiting the Administration, and especially of fastening upon the
Secretary of State the odium of refusing to receive South American Ministers and Consuls-General. I am walking on a rope, with a precipice
on each side of me, and without human aid beyond myself upon which to
rely. ... The policy pursued by the Administration in South American
affairs is, in the general opinion of the public, fixed exclusively upon the
Secretary of State, and, as the popular sentiment is much divided upon it,
no effort is omitted to render it obnoxious."

[14] Bagot to Castlereagh, January 4, 1819. Castlereagh, *Memoirs and Correspondence*, XII, 99.

[15] Polética to Nesselrode, July 12, 1821. Russia, *Correspondence*, XVIII,
327.

often domineering, and an ambition causing unsteadiness in his political career. . . ."[16]

Adams was ambitious politically; but it also seems clear that he had an ambition, a prayerful desire, to use a less flippant term, to achieve something for the good of mankind. He did not want to live on merely as a great man, but he did covet the association of his name with some lasting contribution to the sum total of good in the world, so that men would recall it with gratitude and respect. For Adams, too, was an idealist, a dreamer of dreams; and while the cynical may smile at both the form and the content of Adams's prayer, they may not deride the sincerity of his purpose. He was referring to a projected convention for the regulation of neutral and belligerent rights in time of war.

. . . When I think, if it possibly could succeed, what a real and solid blessing it would be to the human race, I can scarcely guard myself from a spirit of enthusiasm, which it becomes me to distrust. I feel that I could die for it with joy, and that if my last moments could be cheered with the consciousness of having contributed to it, I could go before the throne of Omnipotence with a plea for mercy, and with a consciousness of not having lived in vain for the world of mankind.[17]

*　　　*　　　*　　　*　　　*

Adams had a good deal more than character to bring to bear on the problems of the state department. He possessed, without doubt, more experience in diplomacy and world affairs than any other man who has ever filled the post of secretary. He had moved in diplomatic circles since

---

[16] Stratford Canning's unpublished memoirs, quoted in Lane-Poole, *Life of Stratford Canning*, I, 308.

[17] J. Q. Adams, *Memoirs*, VI, 166.

his early youth. He had been brought up in the tradition of diplomatic usage, and this thorough acquaintance with the science of international relations gave him an almost instinctive sense for the implications of policy. Adams knew perfectly the character of the tools with which he had to work, and this knowledge in itself gave him an assurance and confidence which stood him in good stead.

The long residence of John Quincy in Europe also gave him an opportunity to watch the forces at work and to perceive the actual state of affairs. A man who had served in England, Russia, Prussia, and the Netherlands, and who had thus lived and worked in Europe for years was not at all likely to be misled by wild rumors or the alarmed apprehensions of his less experienced associates. His experience was more recent than that of other Americans connected with the government at the time of his secretaryship. Adams had observed Europe closely during the last years of the Napoleonic wars from the vantage point of Alexander's capital. He gained there a thorough knowledge of the currents of thought which were coursing through the Continent and of the character of the diplomacy which was ruling Europe. He witnessed the episode of the Hundred Days from his residence in Paris, and he concluded his European duties with a stay in London, thus completing his contacts with the three countries whose policies most closely affected the United States.

European diplomacy at this time was peculiarly a personal diplomacy. It was directed and shaped by individuals who gave it character. The names of Tsar Alexander, Nesselrode, Capodistrias, Metternich, and Talleyrand suggest at once this aspect of European affairs. Except for Metternich, Adams knew them all. In an age when individuals dominated diplomacy, the value of these relationships cannot be exaggerated. Adams knew who his adversaries were, not only by reputation but also by social contact. A dispatch read to him by the Russian minister in Washington, for example, setting forth the views of Alexander and signed by Nesselrode, affected him very differently from the way in which it impressed Calhoun or Monroe. Adams had walked along the banks of the frozen Neva with Alexander while they argued over philosophy; and he had often talked with Nesselrode in the course of his routine duties. He could not help having a keener, more accurate judgment in matters involving these men and their countries than could his less experienced colleagues. In short, Adams's thorough knowledge of diplomacy, of the European scene, and of the men in charge of the foreign offices combined to give him a standard for evaluating information which many times was to have an important influence on his decisions and his attitudes toward world affairs.

These factors, however, do not complete a discussion of Adams's background. He had had considerable experience with American politics as his father's son, as a lawyer, and as a Senator. Perhaps the most striking phase of American life which he had the opportunity to observe was faction. It had warped politics from the beginning; it had blasted his father's career; it had removed John Quincy himself from the Senate; and for years its tendency had been to "weaken and distract the public councils."[18] He accused the Virginians of giving impetus to this spirit by their partisan attacks on Washington's administration,[19] and he excoriated the New England Federalists for allow-

---

[18] J. Q. Adams, *Memoirs,* IV, 451.   [19] *Ibid.,* V, 364.

ing it to carry them to the point of treason.[20] He earnestly believed that nothing would save the United States from ruin but the creation of a spirit which would make narrow, intolerant, factional opposition impossible. Before entering upon the office of secretary of state, he wrote a letter to a friend in which he clearly exposed the evil as he saw it and avowed his determination to end it if he could. To Alexander H. Everett he wrote:

. . . But some of the worst features in our composition that it [the war] has disclosed are deformities which, if not inherent in the very nature of our constitution, will require great, anxious and unremitting care to enable us to outgrow them. The most disgusting of them all is the rancorous spirit of faction which drove one part of the country headlong towards the dissolution of the union, and towards a treacherous and servile adherence to the enemies of the country. This desertion from the standard of the nation weakened all its exertions to such a degree that it required little less than a special interposition of Providence to save us from utter disgrace and dismemberment; and although the projects of severing the Union were signally disconcerted by the unexpected conclusion of the peace, they were too deeply seated in the political systems, as well as in the views of personal ambition of the most leading men in our native state, to be yet abandoned. They will require to be watched, exposed, and inflexibly resisted, probably for many years.[21]

The effect of this background on Adams's view is clear. He disliked Europe's methods and traditions, her inability to free herself completely from the enslaving influences of the past, and her tendency to despise the United States. His father had expressed this feeling at Paris a generation earlier, and no doubt John Quincy, too, felt that

---

[20] J. Q. Adams to William Eustis, March 29, 1816. J. Q. Adams, *Writings*, V, 546.

[21] J. Q. Adams to A. H. Everett, March 16, 1816. *Ibid.*, V, 538.

the French and other Europeans were "not a moral people." What he saw in Europe from 1809 to 1815 only confirmed him in his beliefs, and his disgust was manifested on more than one occasion.

The prospects of Europe [he wrote] are not more propitious to the freedom and happiness of its inhabitants than they have been for the last thirty years. Europe has escaped from servitude to France, but it yet remains for France to escape from servitude to Europe. In shaking off the fetters of a French military despotism, Europe is passively submitting to be reshackled with the manacles of feudal and papal tyranny. She has burst asunder the adamantine chains of Bonaparte, to be pinioned by the rags and tatters of monkery and popery. She has cast up the code of Napoleon, and returned to her own vomit of Jesuits, inquisitions, and legitimacy or Divine Right.[22]

John Quincy Adams also felt that the selfish and intriguing policies of Europe were a disturbing influence in American life. Too close a connection with European affairs had given to the internal disputes of the country a bitterness and a hostile character which made unity impossible. European diplomats had freely taken part in American politics for their own purposes, and Adams was shrewd enough to see that this was wholly undesirable.[23]

Adams's experience also gave him a very definite opinion of the attitude of England toward the United States. Although he had encountered friendly receptions in Russia, in Prussia, in the Netherlands, and even in France, his contacts with England and English diplomacy formed a record of determined hostility. During the American Revolution he saw England holding back, refusing to ne-

---

[22] J. Q. Adams to Dexter, April 14, 1816. J. Q. Adams, *Writings*, VI, 15.
[23] J. Q. Adams to William Eustis, March 29, 1816. *Ibid.*, V, 546.

gotiate, and blocking the demands of the United States. While he was in the Senate he witnessed English intrigue in America and had the opportunity to mark the operation of her policy toward neutrals. The war itself was further evidence of English hatred for America, and finally at Ghent he received what to him was complete proof of her duplicity. He was convinced that England was not to be trusted. She would use her dominance in Europe "to inspire prejudices and jealousies against us."[24] Americans could not afford to trust the English; for, while other nations had occasionally exhibited friendship for the United States, England had played the part of an inveterate foe. Therefore it was his opinion that

... although it is to be hoped that the ascendancy which Great Britain has acquired is already waning, and will rapidly decline, we must still be always prepared for self-defence against the aggressions which her interests or her passions may point or excite to effect if possible our ruin. Her language ... is pacific, but the situation of her people is so far from being easy or contented, that it is a prevailing sentiment here that a foreign war is indispensibly necessary to save the nation from internal convulsions. Their animosities against France have been almost satiated by the condition to which they have reduced her, but their feelings against America are keener, more jealous, more envious, more angry than ever.[25]

The influence of the *milieu* on Adams's policies must be obvious. He felt almost instinctively that America should maintain her independence in foreign affairs and preserve a free hand at all times so that she could serve

---

[24] J. Q. Adams to W. Plumer, January 17, 1817. J. Q. Adams, *Writings*, VI, 139.

[25] J. Q. Adams to Abigail Adams, his mother, December 27, 1815. *Ibid.*, V, 454.

her own interests. Coöperation with European Powers was desirable whenever possible, but caution and reserve were necessary lest the United States be hampered in her development. At home, a self-conscious nationalism would do much to end the bad effects of faction and of foreign intrigues. A united front to the rest of the world, an assertion of America's dignity and independence, would strengthen her diplomacy and obtain for the United States of America recognition as a self-respecting member of the society of nations.

In Adams's career as secretary of state many episodes illustrate the definite relation between his feelings and his ideas and policies. If a few of the more striking examples of the nationalist in Adams are selected, a better perspective of his activities will be gained, and many things about his secretaryship, which otherwise seem to be events without causes, will be understandable. It will also be possible to observe the close relation of his outlook to that of the people of the United States and to discover therein a key to his policy in 1823. Adams was a consistent person, and his actions in that year were merely the logical and certain result of deep and permanent currents in his thought.

One of the earliest expressions of Adams's views resulted from the activities of the American peace societies. D. L. Dodge, a Presbyterian merchant of Hartford, formed the first of these organizations in 1815 in New York City.[26] Other groups were quickly organized under the guidance of the Reverend Noah Worcester, a New Hampshire minister. Within two years the number of societies had grown to nearly thirty, situated throughout New Eng-

[26] Whitney, *The American Peace Society,* 10.

land, New York, and Ohio. A publication, *The Friend of Peace*, was launched, and a rather active propaganda on behalf of peace was carried on.

These societies might have continued their work for a long time unnoticed, had not the Reverend Mr. Worcester conceived the grandiose idea of corresponding, on behalf of the Massachusetts group, with the man who was considered by many to be the leading "Friend of Peace" in the world, the Tsar Alexander. The widespread popularity which he enjoyed among all classes in the United States has already been noted, but by none was he more admired and worshiped than by the idealist members of the peace societies. They thought his Holy Alliance sublime and appear to have regarded him with an enthusiasm not unmixed with reverence. This correspondence with Alexander was published in the leading newspapers and reviews as evidence of the activities of Worcester and his colleagues. An excerpt from the epistle to the Tsar will illustrate their attitude.

The friendly disposition which you have manifested in favor of the Christian religion and the peace of the world, has encouraged this address.—The very week in which the holy league of the three sovereigns was officially announced in Russia, a society was formed in Boston, by the name of the Massachusetts Peace Society, the object of which is to disseminate the very principles avowed in the wonderful alliance, and to do whatever may lawfully be done to prevent the recurrence of war, and to promote peace on earth and good will among men.[27]

This uncritical friendship for the Holy Alliance contin-

------

[27] Worcester to Alexander, April 9, 1817. *Niles' Weekly Register*, XIII, 124, October 18, 1817.

ued in the form of an active propaganda which survived even the Congress of Aix-la-Chapelle.[28]

The general reaction of the public to the program of the peace societies was negative. The conservative *North American Review* regretted the lack of interested support and feared that the public was apathetic because the societies had not first been founded in England.[29] This view may have been valid for the readers of that publication but certainly did not apply to the rest of the people.[30] A more typical view was expressed by *The Southern Patriot* with an air of amused tolerance as it pointed out the faintly ridiculous figure cut by the New Englanders and suggested that the dignity of Alexander's position would suffer from his association with the societies.[31]

Biting criticism and denunciation, however, came from both the Adamses, for there was one fatal weakness in the background of the organizations: they were born of the spirit that caused the Hartford Convention. Dodge, the founder, was a Hartford merchant who in 1814 had written a book entitled *War Inconsistent with the Religion of Jesus Christ;* the Reverend Mr. Worcester, too, had written *A Solemn Review of the Custom of War.*[32] As if these antecedents were not enough, the Boston society was formed at a convention of ministers and included in the list of its founders Noah Worcester, Josiah Quincy, Caleb Strong, Christopher Gore, President Kirkland of

---

[28] Thomas, *Russo-American Relations, 1815–1867,* 154.

[29] Review of the first eight numbers of *The Friend of Peace,* in *The North American Review,* VI (1817), 25.

[30] What Republicans thought of *The North American Review* and its political affiliations may be learned from the pungent editorial comments of the *National Intelligencer,* July 18, 1815. See above, p. 60.

[31] *The Southern Patriot,* in the *National Intelligencer,* October 30, 1817.

[32] Whitney, *The American Peace Society,* 10.

Harvard, and other sterling Federalists of the old school.[33] Nor was its program less tainted with defeatist Federalism. Even the Bostonian *North American Review* was constrained to admit the impolitic character of a propaganda which sought to gain converts in the United States to the cause of peace by emphasizing the injustice of the war with England, and which even denied the right of self-defense.[34] It was probably this feature, as well as the politics of the men connected with it, which caused old John Adams to refuse point-blank to become a member and to word the refusal which he sent from Quincy as follows:

> Our beloved country, sir, is surrounded by enemies, of the most dangerous, because the most powerful and most unprincipled character. Collisions of national interest, of commercial and manufacturing rivalries, are multiplying around us. Instead of discouraging a martial spirit, in my opinion it ought to be excited. We have not enough of it to defend us by sea or land.[35]

It is without surprise, therefore, that one reads the judgment which John Quincy passed upon the activities of the peace societies. Fresh from his European experience and from his personal contacts with the Tsar, whom he regarded as the one exception to the rule that Europeans were prejudiced against the United States,[36] he wrote:

> . . . if our Peace Societies should fall into the fashion of corresponding upon the objects of their institutions with foreign Emperors and Kings, they may at some future day find themselves under the necessity of corresponding with attorney gen-

---

[33] Whitney, *The American Peace Society*, 10.

[34] *The North American Review*, VI (1817), 25.

[35] J. Adams to the Massachusetts Peace Society. *Niles' Weekly Register*, X, 328, July 13, 1816.

[36] J. Q. Adams to W. Plumer, January 17, 1817. J. Q. Adams, *Writings*, VI, 139.

erals and petit juries at home. Philip of Macedon was in very active correspondence with a Peace Society at Athens, and with their coöperation baffled and overpowered all the eloquence of Demosthenes. Alexander of the Neva is not so near nor so dangerous a neighbor to us as Philip was to the Athenians, but I am afraid his love of peace is of the same character as was that of Philip of Macedon. . . . While Alexander and his Minister of Religious Worship, Prince Galitzin, are corresponding with the Rev. Noah Worcester upon the blessedness of peace, the venerable founder of the Holy League is sending five or six ships of the line, and several thousand promoters of peace armed with bayonets to Cadiz, and thence to propagate good will to man elsewhere. . . .[37]

Besides being a typical example of Adams's "grand style," which tended to be florid and exaggerated, this letter illustrates several other points. It clearly reflects Adams's independence and sensitive nationalism. It irked him exceedingly to realize that a group of his countrymen had so forgotten their character as Americans that they would correspond with a foreign potentate. It was harmless enough to write letters on idealistic subjects; the fault lay in the fact that, instead of championing their own cause as an American creation, these citizens were fawning upon an outlander as the leader whose ideas they admired. American institutions were not subjects upon which to invoke foreign patronage. Adams's realism is also noticeable. After all, anyone who knew the facts could see that Alexander, great as he was, was a man with very human faults and ambitions. The peace societies, in their enthusiasm for an unattainable ideal, had lost all sight of this earthly side of the Tsar and were fast becoming ridic-

---

[37] J. Q. Adams to A. H. Everett, December 29, 1817. J. Q. Adams, *Writings*, VI, 280.

ulous as a result. It was high time, thought Adams, that they ceased their antics and devoted their energies to better uses. This incident throws light on Adams's views at the beginning of his term of office. He was to express them more clearly in handling his first crisis.

This crisis arose out of the invasion of West Florida by Andrew Jackson. The circumstances of this episode do not concern us here. The protests of the Spanish minister, Onís, however, soon made it necessary for the administration to decide upon a course of action. Was Jackson to be defended or was he to be disavowed? In the cabinet discussions which ensued, Adams found himself ranged against all the others in his defense of Jackson. All except Adams argued that for the administration to take the responsibility for Jackson's actions would be to approve war with Spain, an unconstitutional act which would expose it to bitter criticism.

Adams used every resource at his command to convince his colleagues that a complete justification of Jackson was possible and desirable. He failed, but the reasons which he advanced for his stand are significant. He argued that Jackson had really acted in accordance with his instructions, although they did not order him to seize Spanish forts. Jackson had been told to pursue the Indians into Florida if necessary; the governor of Florida had threatened to drive him out by force; therefore "his only alternative was to prevent the execution of the threat."[38] Adams pointed out that Jackson's motives were not hostile and that "everything he did was *defensive*." This was rather fine logic, and Adams recognized the fact that even the

---

[38] J. Q. Adams, *Memoirs*, IV, 111.

best legal authorities helped his case but little. This was a matter, however, which involved more than legal principles. Here was an American officer who, to say the least, had discretionary powers; to disavow his conduct in the face of foreign criticism was unthinkable.

... I admitted [he wrote] that it was necessary to carry the reasoning upon my principles to the utmost extent it would bear to come to this conclusion. But, if the question was dubious, it was better to err on the side of vigor than of weakness—on the side of our own officer, who had rendered the most eminent services to the nation, than on the side of our bitterest enemies, and against him.[39]

The President and the rest of the cabinet did not agree with this nationalist with his sensitive feeling for the honor of an officer of the United States Army, and Adams was instructed to draw up a reply to Onís which would place the responsibility on Jackson. He confided to his diary that this would be considered "truckling to Spain" by the public at large. That would be bad enough;

... But the mischief of this determination lies deeper: 1. It is weakness, and a confession of weakness. 2. The disclaimer of power in the Executive is of dangerous example and of evil consequences. 3. There is injustice to the officer in disavowing him, when in principle he is strictly justifiable....[40]

There was the rub! It was weakness and a confession of weakness. America could never expect to hold a position of dignity and honor in the world while she pursued a pusillanimous policy in her relations with other Powers. Nor was Adams blind to the political repercussions which would result from a failure to defend Jackson at all hazards. To be sure, the administration would be criticized

---

[39] J. Q. Adams, *Memoirs,* IV, 113.   [40] *Ibid.,* IV, 115.

for whichever course it took, but Adams thought support of Jackson much the preferable policy.

... I glanced at the construction which would be given by Jackson's friends and by a large portion of the public to the disavowal of his acts. It would be said that he was an obnoxious man; that, after having the benefit of his services, he was abandoned and sacrificed to the enemies of his country; that his case would be compared with that of Sir Walter Raleigh.[41]

Adams shrewdly observed that Jackson's friends would be sure to attack the administration, but that the constitutionalists could not be expected to rally to the active defense of the President and the cabinet. "I believe the other would have been a safer, as well as a bolder course."[42] That Adams understood politics as well as diplomacy must be clear from these statements. As a political leader who stood for independent, self-conscious nationalism which would be sensitive to criticism and fearless in the refutation of it, Adams lost the first round of this contest and dispatched a letter to Onís on July 23, 1818, which he characterized as "exactly conformable in substance to the President's original draft—the language only is mine."[43]

Adams's day came four months later. The administration had refused to say that Jackson had acted according to his instructions, but there was nothing in that decision to prevent a defense of Jackson's conduct from being made to the Spanish government. Consequently, in November, with the documents at hand, Adams began the preparation of a comprehensive statement of the American case which would justify the policy and Jackson's acts

---

[41] J. Q. Adams, *Memoirs*, IV, 113.   [42] *Ibid.*, IV, 115.

[43] *Ibid.*, IV, 112. The letter to Onís, the Spanish minister to the United States, is in his *Writings*, VI, 386.

as well. He undertook the responsibility with a clear sense of its importance: "The task is of the highest order: may I not be found inferior to it!"[44] His prayer was answered, for the result was a masterpiece which Jefferson pronounced to be one of the "ablest compositions . . . [he had] ever seen, both as to logic and style. . . ."[45]

Cast in the form of a letter of instructions to George W. Erving, the American minister to Spain, the defense was as complete, and the language as vigorous, as any American could have desired.[46] The dispatch opened with a detailed review of the conditions in Florida which had led to the invasion and of the reasons for Jackson's conduct. Spain must not expect that "the President will [either] . . . inflict punishment, [or] . . . pass a censure upon General Jackson, for that conduct, the motives for which were founded in the purest patriotism; of the necessity for which he had the most immediate and effectual means of forming a judgment; and the vindication of which is written in every page of the law of nations, as well as in the first law of nature—self-defense." Thus the honor of the American officer was defended.

The conduct of the commanders at St. Marks and Pensacola, moreover, had been such that the United States must demand an inquiry into their acts, appropriate punishments, and an indemnification of the United States for the expenses incurred as a result of their inaction. Adams pointed out that violations of international agreements by responsible officers could not be tolerated; and if, as

[44] J. Q. Adams, *Memoirs*, IV, 168.

[45] Jefferson to Monroe, January 18, 1819. Jefferson, *Writings* (P. L. Ford, ed.), X, 123.

[46] J. Q. Adams to Erving, November 28, 1818. J. Q. Adams, *Writings*, VI, 474.

both governors asserted, they acted as they did only because the Spanish force in Florida was too weak to allow them to act otherwise, then Spain herself stood impeached. That fact itself

> ... must carry demonstration irresistible to the Spanish government, that the right of the United States can as little compound with impotence as with perfidy, and that Spain must immediately make her election, either to place a force in Florida adequate at once to the protection of her territory, and to the fulfilment of her engagements, or cede to the United States a province, of which she retains nothing but the nominal possession, but which is, in fact, a derelict, open to the occupancy of every enemy, civilized or savage, of the United States, and serving no other earthly purpose than as a post of annoyance to them.

As if this firm declaration of the right of the United States to respectful consideration were not enough, Adams went on to review the acts of the English in Florida in the war of 1812 and deftly pointed out to the Spanish government that "if a whisper of expostulation was ever wafted from Madrid to London, it was not loud enough to be heard across the Atlantic, nor energetic enough to transpire beyond the walls of the palaces from which it issued, and to which it was borne." Thus the dignified and commanding position of the United States was brought home to Spain, and her batteries turned upon herself.

There was still one more part of Jackson's activities which required defense, and defend it Adams did, though he provoked the ire of England in the process. The execution of Arbuthnot and Ambrister had created quite a furor in the English press, as well as spirited comment at home. Charges of murder and treachery flew back and forth. Nevertheless, Adams did not hesitate. He asserted that these men were leagued with the savages in waging war on the United States; that they were in fact the promoters of a war which would not have occurred without their promises of English support to the Indians; and that "as accomplices of the savages, and, sinning against their better knowledge, worse than savages, General Jackson, possessed of their persons and of the proofs of their guilt, might, by the lawful and ordinary usages of war, have hung them both without the formality of a trial. . . ." With that remark Adams's defense of Jackson and his assertion of the right of the United States and her officers to act according to their interests touched its high point. It was not weak Spain to whom he spoke but to England, a nation with a traditional jealous regard for her citizens the world over.

The conclusion of this remarkable document is a warning to Spain in the same high tone maintained throughout the whole. The restoration of Pensacola and St. Marks is proof of America's

. . . confidence that, hereafter, . . . there will be no more murders, no more robberies, within our borders, by savages prowling along the Spanish line, and seeking shelter within it, to display in their villages the scalps of our women and children, their victims . . . that we shall hear no more apologies from Spanish governors . . . no more excuses. . . .

Peace and order must be maintained by Spain, or else—

. . . if the necessities of self-defense should again compel the United States to take possession of the Spanish forts and places in Florida, [we] declare, with the frankness and candor that become us, that another unconditional restoration of them must not be expected; that even the President's confidence in the good faith and ultimate justice of the Spanish government will yield to the painful experience of continual disappointment; and, that, after unwearied and almost unnumbered appeals to them for the performance of their stipulated duties in vain, the United States will be reluctantly compelled to rely for the protection of their borders upon themselves alone.

Thus Adams closed the most polished state paper he ever wrote, one which alone would serve to make his reputation as a secretary of state secure. Its terms have been analyzed at length because they reflect so perfectly the man who was described in the first part of this chapter, and because they are proof of the effect of his traits of character on his conduct of foreign relations. In the very first test of his ability to handle a delicate international situation, he insisted on defending an attacked American official against all criticism from whatever source, on taking a clear stand for the right of the United States to be treated with respect by other nations, and on asserting in a bold tone the future course of American policy. It is unlikely that he wrote this defense with an eye to the votes of the West, as Bagot charged, but it is no doubt true that he sensed the rising tide of nationalism in the United States and realized that nothing would encourage it so much as a spirited defense of the greatest living American soldier. A more timid man than Adams, one whose spirit was not of the same mold, would have treated the problem very differently. Diplomacy did not require such a thoroughgoing exposition, nor was the language used essential. The secretary of state might, with propriety, have taken no action at all and have allowed the matter to drop. No, it was Adams's spirit and inability to allow criticisms and insults to go unanswered, his nationalism and love of lèadership, even his ambition perhaps, which gave to his defense of Jackson its form and content.

At various times in his dealings with his diplomatic associates Adams felt called upon to assert the leading position of the United States. He did not delude himself by thinking that America was the greatest Power in the world, but there were fields in which she was entitled to leadership, and Adams was quick to assert preëminence where it was justified. The Abbé Corréa, the urbane and witty minister from Portugal, discussed, on several occasions, the idea of an alliance between Portugal and the United States as a guaranty of peace and order in the New World. Adams listened to the Abbé with respect, but the idea appeared to him to be a bit ludicrous when viewed in the light of realities. In a famous passage in his diary he dismissed the project with the words:

. . . I had never disturbed the Abbé in his romancing; but Portugal and the United States are the two great American powers much as a jolly-boat and the Columbus are two great line-of-battle ships; and as to an American system independent of Europe, Portugal is neither American nor independent. So long as Portugal shall recognize the House of Braganza for her sovereign, so long the House of Braganza will be European, and not American—a satellite, and not a primary planet. As to an American system, we have it; we constitute the whole of it; there is no community of interests or of principles between North and South America. . . .[47]

Aside from the fact that the United States *was* the leading Power in the western hemisphere, the idea of associating with a third-rate, semi-European state on terms of equality was very distasteful to Adams. That was not the way to foster the spirit which he felt should dominate America.

---

[47] J. Q. Adams, *Memoirs*, V, 176.

His independence and distrust of the designs of England are clearly brought out in the discussions relating to the slave trade. There is little doubt that England's campaign for the abolition of the slave trade was promoted by disinterested humanitarians and by an aroused public sentiment. All nations had agreed in principle that the traffic should be abolished, but an effective means of combatting it had not been worked out. Obviously, some international police system was necessary, for if slavers could not be searched, the whole movement would fail. From the start, however, Adams so suspected the motives of England that all the overtures, plans, and suggestions of the English came to naught. There was no possibility for an agreement when Adams was so sure that treachery lurked behind her proposals.

... It exactly suited her views to devise an expedient, under color of its necessity for suppressing the slave-trade, which should familiarize other commercial and navigating nations to the practice of submitting to the search of foreign armed ships. All this was to pass to the account of benevolence and humanity. . . .[48]

This was but another proof, Adams felt, of the deep-seated, inveterate, and persistent hostility of England and of her determination to force her policies on other nations by trickery and deception if other means failed.

Not only did he regard the proposals themselves as insincere; he felt that in any case the United States could not with self-respect accede to a belated English suggestion in a field in which America had been a pioneer.

... if we accede to this proposal, the credit of it all goes to her. We follow her lead. We appear to the world as the satellite

---

[48] J. Q. Adams, *Memoirs*, V, 218.

and she the primary planet [again that simile]—a position the more disparaging to us, because in point of fact she was merely following our lead; the first example of prohibiting the trade having been set by us.[49]

So strongly did Adams feel that this whole project should be stripped of its hypocrisy and sham that he wrote to Rush, the American minister to England, an instruction on the subject that ranks with his defense of Jackson for high tone and independence.

... The most noble Marquis [of Lansdowne, he wrote], ... together with Mr. Wilberforce, is laying seige to us with that steam battery the slave trade. As the interferences of those gentlemen in this affair is altogether extra official and not remarkably delicate, I think you would do well to suggest to them that if the British government will begin by stipulating never from this day forth to the end of time to take by force a *white man* from an American merchant vessel on the high seas (unless as a prisoner of war), we will listen to proposals to let them search American vessels for *black men* in time of peace. And so long as their humanity for white freemen stops short of such an engagement for fear it should unman their navy, they may spare themselves the trouble of applying to us to unman our independence by trusting them to search our ships for black slaves to emancipate. I am not partial to the tribe of empirics whose infallible remedies are always worse than the disease.[50]

Sarcasm, dislike of interference in America's affairs, suspicion of England, and a sense of nationalism, all combine here to prove once again the influence of Adams's character and background on his foreign policy. That this challenge to England was consonant with the temper of the people is obvious from the discussion of the subject in an earlier chapter.

---

[49] J. Q. Adams, *Memoirs*, V, 218. See also *ibid.*, V, 182.
[50] J. Q. Adams to Rush, May 2, 1819. J. Q. Adams, *Writings*, VI, 550.

It seems that fate had willed that Adams was to be thrown into close association with men and events which would tend to accentuate his feelings and to draw from him heated declarations in defiance of his adversaries. Adams had to deal with one of the most difficult men who ever graced the English foreign service. Of all the ministers in Washington, Stratford Canning was probably the most high-handed, irritating, and short-tempered. Hyde de Neuville had an unstable disposition, but the tirades of the Frenchman did not disturb Adams greatly, and on the whole their relations were friendly.[51] Stratford Canning, however, was one of those Englishmen who most antagonized Americans. He regarded his stay in America as a sort of exile in the wilderness where his main duty was to keep "the schoolboy Yankees quiet."[52] A man who assumed his position in that spirit was doomed to drive a person like Adams to the verge of frenzy. It must be remembered also that this was the same Stratford Canning whom the Russian government later asked to have recalled from St. Petersburg as *persona non grata,* and who, still later, by his independent and provocative actions at Constantinople, precipitated the Crimean war.[53] It is no wonder then that Adams, who had characterized himself as having a "dogmatical, over-bearing manner . . . harshness of look and expression, and . . . forgetfulness of the courtesies of society . . . ,"[54] found it impossible to avoid clashes with the irascible representative of England.

[51] J. Q. Adams, *Memoirs,* V, 415.

[52] Lane-Poole, *Life of Stratford Canning,* I, 285.

[53] For these later phases of Stratford Canning's career see V. J. Puryear, *England, Russia, and the Straits Question, 1844–1856* (Berkeley, 1932).

[54] J. Q. Adams to Louisa C. Adams, December 16, 1814. J. Q. Adams, *Writings,* V, 239.

Stratford Canning's own testimony reveals one or two interesting aspects of Adams's manner. In his memoirs he wrote of the secretary that

He had a trick when I was with him on some point of difference between the two Governments of leaving open the door into the room occupied by his secretaries and giving them a high opinion of his national spirit by some expression which I could not allow to pass without a corresponding comment.[55]

In justice to Adams it should be remarked that Stratford Canning was the very man to seize upon passing remarks and to reply with interest; Adams's "trick" may have been as much a measure of self-defense as of low political cunning. Indeed, Canning confessed that in arguments with Adams "there was nothing for it but to set my back against the wall," a remark which indicates his inability to understand his adversary's temper.[56] Nay, he even invited trouble. He wrote to one of his friends that, when recognition of South American independence was being considered in Washington, "I accosted him by saying, 'So, Mr. Adams, you are going to make honest people of them?' " That Adams should answer a sarcastic remark like that in kind was inevitable. "Yes, Sir [was the reply], we proposed to your Government to join us some time ago, but they would not, and now we shall see whether you will be content to *follow* us."[57] Apparently Adams could not escape incidents which roused his national spirit and produced statements of American pride.

---

[55] Stratford Canning's memoirs. Lane-Poole, *Life of Stratford Canning*, I, 309. Adams and Canning had each a vivid opinion of the other, and their views may be read conveniently together, *ibid.*, 308–309, where the biographer has quoted Canning in his text, Adams in a note.

[56] S. Canning to Planta, June 15, 1821. *Ibid.*, I, 308.

[57] S. Canning to Planta, April 3, 1821. *Ibid.*, I, 309.

The story of the encounter between these two temperamental individuals has been as much quoted and as little understood as any passage in Adams's diary. It would be dangerous to accept the statements made in the course of it as reliable expositions of either English or American policy toward Oregon. Both men were in a state of high excitement, and each took untenable positions, a fact which Adams later admitted as far as he was concerned.[58] If the circumstances are examined closely, a truer impression of their significance will be gained.[59]

Canning, aroused by remarks in Congress about the American settlement at the mouth of the Columbia River, called upon Adams for an explanation. Adams had none to offer, as he was ignorant of the statements alluded to by his visitor. The discussion immediately became heated as Canning adopted "a tone more peremptory than . . . [Adams] was disposed to endure . . . ," and continued to press his questions, until Adams stopped him with the remark, "Now, sir, if you have any charge to make against the American Government . . . you will please to make the communication in writing." The Englishman then lost his temper completely and drew from Adams the cool statement that "we are as little disposed to submit to dictation as to exercise it." In this vein the argument continued with many pithy remarks on both sides and with the honors about even. Canning made unreasonable statements, and Adams so forgot himself in the oft-quoted passage about claims to Oregon that he denied that the English

[58] The English claim to Oregon in the convention of 1818 was admitted by Adams in his *Memoirs*, V, 259. His remarks, "Keep what is yours, but leave the rest of the continent to us," and the like, cannot be taken literally.

[59] Adams's detailed, practically *verbatim* memoranda of the two conversations of January 26 and 27, 1821, are *ibid.*, V, 243–260.

had any claim whatsoever to any territory on the Pacific Ocean. Canning, in turn, complained of being "treated like a school-boy" and took special exception to Adams's remark that his questions were "captious." For two long interviews on separate days this exchange of pleasantries continued, until Canning withdrew after expressing the deference which he owed to the secretary's years.

Why did Adams let slip his self-control and answer Canning point for point, sarcasm for sarcasm? In somewhat similar circumstances later in the same year, Hyde de Neuville abandoned his diplomatic dignity as completely as did Canning on this occasion, but Adams retained his composure and even managed to see the amusing side of the incident.[60] The reasons are not far to seek. In the first place, there was the personal factor that Canning was an Englishman whose peremptory tone and dictatorial manner were irritating beyond expression. Canning's whole demeanor was one which could not help but strike fire from Adams, as it was calculated to arouse his deepest feelings of independence and nationalism. Adams also suspected that England, through her minister, might be advancing a claim to territory which he considered to be American, for he told Canning at one time "that any chicaning of our right to the mouth of the Columbia River would assuredly not tend to promote...harmony between the two countries." In his apprehension on this point and in his desire to defend the position of the United States, Adams advanced a counterclaim to exclusive dominion over all Oregon which was contrary to the provisions of the convention of 1818. Finally, and this no doubt was

---

[60] J. Q. Adams, *Memoirs*, V, 415.

what touched him most deeply, Canning was interfering in the private affairs of the United States and presuming to criticize things which were no concern of any foreign diplomat. Such interference could not be tolerated for a moment. Adams made this point several times and re-stated it at the conclusion of the conversation as follows:

I said that he [Canning] must consider both the matter and the manner as defensive on *my* part; and then again reminded him of the exceptionable character which, in my situation, must attach to *any* questioning by a foreign Minister founded upon the speeches of members of Congress in their places, or upon proceedings pending in that body; and of my duty to repel at the first instant, and in the most decisive manner, any such enquiry.

Again Adams reflected his nationalism almost involun-tarily. His sensitiveness to criticism from the outside was so keen that when that criticism was offered in a high tone and with almost provocative directness by an Englishman whose motives he distrusted, he lost his poise completely and entered into an exchange of remarks most undignified for a man in his official position. This is the real signifi-cance of this theatrical episode. Considered in relation to what had gone before and what was to follow, it gains meaning and rationality. It was not a mere outburst of peevish temper, but the natural reaction to the circum-stances of the incident.

The episodes thus far reviewed have been chosen be-cause they represent expressions of Adams's feelings over a period of years and in a variety of circumstances. In an intimate diary, in private letters, in formal dispatches, in personal intercourse with diplomats—in all these ways Adams gives unimpeachable proof of the qualities of his mind. Let us now analyze the most interesting example of them all. Adams rarely spoke to the nation directly, for he was not a brilliant orator; but there is one striking exception to this rule in the course of his career as secretary of state. At the invitation of a committee of citizens of the city of Washington, Adams delivered the address at the public celebration of Independence Day, 1821. Ostensibly he was a private citizen speaking to the people of Washington; actually it was Secretary of State Adams talking to the nation and to Europe, for the diplomatic corps was in attendance,[61] and the tone of the oration as well as the immediate printing of thousands of copies of it for distribution gave it more than local significance. It is not too much to say that this speech represents the complete fusion of the personal views of Adams with those of his countrymen. Adams was no demagogue, and the fact that he could allow himself to stand up before the people and express so completely *their* sentiments on that great national holiday is significant. The experiences of the people and those of their secretary of state and "heir-apparent" had done their work; the results were identical.

Adams opened his address with a survey of the origin and development of the English government under which Americans had once lived.[62] He pointed out that the monarchical system there "had been founded in conquest . . . [and] cemented in servitude" from which the people had only partially emerged. It was from this half-free people that the ancestors of his audience had broken away and

---

[61] With the exception of Stratford Canning, who had sufficient perspicacity to visit Harper's Ferry just at this time. Lane-Poole, *Life of Stratford Canning*, I, 309.

[62] The text of the address is in *Niles' Weekly Register*, XX, 326 ff., July 21, 1821.

had come to America, he said, and it was the conflict between a society in which "conquest and servitude had no part" and the older system which caused the Revolution. The orator then proceeded to examine the bases of all true governments and societies and to point out wherein the English colonial system failed. The circumstances preceding the declaration of American independence were reviewed, and then Adams provided that touch of the spectacular which was also characteristic of the man by reading the Declaration of Independence from the original manuscript.

It was not his purpose, however, "to re-kindle . . . angry passion" or to present a "catalogue of alternate oppression and entreaty, of reciprocated indignity and remonstrance." The Declaration of Independence had interest for Americans because

. . . It was the first solemn declaration by a nation of the only *legitimate* foundation of civil government. It was the corner stone of a new fabric, destined to cover the surface of the globe. It demolished, at a stroke, the lawfulness of all governments founded upon conquest. It swept away all the rubbish of accumulated centuries of servitude. . . .

Fortunate it was for Stratford Canning that he was not present, for Adams was unable to keep his denunciation of England on this high plane, and, in describing how the fathers of the Republic expressed their devotion to their principles, his nationalism ran away with him as he recalled the horrors of the war.

. . . While some of the fairest of your fields were ravaged; while your towns and villages were consumed with fire; while the harvests of your summers were blasted; while the purity of virgin innocence, and the chastity of matronly virtue, were violated; while the living remnants of the field of battle were reserved for the gibbet, by the fraternal sympathies of Britons throughout your land, the waters of the Atlantic ocean, and those that wash the shores of either India, were dyed with the mingled blood of combatants in the cause of North American independence.

From this apostrophe, which makes one wonder what Adams would have said had he *planned* to fire public sentiment, he turned quietly to consider the bases of peace and social harmony which characterized the nation in its early years. He spoke of the struggles to form a stable government and of the peaceful transition to the present constitution which was accomplished without "for a moment renouncing or abandoning the great principles consecrated by the declaration of the day."

Up to this point, the oration had been clear, well-worded, and admirably logical but had contained nothing unusual for an address of its kind. It was the unequivocal statement of American policy, the blistering denunciation of England, and the flamboyant assertion of the greatness of the United States in politics, in literature, in science, and in the arts that transformed this somewhat ordinary composition into one which aroused attention, discussion, and interest at home and abroad. The neglect which the speech has received from other writers is adequate excuse for quoting its conclusion at length.

And now, friends and countrymen, if the wise and learned philosophers of the elder world; the first observers of nutation and aberration, the discoverers of maddening ether and invisible planets, the inventors of Congreve rockets and Shrapnel shells, should find their hearts disposed to enquire What has America done for the benefit of mankind? Let our answer be this: America, with the same voice which spoke herself into existence as a nation, proclaimed to mankind the inextinguishable rights of human nature, and the only lawful foundations of government. America, in the assembly of nations, since her admission among them, has invariably, though often fruitlessly, held forth to them the hand of honest friendship, of equal freedom, of generous reciprocity. She has uniformly spoken among them, though often to heedless and often to disdainful ears, the language of equal liberty, of equal justice, and of equal rights. She has, in the lapse of nearly half a century, without a single exception, respected the independence of other nations while asserting and maintaining her own. She has abstained from interference in the concerns of others, even when the conflict has been for principles to which she clings, as to the last vital drop that visits the heart. She has seen that probably for centuries to come, all the contests of that Aceldama, the European world, will be contests of inveterate power, and emerging right. Wherever the standard of freedom and independence has been or shall be unfurled, there will her heart, her benedictions, and her prayers be. But she goes not abroad in search of monsters to destroy. She is the well-wisher to the freedom and independence of all. She is the champion and vindicator only of her own. She will recommend the general cause by the countenance of her voice, and the benignant sympathy of her example. She well knows that by once enlisting under other banners than her own, were they even the banners of foreign independence, she would involve herself beyond the power of extrication, in all the wars of interest and intrigue, of individual avarice, envy, and ambition, which assume the colors and usurp the standard of freedom. The fundamental maxims of her policy would insensibly change from *liberty* to *force*. The frontlet upon her brow would no longer beam with the ineffable splendor of freedom and independence; but in its stead would soon be substituted an imperial diadem, flashing in false and tarnished lustre, the murky radiance of dominion and power. She might become the dictatress of the world. She would be no longer the ruler of her own spirit.

Stand forth, ye champions of Britannia, ruler of the waves! Stand forth, ye chivalrous knights of chartered liberties and the rotten borough! Enter the lists, ye boasters of *inventive* genius! Ye mighty masters of the palette and the brush! Ye improvers upon the sculpture of the Elgin marbles! Ye spawn-ers of fustian romance and lascivious lyrics! Come and en-quire what has America done for the benefit of mankind! In the half century which has elapsed since the declaration of American independence, what have *you* done for the benefit of mankind?

. . . We shall not contend with you for the prize of music, painting or sculpture. We shall not disturb the extatic [*sic*] trances of your chemists, nor call from the heavens the ardent gaze of your astronomers. We will not ask you who was the last president of your Royal Academy. We will not enquire by whose mechanical combinations it was that your steam-boats stem the currents of your rivers and vanquish the opposition of the winds themselves upon your seas. We will not name the inventor of the cotton-gin, for we fear that you would ask us the meaning of the word, and pronounce it a provincial bar-barism. We will not name to you him whose graver defies the imitation of forgery, and saves the labor of your executioner by taking from your greatest geniuses of robbery the power of committing the crime. He is now among yourselves; and, since your philosophers have permitted him to prove to them the compressibility of water, you may perhaps claim him for your own. Would you soar to fame upon a rocket, or burst into glory from a shell! we shall leave you to enquire of your naval heroes their opinion of the steam battery and the tor-pedo. It is not by the contrivance of agents of destruction that America wishes to commend her inventive genius to the admiration and gratitude of aftertimes; nor is it even in the detection of the secrets, or the composition of new modifica-tions, of physical nature.

. . . Her glory is not *dominion*, but *liberty*. Her march is the march of mind. She has a spear and a shield: but the motto upon her shield is—*Freedom, Independence, Peace*. This has been her declaration; this has been, as far as her necessary in-tercourse with the rest of mankind would permit, her practice.

We need not linger over an analysis of the first part of the oration, interesting though that might be. It is the conclusion just quoted that is to be regarded as the climactic statement of American national spirit. It was spoken to a nation whose temper had been steadily rising for years, and whose hostility to England had been worked up by the bitterest of journalistic controversies. It was spoken on the national holiday which was distinguished throughout the country in 1821 by an almost uniform expression of hatred for England and of wild patriotism for the United States.[63] These circumstances give to Adams's conclusion something more than passing interest.

The statement of American foreign policy in the first paragraph throws light on Adams's views. Here he sums up his opinions of America's position in world affairs. The United States has "held forth to . . . [others] the hand of innocent friendship, of equal freedom, of generous reciprocity." She has respected the independence of other nations while asserting and maintaining her own. America sympathizes with the cause of freedom everywhere, "but she goes not abroad in search of monsters to destroy. She is the well-wisher to the freedom and independence of all. She is the champion and vindicator only of her own. She will recommend the general cause by the countenance of her voice, and the benignant sympathy of her example." But the dangers of a different course are too great for her to risk them even in the defense of an ideal.

---

[63] See letter of J. Adams to Sprague, August 4, 1821. *Niles' Weekly Register*, XXI, 11, September 1, 1821. The *National Intelligencer's* account of the banquet which followed the oration, with its forty-one recorded toasts accompanied by three-gun salutes, further gives evidence of the unusual patriotic fervor which characterized this Independence Day. *National Intelligencer*, July 7, 1821.

Here is a declaration of principles which is full of interest to students of the foreign policy of this period. It
reveals Adams's thoughts on the rights and duties of the
United States in the foreign field, and, as the public assertion of those rights and duties by a responsible state
official, it constitutes a document which should be ranked
with those other declarations which from time to time
have both stated and given direction to the foreign policies of the United States. The main principles were traditional; but here, almost for the first time, is an open
recognition of the idea inferred but not expressed in earlier utterances. Adams clearly laid down the proposition
that American policy is governed by the interests of the
United States alone. "She is the well-wisher to the freedom
and independence of all. She is the champion and vindicator only of her own." Those words deserve more prominence than they have hitherto received. There spoke the
realist as well as the patriot.

The challenge to England which follows this statement
of policy needs little comment. It is eloquent of the spirit
which pervaded the speaker and those who heard or read
his words. It was the national reply to the scornful, sneering condescension of the English reviews and newspapers.
It was the affirmation of superior taste, cultivation of mind,
and honesty of heart. There was much to be criticized in
English attitudes and culture, but that a Harvard grad-
uate and scholar of ability could have spoken of Scott,
Byron, and their fellows, even in a Fourth of July address,
as "spawners of fustian romance and lascivious lyrics" reveals much. It reveals how far apart the nations had drifted
and how little sympathy and understanding existed between even their greatest minds.

A few words should be given to the reception of Adams's oration. The Republican press praised it highly, as was to be expected. Niles described its manner as "beautiful—in many instances sublime." He noticed significantly that "There is a warmth and feeling too, in it, that has surprized all who did not recollect his eloquent vindication of general *Jackson* . . . ."[64] The *National Intelligencer* also remarked editorially on the "eloquent vindication of the literary and scientific character of our country from the sarcasms and cavils of European writers. . . ."[65] There were criticisms, to be sure, which the *Intelligencer* thought fit to answer.[66] The speech was attacked by extremists as "too florid," and as "spiritless" [!], and the Richmond *Enquirer* found it not equal to the compositions of Demosthenes and Cicero.

Foreign observers dwelt upon the political implications of the speech and regarded it as cheap demagoguery. Polética transmitted a copy of it to his chief, Nesselrode, and referred to it as follows:

> . . . it is from one end to the other nothing but a virulent diatribe against England interspersed with republican exaggerations addressed not to the informed and enlightened class of the nation but to the numerical majority of the American public.[67]

Polética was right. It *was* an address, not to the intellectual few, but to the American people, who indeed formed that *majorité numérique* which the Russian minister characterized so flippantly. He was astute enough, how-

---

[64] *Niles' Weekly Register*, XX, 305, July 14, 1821.
[65] *National Intelligencer*, July 7, 1821.
[66] *Ibid.*, July 21, 1821.
[67] Polética to Nesselrode, July 12, 1821. Russia, *Correspondence*, XVIII, 327.

ever, to realize that this was no mere occasional speech, but in fact an oration "which gives the key to American policy. It seems . . . to contain the whole system in a few words." Stratford Canning again misunderstood the secretary of state and ascribed only local political significance to the address.

> He [Adams] took advantage of the opportunity [wrote Canning] to ingratiate himself with his new political allies by language offensive to England and altogether averse to that friendly understanding which his Government as well as ours professed a desire to maintain, and of which he was the official organ to one of the parties.[68]

In general, the temper of the country was in tune with the views expressed and the attitude taken by Adams. Niles wrote that he had heard but "one opinion" of its excellence, and John Adams testified that "the proud reflections on us, so perpetually poured forth in England . . . [have] not escaped the notice of any oration I have read this year."[69] While it was not received with universal praise, even the partisan differences which made many hostile to Adams could not obscure the timeliness and appropriateness of his great address.

In concluding this chapter let us again emphasize the consistency of these manifestations of Adams's spirit and national feeling. They delineate not only the character of the man but also his political views. In his relations with foreign statesmen he made a point of asserting American dignity and equality in world affairs. He persistently declared the independence of the United States and its

---

[68] Stratford Canning's memoirs. Lane-Poole, *Life of Stratford Canning*, I, 309.

[69] J. Adams to Sprague, August 4, 1821. *Niles' Weekly Register*, XXI, 11, September 1, 1821.

refusal to tolerate hostile criticism. At home, he tried always to arouse a spirit of national self-consciousness and to expose the selfishness of English policy and the hostility of English spirit. Through it all ran Adams's ambition to give the country the "bold" leadership it needed and desired. He sensed the temper of the nation in some ways as well as Jackson himself. Indeed, the student may see in him the transition from Monroe to Jackson, for he combined in his own spirit elements from the characters of both his contemporaries. Finally, this policy at home and abroad must have given Adams great personal satisfaction when he thought of himself as a loyal servant and defender of his country's honor.

Adams's foreign policy possessed great possibilities. Wrongly or rashly used it would defeat itself; wisely handled it contained definite advantages in the game of diplomacy. What did the future hold for it?

CHAPTER IX

The Monroe Doctrine, an Independent Foreign Policy

\\ THE MONROE DOCTRINE had its immediate origin in the events of the fall of 1823, but it cannot be divorced from the experiences of the preceding years/'It would be very easy to explain the President's message by emphasizing the superficial aspects of the problem, but that would not result in an accurate interpretation.\\The Monroe Doctrine was the result of forces which had been at work in the United States for years, forces whose influence was becoming evident even before 1820./'The developments of the fall of 1823 brought matters to a crisis, revealed the operation of these underlying elements, and made certain a declaration of policy in that year, but they did not "cause" that result. They formed the "incident" which determined the time of the declaration. The important thing to be remembered is that, by June, 1823, the trend of American thought and experience had been so definitely in the direction of an independent, national, republican foreign policy that a formal statement of it was inevitable. Sooner or later, it would have been made. All that was necessary was a provocative "incident."

Let us recall briefly what may be termed the conditioning factors behind the Monroe Doctrine. The unsettled state of Europe, which Monroe likened to that of 1789, was a constant source of concern to Americans. The Continent appeared to be upon the threshold of a new era of internal revolution and international war. There never had been a time in the history of America when war in

Europe had not affected the lives of the people in the western hemisphere. Although Americans did not know how they would become implicated in this new strife, they were haunted by the fear that the old series of developments would be repeated. War in Europe would sooner or later involve England, and, once she entered the fray, the interests of the United States would be threatened. Therefore, the spectacle of Europe at war aroused apprehensions. While America's relations with France and Russia were reasonably satisfactory and while there was no reason to suspect those Powers of hostile designs, problems were pending which required careful diplomacy for their solution. Only by maintaining an attitude of aloofness and impartiality could the United States hope to succeed. Relations with England were much less promising, and her sea power made her a dangerous adversary.

The temper of the public influenced the government at every turn. The steady progress of resentment against England *per se* reached a climax in 1822–1823, and a distinct anti-English bias in the national thought resulted. The course of English policy had increased this tendency. Recent occurrences in Europe had reanimated popular antagonism against Old World principles and reactionary government. American nationalism was of a very emotional type during this period and was easily stirred. The actions of the Powers at Verona and of France in Spain evoked expressions of pride in American institutions and of sympathy for the oppressed peoples of Europe. From this state of mind resulted much inconsistency and uncertainty of purpose. Americans became enthusiastic at the idea of aiding the Greeks to recover their former glories and at the same time demanded increased appropriations for defense against the possible attacks of foreign enemies. This confusion of judgment was increasing in 1823, and the need for directing Americans along the paths of reasonableness was becoming apparent.

Yet another conditioning element is to be found in the fact that, while the United States had declared its policy plainly to France and to Russia, the state of its relations with England made it very difficult to come to any understanding with that Power. England could not be threatened, since America had not the bargaining power which enabled her to be outspoken with France and Russia. *They* did not want to drive the United States into the arms of England, and knowledge of this desire gave the United States considerable influence. But was it possible to convince England that American opposition to her expansion in Oregon or in the areas to the south of the United States would injure English interests? A direct threat might only make matters worse, yet the United States would never be secure so long as there was the possibility of the extension of English political influence in the western hemisphere. The equivocal position of England in world affairs at this time made the need for blocking her power more and more pressing.

The growing preoccupation of the people of the United States with internal affairs also had an influence upon her foreign relations. Westward expansion, the effects of a growing national spirit upon sectional interests, and the complex problems which the Industrial Revolution had produced were directing American development into new channels. The feeling that the United States and the New World were so different from Europe and England that nothing was to be gained from close contact with them was increased by the orientation of internal affairs. In addition, these new problems limited the freedom of action of the United States. Previously, the solution for pressing problems in the areas near the borders had been the seizure or purchase of territory. In this fashion the Louisiana and Florida questions had been settled. But sectional differences, which the admission of Missouri had revealed, precluded the further use of these means. The United States found itself in the very difficult position of a relatively weak nation attempting to maintain the *status quo* in the collapsing colonial empire of another weak Power then engaged in war. Such a situation would have taxed the diplomatic ability of any government. It is indeed a tribute to the diplomacy of the critical decade of the twenties that the interests of the country were protected as well as they were during the nineteenth century.

The unsettled state of European politics, the attitude of the public toward the foreign situation, fear of the power of England, and internal conditions combined to direct the thoughts of American diplomats toward a clear definition of their policy, but certain developments in the fall of 1823 made an immediate declaration a necessity. These determining factors, as they may be called, were three in number. For the first time, the American press began to hint that the peace and happiness of the United States were at stake as a result of the crusade of the French into Spain. Early in 1823, the general view was that there was "nothing to fear" from the aims of the European autocrats.[1] During the summer, however, a change was no-

---

[1] See the *Commercial Advertiser* [New York], in the *National Intelligencer*, March 20, 1823; *Niles' Weekly Register*, XXIV, 33, March 22, 1823; and the *National Intelligencer*, July 16, 1823.

ticeable. The so-called treaty of Verona was published in *Niles' Weekly Register* in August; and in September Niles predicted that "we shall have no small difficulties with the powers of Europe" and that probably American rights would not be respected by the reactionary rulers.[2]

Earlier in the year, *The Edinburgh Review* had published an article which condemned the Holy Alliance and demanded that the English government intervene on behalf of Spain in order to prevent an attack upon its own institutions![3] This partisan dissertation found an echo in the article which appeared in October in *The North American Review*. Interpreting the same collection of documents which had called forth the remarks of its Scottish contemporary, the Boston journal allowed its fancy free rein. It declared that the Holy Alliance planned the destruction of the English constitution and would achieve that end by the same means that had been employed in Naples and in Spain! Assuming, quite logically from this startling premise, that no free nation on earth was safe, the *Review* asked: "Would not the Spanish colonies, as part of the same empire, then demand their parental attention? And might not the United States be next considered as deserving their kind guardianship?" Why not, indeed? The article further expressed the suspicion that Russia had plans for encroaching on American rights on the Northwest Coast as part of a systematic policy directed against the United States. Significantly enough, even in its wildest flights the *Review* did not lose sight of the threat of English action.

---

[2] *Niles' Weekly Register*, XXIV, 347, August 2, 1823, and XXV, 1, September 6, 1823.

[3] *The Edinburgh Review*, XXXVIII (1823), 241.

... If England should join Spain in her contest with France, the chance of this country's remaining at peace will be still more diminished. Great Britain is a greater monopolist of the commerce of the world than even Spain. Her commercial system has extended itself into every quarter, and has been everywhere followed and supported by her wealth, her intrigues, and her arms. In America, Europe, Asia, and Africa, it is seen and felt, grasping and monopolizing the commerce and carrying trade of all nations. Every war has its preservation for an object, and every negotiation tends to extend and perpetuate it. . . .

Just as Calhoun and Jackson exaggerated the power of the Holy Alliance but feared equally the threat of English intervention, so *The North American Review* fell into the same line of thought and, similarly, concluded with an appeal for increased measures of national defense.[4]

These articles happened to coincide with the arrival in America of the news of the fall of Cadiz, with the result that in November a slight panic occurred in some quarters. Calhoun was not the only person who became "moonstruck" at the prospect of French power, and, though there was almost no foundation for the *Review's* statements, they influenced the public. Niles asked his readers the same rhetorical questions which the Boston periodical had proposed,[5] and even the *National Intelligencer* admitted that "The day may come, sooner than we have thought on, when these ['our fortified coast and our gallant navy'] may not only be *our* defence, but a barrier to preserve the remaining liberties of the world."[6] With sounder insight than Niles, however, the organ of the administration de-

[4] *The North American Review*, XVII (1823), 340.
[5] *Niles' Weekly Register*, XXV, 161, November 15, 1823.
[6] *National Intelligencer*, November 18, 1823.

clared that the pent-up volcano in Europe would soon explode with greater fierceness than before.

While the problem of possible interference with the affairs of the New World is being considered, one or two collateral developments may be mentioned. There is no doubt that in October and November there was current in the United States a sense of apprehension of French power, but it is also plain that it was not a deep-seated conviction, but rather a momentary manifestation caused by a few alarmist articles and by the fall of Cadiz. It is also interesting to observe that both Niles and *The North American Review* were strong supporters of the Greek cause and that both argued for active interference in European affairs at the time when they were voicing fears of attacks upon the very existence of the United States. The *Review* had sounded "the clarion call of American Philhellenism" in the same issue which contained the article on the Holy Alliance.[7] Such confusion of thought and judgment was a general phenomenon and throws a great deal of light upon the public spirit. Those who were most inclined to fear attacks upon the United States clamored most loudly for the United States to interfere actively in European affairs by aiding the Greek patriots.

The administration took a saner, more reasoned attitude toward the whole matter and adopted a consistent course. It is significant that when these apprehensions were being aired, one paper steadfastly reiterated its disbelief in them. The editor of *The Enquirer* "repeatedly assured his countrymen that they had nothing to fear from

---

[7] *The North American Review*, XVII (1823), 413. See Earle, "American Interest in the Greek Cause, 1821–1827," *The American Historical Review*, XXXIII (1927), 44.

the tyrants of Europe." Thomas Ritchie was very intimate with the Virginia statesmen and was informed of the progress of diplomatic developments. His conclusions therefore reveal the state of mind of the members of the government. As his biographer rightly notes, "his predictions regarding the intentions of the continental Powers in America must have had a better foundation than the belief that Great Britain would not aid them."[8] In spite of the opinions of *The Enquirer* there was a rather general feeling in the country that all was not well with its foreign relations. This, too, was a matter which required the attention of the government.

While the state of public opinion was thus one of the determining factors, the suggestion which George Canning made to Rush for a joint declaration of policy was a second and even more important one. This English overture further unsettled and complicated the problems of the United States. It raised vague anxieties for the unknown future and misgivings about the real nature of English policy. It forced the United States to act and to act immediately. Canning's proposal could either be accepted or rejected. If it were rejected America would have to make a separate declaration. This implication of a refusal to join England is often overlooked. If England were not bound by her own promises, it was absolutely imperative that the policy of the United States should be placed in a clear light, so that there could be no possible misunderstanding of its character. Canning's action, therefore, was decisive for the United States.

The third factor which made a declaration of American

---

[8] Ambler, *Thomas Ritchie*, 84.

policy certain was the Russian minister's communications to Adams in October and November. These impersonal statements of the essential soundness of monarchical principles and the resolution of the Tsar not to recognize the South American republics were received when there was little chance of their being disregarded by the administration. They were not threats, and none of the members of the government so regarded them. The spirit of the country, however, made a reply, a counterstatement, natural and indispensable. Above all, the Russian notes afforded a magnificent opportunity to make the statement general. It could be an answer to Russia as well as to England, and it could be couched in terms which would include the Old World as a whole.

These three developments, added to the more general forces already discussed, made necessary the declaration of policy which Monroe included in his message to Congress. It is not surprising, therefore, that the reaction of the administration and its advisers to the events of October and November reflected quite accurately the currents of thought which had so long been gathering force. It is unnecessary to narrate again the details of the correspondence between Canning and Rush and the reports of the American minister to the secretary of state. If the phases of English policy are sketched briefly and the reaction of American statesmen to those developments is emphasized, the connection between the history of the postwar years and the Monroe Doctrine will be established, and a truer understanding of that policy will be obtained.[9]

⁹ Footnotes are superfluous, as the sources are well known. They are (1) W. C. Ford, ed., "Genesis of the Monroe Doctrine," *in* Massachusetts Historical Society, *Proceedings*, Second series, XV, 373; (2) W. C. Ford,

In August, 1823, Rush had expressed to Canning his understanding that it was the policy of England to prevent any interference by France in the New World. To his surprise, the foreign secretary replied by suggesting an Anglo-American declaration to that effect. No mention was made of any immediate danger of French action, nor was it even affirmed that France had any intention of interfering in the New World. At the same time, moreover, Canning refused to state definitely that the colonies were irrevocably lost to Spain. A few days after this interview, he wrote the communication to Rush in which he outlined the form of the proposed declaration.[10] Again he did not say positively that any European Power had plans for the reduction of the revolted colonies. However, Rush's steadfast refusal to act in concert apparently led Canning to intimate that a congress was planned for the near future. But this report was suspiciously indefinite.

I have received notice . . . [he wrote] that so soon as the military objects in Spain are achieved . . . a proposal will be made for a Congress, or some less formal concert and consultation, specially upon the affairs of Spanish America.[11]

ed., "John Quincy Adams and the Monroe Doctrine," *The American Historical Review,* VII (1902), 676, and VIII (1902), 28; (3) Rush, *Memoranda,* Second series; and (4) J. Q. Adams, *Memoirs,* VI.

[10] Canning suggested that the declaration include these principles:

"1. We conceive the recovery of the colonies by Spain to be hopeless.

"2. We conceive the question of the recognition of them, as independent States, to be one of time and circumstances.

"3. We are, however, by no means disposed to throw any impediment in the way of an arrangement between them and the mother country by amicable negotiation.

"4. We aim not at the possession of any portion of them ourselves.

"5. We could not see any portion of them transferred to any other power with indifference."

[11] Canning to Rush, August 23, 1823. W. C. Ford, ed., "John Quincy Adams and the Monroe Doctrine," *The American Historical Review,* VII (1902), 683.

Even Rush realized that this information did not impose the necessity of instant action and adhered firmly to his demand for English recognition of South American independence *first* and for a joint declaration second.

The information revealed by the interview of August 16 and by the letters of August 20 and 23 was sent to Washington by Rush with explanations of his stand. These dispatches were received on October 9 and formed the basis of the first steps taken by Monroe. The President felt that the time had arrived when England must make a decision between despotism and liberty and that she had adopted this means of announcing her choice. He assumed that this was an occasion on which a European connection might safely be made by the United States and was inclined to believe that an attack on the colonies would be followed by a move against the United States. These impressions were recorded in the letter of October 17 in which Monroe asked Jefferson and Madison for their advice on the subject.[12]

Madison's reply was cautious. He regarded Canning's move as a confirmation of the current idea that a "crusade" against South America was planned. He approved the project for a joint declaration and thought it "particularly fortunate" that England was ready to coöperate, for with her support "we have nothing to fear from the rest of Europe." But Madison, admittedly uninformed on the details of foreign relations, misunderstood the extent of England's conversion to liberal principles when he suggested that she might be induced to condemn the invasion of Spain by France and to declare her support of

---

[12] Monroe to Jefferson, October 17, 1823. Monroe, *Writings*, VI, 323.

the Greeks. Although his thought was confused about the consistency of such action, it is clear that he regarded England as the key to the future and that he esteemed the chance to draw her over to the side of free government as worth the abandonment of America's policy of independent action. Significantly, he raised the question of the effect which an acceptance of Canning's proposal would have on the future of Cuba and Porto Rico. His views were rather vague and general, however, and he asked as many questions as he answered.[12]

Jefferson was better informed upon the subject of world politics than was Madison, and his reply to Monroe gained definiteness as a result. In a letter which has rightly become a classic of American political literature, Jefferson formulated the principles on which the foreign policy of the United States should be based: the noninterference of America in European affairs, and the prevention of European intervention in the affairs of the New World. At the outset, Jefferson avoided the confusion of thought which misled every member of the administration except John Quincy Adams. If America desired to maintain the *status quo* in the western world, consistency demanded that she take no part in attempts to upset the existing order in Europe.

It is of the greatest interest to notice what Jefferson regarded as the advantage and the disadvantage of an acceptance of Canning's plan. The chief benefit would *not* be the opportunity to block the Holy Alliance, but the chance to limit the danger of *English* hostility.

. . . One nation, most of all [he wrote], could disturb us in this

---

[12] Madison to Monroe, October 20, 1823. Madison, *Writings,* IX, 157.

pursuit [of freedom]; she now offers to lead, aid, and accompany us in it. By acceding to her proposition, we detach her from the bands, bring her mighty weight into the scale of free government, and emancipate a continent at one stroke, which might otherwise linger long in doubt and difficulty. Great Britain is the nation which can do us the most harm of any one, or all on earth; and with her on our side we need not fear the whole world. With her then, we should most sedulously cherish a cordial friendship; and nothing would tend more to knit our affections than to be fighting once more, side by side, in the same cause. . . . And if, to facilitate this, we can effect a division in the body of the European powers, and draw over to our side its most powerful member, surely we should do it. . . . With Great Britain withdrawn from their scale and shifted into that of our two continents, all Europe combined would not undertake such a war. For how would they propose to get at either enemy without superior fleets? Nor is the occasion to be slighted which this proposition offers, of declaring our protest against the atrocious violations of the rights of nations, by the interference of any one in the affairs of another, so flagitiously begun by Bonaparte, and now continued by the equally lawless Alliance, calling itself Holy.

This clear recognition of England's sea power and the value to the United States of removing it as a threat is of the greatest importance, for it reveals the way in which a very influential and very experienced American interpreted the foreign scene. *Only* in the event of a combination of England with the European Powers would the New World be seriously endangered.

The disadvantage of participating in a declaration of the sort suggested by Canning lay in the fact that that would prevent the United States from acquiring Cuba. But even the sacrifice of this valuable island was of secondary significance. The greatest danger which confronted the United States, the occupation of Cuba by England, would be averted.

Yet, as I am sensible that this can never be obtained [American possession of Cuba], even with her own consent, but by war; and its independence, which is our second interest, (and especially its independence of England,) can be secured without it, I have no hesitation in abandoning my first wish to future chances, and accepting its independence, with peace and the friendship of England, rather than its association, at the expense of war and her enmity.

To tie the hands of England in the New World was worth the abandonment of Cuba, the surrender of the principle of independent action, and the limitation of freedom to expand southward and westward. This was a high price; that Jefferson was willing to pay it is proof of his respect for the power of England in world affairs.[14]

Hardly had Monroe received the replies of Jefferson and Madison when additional dispatches arrived from Rush which completely changed the earlier aspect of the negotiation. Canning had refused to recognize South America, Rush reported, and had also declined to wait until the American minister could receive instructions from his government. The foreign secretary had therefore asked Rush to forget the whole affair and to consider the proposal nonexistent. In a letter to the secretary of state, Rush related in detail the arguments which Canning had used to induce him to act immediately. The tone of the dispatch makes it clear that Rush suspected ulterior motives for the haste displayed by Canning. This distrust was further revealed in a private letter to Monroe which reached Washington on November 3 with the second set

[14] Jefferson to Monroe, October 24, 1823. Jefferson, *Works* (P. L. Ford, ed.), XII, 318.

of dispatches. Rush was in the habit of writing private notes to his friend, and there is no doubt that they influenced the President. All the ingrained suspicion of England so characteristic of American thought is here.

I am bound to own that I shall not be able to avoid, at bottom, some distrust of the motives of all such advances to me, whether directly or indirectly, by this government, at this particular juncture of the world.

We have seen her wage a war of 20 years at a cost of treasure and blood incalculable, in support of the independence of other states (as she said) when that independence was threatened by a movement proceeding from the *people* of France. We have seen her at the close of that contest abandoning the great interests of the people of other states, anxious apparently only about monarchs and thrones. We have seen her at the same epoch become in effect a member of the Holy Alliance; though she could not in form, and continue to abet its principles up to the attack on Naples. Even then the separation was but partial, and, true to her sympathy with the monarchical principle, we find her faith pledged and her fleets ready to interpose not on any new extremity of wrong or oppression to the *people* of Naples, but on any molestation to the royal family. . . .

The estimate which I have formed of the genius of this government, as well as of the characters of the men who direct, or who influence, all its operations, would lead me to fear that we are not as yet likely to witness any very material changes in the part which Britain has acted in the world for the past fifty years, when the cause of freedom has been at stake; the part which she acted in 1774 in America, which she has since acted in Europe, and is now acting in Ireland. I shall therefore find it hard to keep from my mind the suspicion that the approaches of her ministers to me at this portentous juncture for a concert of policy which they have not heretofore courted with the United States, are bottomed on their own calculations. I wish that I could sincerely see in them a true concern for the rights and liberties of mankind. Nevertheless, whatever may be the *motive* of these approaches, if they give promise of leading to good *effects* . . . [I shall listen to them].[15]

Despite the last sentence, this letter presents no encouraging picture of English policy. If five years' experience at the English court led Rush to express such sentiments in private correspondence with the President, one may be sure that the general opinion in America was equally skeptical. The way in which Canning dropped the negotiation rankled in the heart of the American minister and made him unusually watchful. He was an admirer of England, as his memoirs indicate, but he had no confidence in the honesty of English policy. In a dispatch to Adams, which was received in the United States on November 19 and which completed the information in the hands of the government, Rush repeated his indictment of England in even stronger terms.

. . . That the British cabinet, and the governing portion of the British nation, will rejoice at heart in the downfal of the constitutional system in Spain, I have never had a doubt and have not now, so long as this catastrophe can be kept from crossing the path of British interests and British ambition. This nation in its collective, corporate, capacity has no more sympathy with popular rights and freedom now, than it had on the plains of Lexington in America. . . . With a king in the hands of his ministers, with an aristocracy of unbounded opulence and pride, with what is called a house of commons constituted essentially by this aristocracy and always moved by its influence, England can, in reality, never look with complacency upon popular and equal rights, whether abroad or at home. She therefore moves in her natural orbit when she

---

[15] Rush to Monroe, September 15, 1823. W. C. Ford, ed., "John Quincy Adams and the Monroe Doctrine," *The American Historical Review*, VII (1902), 687.

wars, positively or negatively, against them. For their own sakes alone, she will never war in their favor.[16]

Rush questioned English policy in principle and also felt that concrete reasons for alarm existed. In this same dispatch he told Adams that Canning had informed him that English commissioners (one of whom had ministerial credentials) had been sent to Mexico and that the English government expected that closer relations between the two countries would result. This move, together with others which Canning revealed, made the future dark indeed. The picture of English policy which Rush gave to Adams is best painted in his own words.

It may perhaps afford room for conjecture what had led to the preference of Mexico over the other ex-colonies for such a provisionary diplomatic representation. I have heard a rumour, that an eye to some immediate advantage from the mines of that country has been the motive. . . . Mr. Canning himself in one of our conversations thought fit to select Mexico as affording a prominent illustration of interior disquiet. Whether then the above rumour is the key to this early preference, or the proximity of this new state to the territories of the United States—or what considerations may have led to it, a little more time will probably disclose. It may rest on the mere fact of her greater population and riches.

Mr. Canning also informed me, that orders would be given by this government to its squadron in the West Indies, to protect the trade of British subjects (to the extent of making reprisals if necessary) with the Spanish colonies, in case the licence for this trade which the Cortes granted in January last was not renewed. It will be recollected, that the same decree of the Cortes in that month which settled, under a threat of reprisals, the British claims upon Spain for captures, laid

---

[16] Rush to J. Q. Adams, October 10, 1823. W. C. Ford, ed., "John Quincy Adams and the Monroe Doctrine," *The American Historical Review*, VII (1902), 690.

open the trade of the ultra marine provinces to Britain for ten years. . . .

. . . It will next be seen that her ex-colonies come in for their share of this prompt and summary species of remedy of which Britain is setting other nations the example, for Mr. Canning also informed me that if the Colombian government did not make speedy reparation for the alleged aggression committed upon a British ship by the fort at Bocachica at the entrance of the bay of Carthagena, orders would be given to blockade that port. . . . From the account I have had of it from the Colombian minister in this city, Mr. Ravenga, I infer and believe that the offence was on the side of the British ship.

This was definite information from the foreign secretary himself. No rumors were these, but statements of fact. England had sent agents to Mexico to work for closer relations; she had announced her determination to maintain her privileged position in the trade with Cuba and Porto Rico by reprisals (a euphemistic term for undeclared war); and she had avowed the purpose of coercing one of the independent republics by means of a blockade. England had long been suspected of designs on Mexico, and she had long been charged with seeking to dominate the economic life of Spanish America. Here was proof of her plans, of the actual steps which she had taken toward their execution, and of her supreme indifference to the views of the United States. Canning's very boldness in informing the American minister was disquieting, for the imagination of Americans might wander at will over the possibilities of what had *not* been disclosed. What Power was it, then, that was about to interfere in the New World in 1823? Was it France, who had given every indication that she did not wish to antagonize the United States, who was then engaged in a European war, and concerning whose "plans" only the vaguest rumors in the press and the hints of an *English* diplomat had reached America? Or was it England, who had never once satisfactorily assured the United States of her friendly spirit, who had pursued a uniformly hostile course, and who now added to a suspicious proposal for joint action the announcement that she contemplated armed interference in the Spanish colonial trade and the actual blockade of the port of an independent South American republic?

It was a foregone conclusion that the cabinet would decline to act with England when it became clear that her proposals lacked sincerity. Adams regarded Canning's moves as attempts to trap the United States into a renunciation of Cuba, and the secretary opposed the making of any such self-denying statement. The future of the United States should be unhampered by inconvenient declarations. The refusal of England to recognize the republics of the south and her reluctance to break completely with the Continental Powers made joint action impossible. Instructions to Rush on November 30 made this view of the American government plain.

... Great Britain negotiating at once with the European Alliance, and *with us,* concerning America, without being bound by any permanent community of principle ... would still be free to accommodate her policy to any of those distributions of power, and partitions of Territory which have for the last half century been the ultima ratio of all European political arrangements. ... [17]

That sentence is an interesting echo of the past experience of the secretary of state, for he was convinced years before

[17] J. Q. Adams to Rush, November 30, 1823. W. C. Ford, ed., "Genesis of the Monroe Doctrine," *in* Massachusetts Historical Society, *Proceedings,* Second series, XV, 391.

that the early failure of the administration's South American policy had resulted in part from Monroe's willingness to confide in England and to act with her, rather than independently.

The effect of a joint declaration on world politics did not escape the keen eyes of the members of the administration. To range the United States with England would antagonize France and Russia and would deprive American diplomacy of one of its strongest weapons in the important negotiations which were then being conducted with those Powers. England was a dangerous friend, and the "threat" of Continental action was not real enough to induce the Americans to accept the unpleasant aspects of an *entente* with her.

. . . By taking the step here [wrote Monroe to Jefferson early in December], it is done in a manner more conciliatory with, & respectful to Russia, & the other powers, than if taken in England, and as it is thought with more credit to our govt. Had we mov'd in the first instance in England, separated as she is in part, from those powers, our union with her, being marked, might have produced irritation with them. We know that Russia, dreads a connection between the UStates.& G. Britain, or harmony in policy. Moving on our own ground, the apprehension that unless she retreats, that effect may be produced, may be a motive with her for retreating. Had we mov'd in England, it is probable, that it would have been inferr'd that we acted under her influence, & at her instigation, & thus have lost credit as well with our southern neighbours, as with the allied powers.[18]

This is the best commentary on the background of the Monroe Docrine that has ever been written, for its im-

---

[18] Monroe to Jefferson [no date; inscribed "received December 11"]. W. C. Ford, ed., "Genesis of the Monroe Doctrine," in Massachusetts Historical Society, *Proceedings*, Second series, XV, 412.

plications touch the foundations of that policy. Monroe's failure to mention France, his able discussion of the effect of the Balance of Power on American diplomacy, his assumption that the Continental Powers would not force any issue with the United States, and his concluding phrase, "& thus have lost credit as well with our southern neighbours, as with the allied powers," are of the utmost significance. For these very excellent reasons, the administration determined to act alone. All the factors which prompted this decision are related to the central idea that England was not sincere in her offer and that too close a connection with her would injure the foreign relations of the United States.

Coincident with these developments were two communications from Tuyll to Adams. They were circular letters which the Tsar had sent to all his diplomats and they expressed the views of monarchy and of Russian policy which were mentioned above. That Adams should demand the opportunity to answer these declarations of Old World principles with an equally plain statement of the foundations of American institutions is obvious. To him, a proud, clear, and bold utterance of her ideals was a sacred obligation which could not be avoided without dishonor. Neither he nor Monroe regarded the Russian notes as threats to the United States, and both welcomed the opportunity to reply. All the nationalism which had been growing in intensity during the preceding years found expression in the paragraphs of the message which dealt with American principles.

The cabinet discussions which resulted in the Monroe Doctrine have often been analyzed by those who desired to ascertain the authorship of its provisions. As a foreign policy, it is immaterial whether Monroe or Adams enunciated it, for it was a *national* policy decided upon after the fullest consideration by the leaders of the government. What *is* significant about these cabinet meetings is that the views of the active members, Adams, Calhoun, and Monroe, reflected all the conflicting currents of thought which filled the minds of their countrymen.[19] Calhoun's panic at the ostensible power of the Holy Alliance, his interest in the cause of the Greeks, and his inconsistent, emotional statements of the position of the United States are typical of one aspect of public opinion. Adams's nationalism, self-assurance, shrewd judgment, and more harmonious suggestions represent the other phase of the national spirit. Between these two men stood Monroe, exerting a moderating influence on both, reflecting at times the views of each, and ultimately making the decision upon which the policy was to be based. That he chose the more independent, the more nationalistic, and the more fearless course is a tribute both to his own insight and to Adams's arguments. Finally, these cabinet discussions reveal in the clearest way how considerations of American foreign policy at this time revolved around the question of English policy. That she might become involved through fear or self-interest, that her action might injure the United States, and that trouble of any sort between the Old World and the New might result in the complete commercial and political dominance of England, were possibilities which colored all the conversations.

It is now time to place the Monroe Doctrine in its proper setting in the national life of America. In the de-

---

[19] Crawford was too ill to attend the meetings, and Southard and Wirt ventured few opinions on the foreign situation.

velopment of this study the relation to foreign policy of many factors which are not usually considered in that connection has been indicated. In this new light, the Monroe Doctrine appears as the logical culmination of the thought and experience of the American nation from 1815 to 1823 and it cannot be separated from the history of those years. It was a truly national policy which could serve the United States as a guide and a defense. It was, on the one hand, a declaration of principles; on the other, a protective measure designed to shield the United States from any disturbance of the *status quo* in the New World. Its aim was to prevent all interference in the western hemisphere by any Power whatsoever. An extension of political or commercial control by England would have violated its provisions in letter as well as in spirit.

England was the key Power in the formation of American foreign policy. This idea has been traced in some detail, and it should be recalled here that even those who advocated joining her in a declaration of policy did so principally because they sought a means of protecting their country from her hostility. The Holy Alliance was hardly an active menace, and the statements concerning it were motivated more by American nationalism than by fear.

It has been the fashion of late to minimize the importance of the Monroe Doctrine, to rank it as a less brilliant achievement than the Florida treaty of 1819 or the recognition of South America in 1822. Viewed in the light of world politics and the realities of America's position, it appears in a different guise. Regarded for what it really was, it represents the outmaneuvering of a strong Power by a weak one. It made plain to England that war would probably result from further extensions of her political

influence in the New World. Either she must fight or re-
nounce the idea of possessing Cuba and establishing new
posts in the Oregon country. The Monroe Doctrine was
no guaranty of protection to the United States, but it did
make the policy of this country clear to all who chose to
read. The dangers of foreign connections were avoided,
the United States remained free, and England was caught
in the mesh of her own tangled policy. The English government was blocked not only by the threat contained in
the Monroe Doctrine but also by the fact that the declaration appealed to the widespread sentiments of the masses
of the English people. When it is compared with earlier
diplomatic successes, the Monroe Doctrine does not suffer. Previously, the United States had been dealing with
weak Powers like Spain, or with land Powers like France
and Russia. Now, she was primarily concerned with a great
sea Power which had no strong motives for placating
its weaker rival. The Monroe Doctrine did not produce
all the effects which ardent but uncritical writers have
claimed for it, but it did accomplish more than recent
critics admit. It was no fourth-rate diplomatic move, but
a decisive declaration of fundamental policies.

There is no simple explanation of so important a land-
mark in the history of American foreign policy as the
Monroe Doctrine. This comprehensive statement of the
position of the United States in world affairs was the product of past history and tradition, of internal conditions
and social outlook, and of the coincidence of events. In
the social and spiritual development of the United States,
its significance is great. It reflects the deepest convictions
of the people as a whole toward the Old World and is the
expression of the fact that the United States had turned

its back upon Europe and was henceforth to be occupied primarily with its own domestic problems, with the issues raised by westward expansion, and with the serious complications created by a growing spirit of nationalism.

The principles which the President laid down in his message of December 2, 1823, reflect this background. The declaration that "the American continents . . . are henceforth not to be considered as subjects for future colonization by any European powers" is both a statement of fact and a warning. No portion of those continents remained unclaimed. Russia was about to withdraw her claim to influence south of the fifty-fifth parallel. The noncolonization principle, therefore, was merely a restatement of a proposition upon which both countries had tentatively agreed. The warning was made to England. She alone of all the European Powers had in contemplation the establishment of new colonial settlements. The Oregon question was far from solved, and Americans had a decided impression that England hoped to found new posts on the Columbia River. The joint occupation of Oregon was to continue for five years, and it was the task of the United States to prevent any extension of English control that would threaten American interests in the Columbia River basin. To preserve the *status quo* in Oregon and to block new undertakings by England constituted the real purpose of the noncolonization clause.

The second principle, "With the existing colonies or dependencies of any European Power we have not interfered and shall not interfere," is plain. But it should be noticed particularly that it is more narrow in its application than was Canning's proposed disclaimer, which had included all the Spanish colonies, past and present. The reasons for this distinction are manifest. As long as Cuba and similar areas near the United States remained Spanish, the United States would be satisfied. But should they become independent and their free existence precarious, the United States must not be bound to stand aside. There was nothing in this provision which would in any way affect the relations between the United States and *independent* areas in the New World. Again Monroe went on record as favoring the maintenance of the existing order.

The third provision of the Monroe Doctrine has aroused the most interest and comment. At one point in his message Monroe declared that the system of Europe was different from America's and that "we should consider any attempt on their part to extend their system to any portion of this hemisphere as dangerous to our peace and safety." Referring to the independent states which had already been recognized by the United States, he added, "we could not view any interposition for the purpose of oppressing them, or controlling in any manner their destiny, by any European power in any other light than as the manifestation of an unfriendly disposition toward the United States." Taken together, these phrases are a blanket warning to the Old World to leave the Americas alone. They included England as well as the Continental Powers. Indeed, in the light of the experience of the preceding years, it would be more nearly correct to say, "the Continental Powers as well as England." To Americans, the European "system" was both commercial and political; and it was the former phase, the *English* phase, which touched them more closely. This principle was a reply to Russia, but the blow was struck at England. Canning's proposed blockade of a Colombian port came within its scope.

The prohibition of the transfer of territory from one European Power to another is usually considered as the first extension of the Monroe Doctrine. It is appropriate to suggest that this assumption is not correct. In view of the fact that throughout these years the possible transfer of Cuba to England was ever-present in American thought, such a prohibition is implicit in the very spirit of the doctrine. Since Canning had avowed his readiness to give up the idea of acquiring Cuba, and since the United States had received similar assurances from France, a direct statement was not necessary. America's own promise not to interfere was enough to remove Canning's fears. But it is inconceivable that a transfer of Cuba to England in 1824 would not have been resisted by the United States as an act contrary to the policy enunciated by Monroe in December, 1823. The purpose of that policy was to maintain the *status quo* in the New World. A change in the condition of Cuba and Porto Rico would have been the most threatening modification possible.

The fourth principle which forms a part of the Monroe Doctrine is that of noninterference by the United States in the affairs of Europe. This was an expression of a traditional idea, but in 1823 it was also a triumph for consistency and wisdom. In the face of a strong public clamor for aid to the Greeks, the administration sought to direct the people along saner lines. The problems of the United States must receive undivided attention, undisturbed by enthusiastic tilting at windmills in the Old World.

These statements *were* the Monroe Doctrine. They expressed in the truest sense the republican, national spirit of the times—that pride in American institutions and that confidence in America's destiny which permeated the spiritual life of the United States and which John Quincy Adams voiced in his oration in 1821. Time has made strange additions to their number. The Monroe Doctrine is no longer what it was, for, as it reflected the spirit of America in 1823, so has it ever since mirrored the changes in American thought. Never did a statesman more nearly fill the rôle of seer than did Adams when he warned his countrymen that a departure from these fundamental ideals would mark the end of the America he loved so well. The future of American foreign policy and particularly of the Monroe Doctrine was forecast in the words of the secretary of state:

The frontlet upon her brow will no longer beam with the ineffable splendor of freedom and independence; but in its stead will soon be substituted an imperial diadem, flashing in false and tarnished lustre, the murky radiance of dominion and power. She may become the dictatress of the world. She will be no longer the ruler of her own spirit.

The Historiography of the Monroe Doctrine

THE USUAL EXPLANATION of the Monroe Doctrine, that fear of the Holy Alliance and of Russian aggressions on the Northwest Coast called it forth, has exercised a deadening influence on the writing of histories of American foreign policy. The simplicity of this explanation and the engaging facility with which it may be presented have led nearly all writers to adopt it as historically true. It would be a most valuable and illuminating study that would trace in detail the steps by which this formula has become fixed. The limits of this essay will permit only a brief indication of the way in which this idea has gained currency and a general criticism of the best-known accounts of the formation of the Monroe Doctrine with reference to the false assumptions based upon this erroneous premise.

The sources of the conventional interpretation are English. The first suggestions that the United States and the New World were in danger of attacks by the Holy Alliance appear in the English press in 1823, particularly in the article in *The Edinburgh Review* in February. The text of the notorious "Treaty of Verona" which seemed to confirm the reality of Continental designs was first printed in the London *Morning Chronicle,* a Tory publication, and was copied into the American press from that source. These views were soon reflected in the United States, and the essay which appeared in *The North American Review* in October presented them to the public. The effectiveness of this article was enhanced by the hints which Canning had made to Rush in August and September, and Clay's attempt to obtain Congressional confirmation of the so-called "danger" emphasized the apparent reality of European designs upon the western world. The partisan debates upon the proposed mission to Panama in 1826 gave further impetus to the idea that Monroe's declaration was purely *ad hoc,* and decades later Calhoun advanced in an authoritative manner a similar explanation of the events of the year 1823.

By 1850, therefore, a definite theory of the origin of the Monroe Doctrine had been established. Significantly, it was the work of the pro-English *North American Review* and of such emotional statesmen as Clay, Webster, and Calhoun. These were not reliable sources of information, but they had the appearance of authority, and the first published accounts of the diplomacy of 1823 were of a type which reënforced their statements. The works of Rush and Stapleton, the debates in Congress and in Parliament, created a false impression, so that the earlier declarations seemed to be confirmed. In April, 1856, there appeared in *The North American Review* an article on the genesis of the Monroe Doctrine which was based upon these sources and which first presented the conventional interpretation in its complete form. By that year the threat of English expansion in Oregon, in California, in Texas, and in Cuba had been removed, and the experience of thirty years of peaceful relations had lessened the tension between the two Powers. Eleven treaties or agreements with England were concluded between 1824 and 1856, and as a result the American public became less convinced of English hostility and duplicity. The stage was set for an explanation of the Monroe Doctrine such as the *Review* presented.

In brief, these were the steps by which the formula became fixed in American thought. It had everything to recommend it. It was simple and understandable. It could be expressed in a few words, and it appeared to be based on sound historical evidence. It appealed to America's national pride and flattered her growing vanity. As a result of all these elements, the formula has influenced the writing of American history to this day. Historians of American foreign policy have universally admitted the premise that the United States feared the Holy Alliance and the designs of Russia. They have distorted their interpretations in order to make them fit this theory and they have resorted to almost fantastic explanations of the evidence before them so that it will support their primary assumption. The ablest writers have succumbed to the blinding influence of this idea. They have persistently approached the problem of the origin of the Monroe Doctrine from a European rather than from an American point of view. They have analyzed the history of *Europe* from 1815 to 1823 in order to explain the *American* Monroe Doctrine. They have ascertained the intentions of the European Powers, but have never for a moment considered the possibility that the origin of the foreign policy of the United States was to be found in American conditions and in American thought.

There is a large group of works, therefore, which almost completely overlook the fundamental aspects of the problem. Schouler's *History of the United States* presents the conventional view. The account is based chiefly on Rush's memoirs, and the author appears to be more interested in minimizing the part which Adams played than in attacking the question in a penetrating manner. The same criticism may be made of the explanation by McMaster in his *History of the People of the United States*. . . . The activities of the Holy Alliance are stressed, the American phase is neglected, and the position and attitude of England are not discussed at all. Channing's *History of the United States* is likewise superficial and stereotyped in its treatment of the origins of the Monroe Doctrine.

Similar thoughts are encountered in books which deal primarily with the Monroe Doctrine. In 1885, George F. Tucker published *The Monroe Doctrine: a Concise History of its Origin and Growth,* one of the earliest books upon that subject. He was more interested in the later developments of the doctrine than in its background and did not depart from the established theory. Maurice de Beaumarchais presents in his work, *La Doctrine de Monroë* (1898), only a short chapter on its origins in which he repeats the old tale again. The influence of the patriotic fervor of the Spanish-American War period is evident in *Cuba and International Relations,* by James M. Callahan. Published in 1899, this work adds to the usual explanation of the Monroe Doctrine the idea of the divinely inspired mission of the United States in the New World. The highly colored and flamboyant style in which it is written detracts from its effectiveness. The first book on the Monroe Doctrine which utilized the article by W. C. Ford in the *Proceedings* of the Massachusetts Historical Society was that by Thomas B. Edgington, *The Monroe Doctrine* (1904). In attempting to present a complete history of the doctrine, Mr. Edgington followed the path of his predecessors. His account of the origins is wholly conventional, and his lack of knowledge of European conditions from 1815 to 1823 makes his book quite unreliable. William F. Reddaway improved considerably upon earlier works in *The Monroe Doctrine* (1905). He understood English policy fairly well and grasped the diplomatic skill with which Adams handled the problem. But any consideration of Anglo-American relations or of the Caribbean question as factors in the formation of the doctrine is omitted, and Reddaway concludes that the United States "opposed it chiefly to the Holy Alliance."[1]

The first scientific treatment of the Monroe Doctrine appeared in 1913 when Herbert Kraus published his book, *Die Monroedoktrin in ihren Beziehungen zur amerikanischen Diplomatie und zum Völkerrecht*. His work is juristic in character, clear and definite in style, and neat in construction. The discussion of the origins of the doctrine is brief and conventional. He does note the traditional character of the policy, but he accepts the usual theory of its background. Two events evoked it:

> On the one hand was the dispute between the United States and Russia on their frontier on the Northwest Coast. On the other hand was the Holy Alliance and its preparations to interfere with the struggle of the Latin American colonies for freedom.[2]

He also argues that the prohibition of the transfer of territory from one European Power to another should be termed the Madison Doctrine, since it was first enunciated by Madison in 1811. Kraus maintains that this policy was not in any way a part of the Monroe Doctrine and that it was first united with it in 1845. Admirable as his book is in some respects, it is inadequate as a discussion of the origins of Monroe's policy, for it fails to develop the part which *Realpolitik* (as Kraus would have termed it) and sentiment played in its formation.

---

[1] P. 12. [2] P. 41.

This book was soon followed by Albert B. Hart's *The Monroe Doctrine: an Interpretation* (1916). This supposedly complete account of the history of the doctrine disregarded the effect of world politics upon American thought. No violence was done to the previous explanations of the background, the alleged friendly attitude of England was stressed, and this extraordinary interpretation of the Monroe Doctrine was advanced:

Nevertheless it is to this day a wonder that the United States of America felt strong enough to protest, and to take the position of the one power in the world that had a right to lay down a permanent principle regulating the affairs of the western hemisphere. This boldness was due in part to the lively national spirit of Monroe and Adams, Clay and Calhoun, and their fellow statesmen; in part it was called out by a real danger that Europe might settle the affairs of the southern Americans and take the northern Americans later; in part the "Special Providence for little children and the United States," aroused Americans to impress on the world their conviction that whatever the United States vigorously opposed must be given up. No success on those lines was then possible, without the enlightened policy of England under the guidance of George Canning.[3]

There was nothing marvelous or supernatural in the declaration of Monroe, and for an American historian so to misread the spirit of English policy that he can give the credit for the Monroe Doctrine to "the enlightened policy of England under the guidance of George Canning" is ironical in the extreme. True it is that histories often reflect the times in which they are written, rather than those which they affect to describe.

Two doctoral dissertations next claim attention. Little need be said of William P. Cresson's *The Holy Alliance:*

---

[3] P. 56.

American Relations (1930)
t Alexander that the Mon-

en discussed are thus rend-
: who wishes to gain a fair
Monroe Doctrine. The view-
: inability to shake off the
mited the accuracy of their
ot considered the play of
States, nor have they ana-
of which the doctrine rose.
ention to the relation of
octrine was Georg Heinz,
ungen zwischen Russland,
n Jahre 1823 (1911). His
ls with the broad outlines
to state occasionally that
ly Alliance, but he places
wer, the Cuban question,
not touch upon the atti-
as a study in the interna-
ok is excellent. Heinz pen-
lem when he wrote:

ended her interests against
: United States also have to
: in the year 1823, but not
d Russia, but also against
her colonies, and her fleet,
chtfaktor] in America."[13]

, in his book, *The United*
, points out that through-

the European Background of the Monroe Doctrine (1922).
The very title is eloquent of the author's point of view.
As a study in European history it is of interest, but it fails
to explain the Monroe Doctrine in an adequate manner.
The second dissertation disappoints the reader. Leonard
A. Lawson chose a significant subject, *The Relation of
British Policy to the Declaration of the Monroe Doctrine*
(1922). His discussions of English commercial interests in
the New World are revealing and give weight to the idea
that the most powerful force in South American politics
was English economic influence. When Mr. Lawson attempts to explain the Monroe Doctrine, however, he falls
into the most grievous errors. So strong was the conventional theory of its origin that the most obvious evidence
to the contrary has been disregarded. The threat of the
Holy Alliance is conjured up in terrifying form. With
more enthusiasm than judgment, the author declares that,
as a result of French success in Spain, there

. . . might occur the very event which both the government of
Great Britain and that of the United States had long suspected—European intervention in South America. King Ferdinand, emboldened by success, would give such an enterprise
his most active encouragement. France would profit, the old
order would be victorious, and probably the old colonial system would be restored.[4]

Similarly, the communications which the Russian minister had made to Adams "must be answered immediately,
lest the Alliance should actually intervene in Latin America, and there should take place . . . political changes and
the transfer of territory. . . ."[5] Faced with these threatening
prospects, England and the United States stood side by
side and repelled the threats of the autocrats. Lawson ad-

[4] P. 106.   [5] P. 132.

vances the most interesting reasons for this Ar
ican *rapprochement*. Because they were both s
because they both possessed territory in Amer
had a common interest in the preservation of
tories against possible attacks by other power
mentions *Canada* as a possible victim), and be
were conscious of a common heritage, the Ur
and England presented a united front to Europ
three factors explain perfectly why the United
England were as antagonistic to each other as
his interpretation is extremely questionable.

Finally, in his excess eagerness to give Er
Canning credit for the formulation of the M
trine, Mr. Lawson writes: "The principles of
Doctrine had not yet been formulated when tl
Polignac conference took place. Indeed, whe
there was to be a Monroe Doctrine seems
pended largely upon the outcome of that
Canning's blunt warning to the French aml
made in October, and the secret memorandu
France promised not to interfere in the Nev
drawn up at that time. But Rush knew noth
until *November 27*, and all the evidence av
cates that knowledge of the affair was not re
United States until February, 1824. It is ac
that the American government was entirely
the Canning-Polignac conference until long
ber 2, 1823. Lawson gives no proof for his co
it is hard to see upon what basis it could
However, it is typical of the way in which h
ored by preconceived ideas and unquestio

---

⁶ P. 16.   ⁷ P. 138.

P. Thomas states in his *Russo-
that "it had been mainly agair
roe Doctrine had been issued.

All the books which have b
ered more or less useless to or
idea of the background of the N
points of the authors and the
traditional explanation have l
interpretations. They have r
world forces upon the United
lyzed the American *milieu* out

The first writer to draw a
world politics to the Monroe I
in his thesis entitled *Die Bezie*
England, und Nordamerika
work is the only one which de
of the situation. He is incline
the United States feared the H
emphasis on the Balance of P
and English interests. He doe
tude of the United States, but
tional relations involved his bo
etrated to the heart of the prol

Just as in Europe England de
Russia and the alliance, so did t
look to their threatened interes
only against the Holy Alliance
England who, through her trade
represented a powerful factor [M

The late Professor Latané al
States and Latin America (192

---

¹² P. 175.   ¹³ P. 12.

the European Background of the Monroe Doctrine (1922). The very title is eloquent of the author's point of view. As a study in European history it is of interest, but it fails to explain the Monroe Doctrine in an adequate manner. The second dissertation disappoints the reader. Leonard A. Lawson chose a significant subject, *The Relation of British Policy to the Declaration of the Monroe Doctrine* (1922). His discussions of English commercial interests in the New World are revealing and give weight to the idea that the most powerful force in South American politics was English economic influence. When Mr. Lawson attempts to explain the Monroe Doctrine, however, he falls into the most grievous errors. So strong was the conventional theory of its origin that the most obvious evidence to the contrary has been disregarded. The threat of the Holy Alliance is conjured up in terrifying form. With more enthusiasm than judgment, the author declares that, as a result of French success in Spain, there

... might occur the very event which both the government of Great Britain and that of the United States had long suspected—European intervention in South America. King Ferdinand, emboldened by success, would give such an enterprise his most active encouragement. France would profit, the old order would be victorious, and probably the old colonial system would be restored.[4]

Similarly, the communications which the Russian minister had made to Adams "must be answered immediately, lest the Alliance should actually intervene in Latin America, and there should take place . . . political changes and the transfer of territory. . . ."[5] Faced with these threatening prospects, England and the United States stood side by side and repelled the threats of the autocrats. Lawson ad-

---

[4] P. 106.　　[5] P. 132.

vances the most interesting reasons for this Anglo-American *rapprochement.* Because they were both sea Powers, because they both possessed territory in America ("They had a common interest in the preservation of these territories against possible attacks by other powers." Lawson mentions *Canada* as a possible victim), and because they were conscious of a common heritage, the United States and England presented a united front to Europe.[6] As those three factors explain perfectly why the United States and England were as antagonistic to each other as they were, his interpretation is extremely questionable.

Finally, in his excess eagerness to give England and Canning credit for the formulation of the Monroe Doctrine, Mr. Lawson writes: "The principles of the Monroe Doctrine had not yet been formulated when the Canning-Polignac conference took place. Indeed, whether or not there was to be a Monroe Doctrine seems to have depended largely upon the outcome of that conference."[7] Canning's blunt warning to the French ambassador was made in October, and the secret memorandum in which France promised not to interfere in the New World was drawn up at that time. But Rush knew nothing about it until *November 27,* and all the evidence available indicates that knowledge of the affair was not received in the United States until February, 1824. It is accurate to say that the American government was entirely ignorant of the Canning-Polignac conference until long after December 2, 1823. Lawson gives no proof for his conclusion, and it is hard to see upon what basis it could possibly rest. However, it is typical of the way in which his book is colored by preconceived ideas and unquestioned theories.

---

[6] P. 16.   [7] P. 138.

Harold Temperley has done much to explain the foreign policies of Canning, but his estimate of the origin of the Monroe Doctrine suffers from the fact that he, too, approaches it from the European side. The United States feared Russia, and the Monroe Doctrine solved the Russian problem, he writes in *The Foreign Policy of Canning* (1925).[8] In *The Cambridge History of British Foreign Policy* he expresses the same view and contradicts himself in the process. At one point he declares: "Canning was not, in fact, afraid of the Tsar's pretensions, for he knew their emptiness. Alexander was not dangerous. . . ."[9] Five pages later he states: "The case of Russia was different; she might intervene as a land Power in America. . . ."[10] Again the idea that a Continental Power might interfere rises to plague the historian. If Alexander was not dangerous, there was no possibility of his intervening in America—both statements cannot be true. Temperley realized that the French menace did not terrify Adams; but, since America must unquestionably have feared *some* Power, he chose Russia and left England out of the picture. That is a serious mistake, as fear of Russia was almost nonexistent in the United States in 1823, and Adams understood the Tsar as well as did Canning. The effect which this line of reasoning had on Temperley's conclusions is revealed when he writes, "the Monroe Doctrine was a vague statement of policy, a lecture, a doctrine, an ideal; it was not a rule of action that the Government was prepared to enforce."[11] Two other writers agree with Temperley in this conclusion. Charles K. Webster expresses similar views in *The Foreign Policy of Castlereagh* (1925), and Benjamin

---

[8] Pp. 104 and 107.   [9] Vol. II, p. 66.   [10] Vol. II, p. 71.   [11] Vol. II, p. 72.

P. Thomas states in his *Russo-American Relations* (1930) that "it had been mainly against Alexander that the Monroe Doctrine had been issued."[12]

All the books which have been discussed are thus rendered more or less useless to one who wishes to gain a fair idea of the background of the Monroe Doctrine. The viewpoints of the authors and their inability to shake off the traditional explanation have limited the accuracy of their interpretations. They have not considered the play of world forces upon the United States, nor have they analyzed the American *milieu* out of which the doctrine rose.

The first writer to draw attention to the relation of world politics to the Monroe Doctrine was Georg Heinz, in his thesis entitled *Die Beziehungen zwischen Russland, England, und Nordamerika im Jahre 1823* (1911). His work is the only one which deals with the broad outlines of the situation. He is inclined to state occasionally that the United States feared the Holy Alliance, but he places emphasis on the Balance of Power, the Cuban question, and English interests. He does not touch upon the attitude of the United States, but as a study in the international relations involved his book is excellent. Heinz penetrated to the heart of the problem when he wrote:

Just as in Europe England defended her interests against Russia and the alliance, so did the United States also have to look to their threatened interests in the year 1823, but not only against the Holy Alliance and Russia, but also against England who, through her trade, her colonies, and her fleet, represented a powerful factor [*Machtfaktor*] in America.[13]

The late Professor Latané also, in his book, *The United States and Latin America* (1920), points out that through-

[12] P. 175.   [13] P. 12.

out the nineteenth century the connection between the Monroe Doctrine and the Balance of Power in Europe was very close. He does not emphasize sufficiently, however, the part which England played, and he argues that the transfer of territory from one European Power to another was in no way prohibited by the Monroe Doctrine. The statements made by Clay in 1825 were an extension of the original doctrine, for Monroe "had made no declaration against the transfer of sovereignty in America from one European power to another. In fact he positively renounced any such idea, when he said: 'With the existing colonies. . . ' "[14] It should be suggested that this is a misinterpretation of the facts. Monroe's disclaimer applied only to existing colonies as they stood in 1823. Adams had said plainly that he did not want to make any declarations which would limit the freedom of action of the United States if the status of any of the existing colonies should be altered. An independent Cuba, or a Cuba in the hands of England, was not an "existing colony" within the sense of the Monroe Doctrine. The United States was bound to inaction only as long as the *status quo* in the western hemisphere should be preserved.

In passing, tribute should be paid to the sound judgment of A. P. Newton. Writing in *The Cambridge History of British Foreign Policy,* not upon the Monroe Doctrine, but upon another subject entirely, he makes a statement which is far more accurate than those in special treatises. In England, he writes, the Monroe Doctrine was regarded as a carrying out of Canning's suggestions,

. . . But to the United States the Message made a different appeal. . . . The United States seemed to stand forth and claim

---

[14] P. 324.

the place of leader among the American peoples, and to the ordinary citizen the ban upon adventures in the New World appeared to be directed at least as much against Great Britain and her supposed designs upon Cuba as against the Continental Powers of whom much less was known.[15]

Strangely enough, the most penetrating comments on the Monroe Doctrine are to be found in monographs upon other subjects.

A most interesting article on the origins of the Monroe Doctrine is that by Samuel E. Morison in the *Revue des sciences politiques* (1924). He discounts completely the danger of French interference in the New World and disagrees with Temperley's assertion that such a move was contemplated. Morison emphasizes the part which Adams played in shaping American foreign policy in 1823 and minimizes the seriousness of the Russian notes. But he goes to an extreme when he declares that England and the United States were essentially friendly at that time. He disregards the facts when he says:

> No one can fail to note the friendly attitude of American statesmen toward Great Britain, ten years after the burning of Washington. None of the statesmen responsible for the Monroe Doctrine believed it to be incompatible with Anglo-American coöperation in America.[16]

Rush, Monroe, Jefferson, and Calhoun, to say nothing of Adams, were all suspicious of England and were willing to join her in a declaration of policy only as a means of blocking her hostile activities. Finally, Morison seems to have misjudged the entire spirit and purpose of American foreign policy during these years, for he concludes:

> Perhaps the most interesting feature in the history of Am-

[15] Vol. II, p. 231.   [16] Vol. XLVII, p. 83.

erican foreign policy . . . [1818–1823] was its tendency to become, on the one hand, a simple echo of the foreign office, and, on the other hand, to attempt the fanciful plan of undertaking a crusade in favor of liberty.[17]

On what conceivable grounds it can be said that the policy of Adams and Monroe from 1818 to 1823 was "a simple echo of the foreign office," is a mystery. The general excellence of Mr. Morison's article makes his conclusions difficult to understand. He has escaped from the usual pitfall which besets writers on the Monroe Doctrine, but he appears to have blundered into another equally deep.

One of the studies which throw considerable light upon the Monroe Doctrine is J. Fred Rippy's *Rivalry of the United States and Great Britain over Latin America* (1929). Rippy has realized clearly that Anglo-American rivalry and mutual suspicion are the keys to an understanding of the problem. He points out the importance of Cuba and of naval and commercial competition, while he rightly concludes that "the rivalry of the two powers represented a continuation of the contest which had begun decades before and was left unsettled by the War of 1812 and the Treaty of Ghent."[18] But even Rippy cannot shake off the spell of the traditional explanation of the Monroe Doctrine. After an excellent paragraph in which he points out the American fear of English aggressions, he weakens and pays homage to the formula: "Of course, this was not the only motive which led Adams to advocate the message of Monroe—Russia and the other 'Holy Allies' were also feared. . . ."[19] However, Mr. Rippy's book is one of the most illuminating that has been written upon

---

[17] Vol. XLVII, p. 84.   [18] P. 111.   [19] P. 118.

this period and will do much to remove misconceptions about the foreign relations of the United States.

Carl R. Fish was another historian whose writings point the way to sound interpretations. Brief though they are, mention must be made of the paragraphs in his *American Diplomacy* (1929) which deal with the Monroe Doctrine. There he minimizes the threat of the Holy Alliance and shows that the Monroe Doctrine "bore more heavily" upon England than upon the Continental Powers. Mr. Fish has also expressed these views succinctly in his essay in the volume, *American Policies Abroad: The United States and Great Britain* (1932), where he declares that the Monroe Doctrine "was a warning not to Europe as Canning conceived it but to the Europe of American thought which included Canning."[20] The soundness of these views makes one regret that they were not presented in more detail.

The writings of Dexter Perkins are generally considered the best that have yet appeared on the Monroe Doctrine. They are the result of much research and careful investigation. Yet their viewpoint is essentially the same as that of the conventional works. Deliberately, Mr. Perkins emphasizes the European aspect of affairs, with the result that his conclusions are open to question. He is concerned almost entirely with the diplomatic background and omits any consideration of the general American attitude toward Europe. This leads him to accept without question the conventional premises. In the first paragraph of *The Monroe Doctrine, 1823–1826* (1927), he writes:

The famous declaration . . . had a dual origin and a dual purpose. On the one hand, it was the result of the advance of Russia on the northwest coast of America, and was designed

---
[20] P. 33.

to serve as a protest against this advance and to establish a general principle against Russian expansion. . . . On the other hand, the message was provoked by the fear of European intervention in South America to restore to Spain her revolted colonies, and was intended to give warning of the hostility of the United States to any such intervention.

His treatise, therefore, is directed to an examination of those two factors. Their influence leads him to relate to the Monroe Doctrine only such evidence as supports their validity. For example, he declares that the dispatch to Hugh Nelson of April 28, 1823, "stands a little aside from the main line of events which led up to the President's message," because it deals with England and Cuba rather than with the Holy Alliance and South America.[21] Another example of the way in which his conclusions are shaped by his premises is his argument that relations between the United States and England improved steadily during Monroe's administrations and that the two countries were positively friendly in 1823.

Mr. Perkins's works suffer from the limitations of his viewpoint. He does not develop the relationship between the Balance of Power and American diplomacy, and he pays little attention to the condition of public opinion as it influenced the actions of the government. The central position of England and the direction of her policy are not stressed, nor are the internal affairs of the United States related to the Monroe Doctrine. As a result of this explanation of the doctrine, Mr. Perkins concludes that its contemporary results were practically nonexistent, and he ranks it as a diplomatic achievement inferior to the treaty with Spain in 1819, to the treaty with Russia in 1824, and to the recognition of the South American re-

[21] P. 54.

publics in 1822. If his premise is accepted, these conclusions are sound, but if his assumption is questioned, they must be altered accordingly.

ᴸ It is hoped that this brief sketch will have pointed out the weaknesses of the existing accounts of the background of the Monroe Doctrine. Practically all of them fall short of being satisfactory explanations because they have embodied a narrow view and have failed to include obvious elements which shape all American foreign policy. Some writers have hinted that another interpretation might be more accurate. This book has explored that possibility in detail. ᶜᵧ

*   *   *   *

SINCE this book was written in the winter of 1933–1934, three additions to the list of writings on the origin of the Monroe Doctrine have appeared.

The Idea of National Interest, by C. A. Beard, does not deal directly with American policy from 1815 to 1823, but the general theme is very much to the point. Beard's analysis of the basic elements in the foreign policies of the United States coincides with that which has been presented here with reference to the origin of Monroe's declaration.

In an article entitled, "Jeffersonian Origins of the Monroe Doctrine," in *The Hispanic American Historical Review,*[22] T. R. Schellenberg advances Jefferson's claim to credit for shaping the "basic doctrine" of the message and relegates Adams to a secondary, negative rôle. Unquestionably, Jefferson's part in the creation of the Monroe Doctrine is greater than is usually assumed; but attempts to determine exactly the relative position of those responsible for that policy is dangerous, for no one man made

[22] Vol. XIV (1934), p. 1.

the positive contributions and another the negative ones. Mr. Schellenberg seems to infer that Monroe's declaration was primarily concerned with South America and the western hemisphere as a whole rather than with the direct national interests of the United States. As a result, he emphasizes the importance of Jefferson's "doctrine of the two spheres" and minimizes the contribution of Adams. This interpretation implies a tacit acceptance of the conventional account of the origins of the Monroe Doctrine and is therefore open to criticism. The secondary thesis, that Jefferson derived the "doctrine of the two spheres" in its developed form from the writings of the Abbé de Pradt, falls into the class of those arguments which present French sources for Jefferson's ideas on agricultural democracy, representative government, and the rights of man. It is more likely that the Abbé's works analyzed existing American ideas than that they created new ones. The conviction that the New World and the Old should remain separated was current in the United States long before the Abbé began to write in 1817. Naturally, men like Jefferson approved these ideas when they appeared in print. However, the "doctrine of the two spheres," as it was presented to Monroe in 1823, resulted from the influence of the events of the preceding fifteen years on Jefferson's lifelong belief that the republican United States should be independent of Europe in thought as well as in reality. It was not an importation from France in 1817.

Gaston Nerval's *Autopsy of the Monroe Doctrine* presents a Latin American indictment of that policy in all its forms. In dealing with the origin of the doctrine, his arguments are to be questioned because they do not emphasize conditions in the United States and do not an-

alyze the point of view of the leaders of the country. No
mention is made of the American attitude toward England or of Anglo-American rivalry. The old interpretation of the doctrine leads him to state that Monroe feared
the designs of the Holy Alliance on Latin America and of
Russia on the Northwest Coast.[28] He assumes that England was the friend of South America and that therefore
the Monroe Doctrine accomplished very little. The conventional interpretation of the origin of the doctrine does
expose it to the charges which Nerval makes. So regarded,
its immediate results were negligible, it has had no relation to conditions since its birth, and violations of its principles have been numerous. But if the Monroe Doctrine
was a national policy conceived by realists in the interests
of the United States, if it was designed to protect those
interests from any alteration of the *status quo* in the New
World which threatened them, if it was enunciated so as
to preserve the freedom of action of the United States,
then it was not useless in 1823, nor is it obsolete today.
Thus interpreted it may be diabolical from Mr. Nerval's
point of view, but its vitality as a national policy is un-
impaired.

[28] P. 42.

Bibliography

PRINTED SOURCES

ADAMS, JOHN QUINCY
Writings (W. C. Ford, ed.). 7 v. New York, 1913–1917.
*Memoirs of John Quincy Adams, comprising Portions of his Diary from
1795 to 1848* (C. F. Adams, ed.). 12 v. Philadelphia, 1874–1877.

ALASKAN BOUNDARY TRIBUNAL
Proceedings. . . . 7 v. in 3. Washington, 1904. (Also printed as: 58 Cong.,
2 sess., Senate executive document No. 162.)

ANONYMOUS
*The Colonial Policy of Great Britain, considered with Relation to her
North American Provinces, and West India Possessions; wherein the
Dangerous Tendency of American Competition is Developed, and the
Necessity of Recommencing a Colonial System on a Vigorous and Ex-
tensive Scale, Exhibited and Defended; with Plans for the Promotion of
Emigration, and Strictures on the Treaty of Ghent.* Philadelphia, 1816.

BENTON, THOMAS HART
Thirty Years' View . . . from 1820 to 1850. . . . 2 v. New York, 1865.

BERING SEA CONTROVERSY
Fur Seal Arbitration: Proceedings of the Tribunal of Arbitration. (53
Cong., 2 sess., Senate executive document No. 177.) 9 v. Washington,
1894.

CALHOUN, JOHN CALDWELL
Works (R. K. Crallé, ed.). 6 v. New York, 1851–1870.
"Correspondence (J. F. Jameson, ed.)," in American Historical Associa-
tion, *Annual Report*, 1899, II.

CANNING, GEORGE
The Speeches of the Right Honourable George Canning (R. Therry,
ed.). Third edition. 6 v. London, 1836.
Some Official Correspondence of George Canning (E. J. Stapleton, ed.).
2 v. London, 1887.

CASTLEREAGH, VISCOUNT
*Memoirs and Correspondence of Viscount Castlereagh, second Mar-
quess of Londonderry* (W. Stewart, ed.). 12 v. London, 1848–1853.

CHATEAUBRIAND, FRANÇOIS A. DE
Congrès de Verone: guerre d'Espagne: negociations: colonies Espagnoles.
2 v. Bruxelles, 1838.

CLAY, HENRY
Works (C. Colton, ed.). 10 v. New York and London, 1904.

[DWIGHT, TIMOTHY]
Remarks on the Review of Inchiquin's Letters, published in the Quarterly Review; addressed to the Right Honorable George Canning, Esquire. Boston, 1815.

The Edinburgh Review, or Critical Journal. Edinburgh, 1802–

FEARON, HENRY
Sketches of America. A Narrative of a Journey of Five Thousand Miles through the Eastern and Western States of America. . . . London, 1818.

FORD, W. C., ed.
"Genesis of the Monroe Doctrine," in Massachusetts Historical Society, *Proceedings,* Second series, XV (1902), 373.

"John Quincy Adams and the Monroe Doctrine," *The American Historical Review,* VII (1902), 676, and VIII (1902), 28.

GALLATIN, ALBERT
Writings (H. Adams, ed.). 3 v. Philadelphia, 1879.

GREAT BRITAIN. FOREIGN OFFICE
British and Foreign State Papers. London, 1841–

"Select Dispatches from the British Foreign Office Archives relating to the Third Coalition against France, 1804–1805" (J. H. Rose, ed.), *in* Royal Historical Society, *Publications,* Third series, VII (1904).

HYDE DE NEUVILLE, GUILLAUME, BARON
Mémoires et souvenirs du Baron Hyde de Neuville. Third edition. 3 v. Paris, 1912.

[IRVING, WASHINGTON]
The Sketch Book of Geoffrey Crayon, Gent. Many editions, 1819 ff.

JACKSON, ANDREW
Correspondence (J. S. Bassett, ed.). 6 v. Washington, 1826–1934.

"Letter of Andrew Jackson to Maj. W. B. Lewis," *in* New York Public Library, *Bulletin: Astor, Lenox, and Tilden Foundations,* IV (1900), 193.

JAMES, E., COMP.
Account of an Expedition from Pittsburg to the Rocky Mountains, performed in the Years 1819 and '20 . . . under the Command of Major Stephen H. Long. 2 v. Philadelphia, 1823.

JEFFERSON, THOMAS
Works (P. L. Ford, ed.). Federal edition. 12 v. New York, 1905.

Writings (A. A. Lipscomb, ed.). Memorial edition. 20 v. Washington, 1903.

JEFFERSON, THOMAS, and MARQUIS DE LAFAYETTE
The Letters of LaFayette and Jefferson (G. Chinard, ed.). Baltimore, Paris, 1929.

KING, RUFUS
Life and Correspondence . . . (C. R. King, ed.). 6 v. New York, 1894–1900.

LANE-POOLE, STANLEY
The Life of the Right Honourable Stratford Canning. . . . 2 v. London and New York, 1888.

MADISON, JAMES
Letters and Other Writings. 4 v. Philadelphia, 1865.
Writings (G. Hunt, ed.). 9 v. New York, 1900–1910.

MARTENS, G. F., ed.
Nouveau recueil de traités d'alliance, de paix, de neutralité, de commerce, d'échange, . . . *des puissances et états de l'Europe depuis 1808 jusqu'à present.* 16 v. in 20. Gottingue, 1817–1842.

MONROE, JAMES
Writings (S. M. Hamilton, ed.). 6 v. New York, 1898.

MOORE, J. B., ed.
A Digest of International Law . . . (52 Cong., 2 sess., House document No. 551). 8 v. Washington, 1906.

National Intelligencer. Washington, 1800–1861.

Niles' Weekly Register. Baltimore, 1811–1845.

The North American Review. Boston, 1815–

The Pamphleteer: Dedicated to Both Houses of Parliament. London, 1813–1828.

PLUMER, WILLIAM, JR.
"Extracts from the Journal of William Plumer, Jr.," *Pennsylvania Magazine of History and Biography,* VI (1882), 357.

[POINSETT, JOEL ROBERTS]
Notes on Mexico, made in the Autumn of 1822. Philadelphia, 1824.

PRADT, DOMINIQUE, ABBÉ DE
Vrai système de l'Europe relativement à l'Amérique et à la Grèce. Paris, 1825.

The Quarterly Review. London, 1809–

RATTENBURY, J. FREEMAN
"Remarks on the Cession of the Floridas to the United States of America, and on the Necessity of Acquiring the Island of Cuba by Great Britain," *The Pamphleteer,* XV (1819), 261.

RUSH, RICHARD
Memoranda of a Residence at the Court of London. Philadelphia, 1833.
Memoranda of a Residence at the Court of London, comprising Incidents Official and Personal from 1819 to 1825 . . . [usually known as *Memoranda,* Second series]. Philadelphia, 1845.
Recollections of a Residence at the English and French Courts (B. Rush, ed.). London, Philadelphia, 1872.

RUSSIA. FOREIGN OFFICE
"Correspondence of the Russian Ministers in Washington, 1818–1825,"
The American Historical Review, XVIII (1913), 309, 537.

TEMPERLEY, H. W. V., ed.
"Documents Illustrating the Reception and Interpretation of the Monroe
Doctrine in Europe, 1823–24," *The English Historical Review*, XXXIX
(1824), 590.

UNITED STATES. CONGRESS
American State Papers:
   Series I Foreign Relations. 6 v. ⎱ Washington, 1832–1861.
   Series II Naval Affairs. 4 v.   ⎰
The Congressional Globe. Washington, 1833–1873.
Debates and Proceedings of the Congress of the United States . . . [cover
title, *Annals of Congress*]. 42 v. Washington, 1834–1856.
Register of Debates in Congress. . . . 14 v. in 29. Washington, 1825–1837.
*Treaties, Conventions, International Acts, Protocols, and Agreements
between the United States of America and other Powers* (W. M. Malloy,
ed.). 3 v. Washington, 1910–1923.

UNITED STATES. DEPARTMENT OF STATE
*Diplomatic Correspondence of the United States concerning the Inde-
pendence of the Latin American Nations* (W. R. Manning, ed.). 3 v.
New York, 1925.

UNITED STATES. PRESIDENT
A Compilation of the Messages and Papers of the Presidents (J. D.
Richardson, comp.). 20 v. New York [1897–1916].

WALSH, ROBERT, JR.
*An Appeal from the Judgments of Great Britain respecting the United
States of America.* . . . Part One. Philadelphia, 1819.

WEBSTER, C. K., ED.
British Diplomacy, 1813–1815. London, 1921.

WEBSTER, DANIEL
The Private Correspondence of Daniel Webster (F. Webster, ed.). 2 v.
Boston, 1875.
Writings and Speeches. National edition. 18 v. Boston, 1903.

WELLESLEY, HENRY
*The Diary and Correspondence of Henry Wellesley, First Lord Cowley,
1790–1846* (F. A. Wellesley, ed.). London [n.d.].

WELLINGTON, ARTHUR, DUKE OF
Supplementary Dispatches and Memoranda (second Duke of Wellington, ed.). 15 v. London, 1858–1872.
Dispatches, Correspondence and Memoranda (second Duke of Wellington, ed.). 8 v. London, 1867–1880.

SECONDARY WORKS

ADAMS, CHARLES F.
The Monroe Doctrine and Mommsen's Law. Boston and New York, 1914.

AMBLER, CHARLES H.
Thomas Ritchie, a Study in Virginia Politics. Richmond, 1913.

AMERICAN SOCIETY OF INTERNATIONAL LAW
Proceedings, 1914. Washington, 1914.

ARTZ, FREDERICK B.
France under the Bourbon Restoration, 1814–1830. Cambridge, 1931.

BEAUMARCHAIS, MAURICE D. DE
La Doctrine de Monroë, l'évolution de la politique des Etats-unis au XIXᵉ siècle. 2d ed. Paris, 1898.

BEMIS, S. F., ED.
American Secretaries of State and their Diplomacy. 10 v. New York, 1927–1929.

BRADLEY, PHILLIPS
A Bibliography of the Monroe Doctrine, 1919–1929. London, 1929.

CALLAHAN, JAMES M.
Cuba and International Relations: a Historical Study in American Diplomacy. Baltimore, 1899.

CLARK, BENNETT C.
John Quincy Adams: "Old Man Eloquent." Boston, 1932.

COOLIDGE, ARCHIBALD C.
The United States as a World Power. New York, 1909.
"La Doctrine de Monroë," *La Revue de Paris,* XIV:2 (1907), 650.

CORTI, EGON C., COUNT
The Rise of the House of Rothschild (B. and B. Lunn, trs.). New York, 1928.

CRESSON, WILLIAM P.
The Holy Alliance: the European Background of the Monroe Doctrine. New York, 1922.

EARLE, EDWARD M.
"American Interest in the Greek Cause, 1821–1827," *The American Historical Review,* XXXIII (1927), 44.

EDGINGTON, THOMAS B.
The Monroe Doctrine. Boston, 1904.

FISH, CARL R., SIR NORMAN ANGELL, and REAR ADMIRAL CHARLES L. HUSSEY
American Policies Abroad: The United States and Great Britain. Chicago [1932].

GILMAN, DANIEL C.
James Monroe. New York, 1898.

HART, ALBERT B.
"The Monroe Doctrine in its Territorial Extent and Application," *in* United States Naval Institute, *Proceedings*, XXXII (1906), 753.
The Monroe Doctrine: an Interpretation. Boston, 1916.

HEINZ, GEORG G. H.
Die Beziehungen zwischen Russland, England, und Nordamerika im Jahre 1823: Beitrage zur Genesis der Monroedoktrin. Berlin, 1911.

HILDT, JOHN C.
"Early Diplomatic Negotiations of the United States with Russia," *in* Johns Hopkins University, *Studies in Historical and Political Science*, XXIV (1906), 251.

KRAUS, HERBERT
Die Monroedoktrin in ihren Beziehungen zur amerikanischen Diplomatie und zum Völkerrecht. Berlin, 1913.

LATANÉ, JOHN H.
The United States and Latin America. Garden City, 1920.

LAWSON, LEONARD A.
The Relation of British Policy to the Declaration of the Monroe Doctrine. New York, 1922.

LLOYD, COLONEL E. M.
"Canning and Spanish America," *in* Royal Historical Society, *Transactions*, New series, XVIII, 77.

MACCORKLE, WILLIAM A.
The Personal Genesis of the Monroe Doctrine. New York and London, 1923.

MANNING, WILLIAM R.
Early Diplomatic Relations between the United States and Mexico. Baltimore, 1916.

MEIGS, WILLIAM M.
The Life of Charles Jared Ingersoll. Second edition. Philadelphia, 1900.

MESICK, JANE L.
The English Traveller in America, 1785–1835. New York, 1922.

MILLER, HUGH G.
The Isthmian Highway: a Review of the Problems of the Caribbean. New York, 1929.

MOORE, JOHN B.
"The Monroe Doctrine," *Political Science Quarterly*, XI (1896), 3.

MORISON, SAMUEL E.
The Maritime History of Massachusetts, 1783–1860. Boston and New York, 1921.
"Les Origines de la doctrine de Monroë, 1775–1823," *Revue des sciences politiques*, XLVII (1924), 52.

PAXSON, FREDERIC L.
The Independence of the South American Republics: a Study in Recognition and Foreign Policy. Second edition. Philadelphia, 1916.

PERKINS, DEXTER
"Europe, Spanish America, and the Monroe Doctrine," *The American Historical Review,* XXVII (1922), 207.
"Russia and the Spanish Colonies, 1817–1818," *ibid.,* XXVIII (1923), 656.
The Monroe Doctrine, 1823–1826. Cambridge, 1927.
The Monroe Doctrine, 1826–1867. Baltimore, 1933.

PHILLIPS, W. ALLISON
The Confederation of Europe: a Study of the European Alliance, 1813–1823, as an Experiment in the International Organization of Peace. London and New York, 1914.

PRATT, E. J.
"Anglo-American Commercial and Political Rivalry on the Plata, 1820–1830," *The Hispanic American Historical Review,* XI (1931), 302.

PRATT, JULIUS W.
The Expansionists of 1812. New York, 1925.

REDDAWAY, WILLIAM F.
The Monroe Doctrine. New York, 1905.

REZNECK, SAMUEL
"The Depression of 1819–1822, a Social History," *The American Historical Review,* XXXIX (1933), 28.

RIPPY, J. FRED
Rivalry of the United States and Great Britain over Latin America (1808–1830). Baltimore, 1929.

ROBERTSON, WILLIAM S.
"The United States and Spain, 1822," *The American Historical Review,* XX (1915), 781.

SCHOULER, JAMES
"The Authorship of the Monroe Doctrine," *in* American Historical Association, *Annual Report,* 1905, I.

SHIPP, JOHN E. D.
Giant Days, or the Life and Times of William H. Crawford. . . . Americus, Ga., 1909.

SRBIK, HEINRICH, RITTER VON
Metternich der Staatsmann und der Mensch. 2 v. München [1925].

TEMPERLEY, HAROLD W. V.
"The Later American Policy of George Canning," *The American Historical Review,* XI (1906), 779.
"French Designs on Spanish America, in 1820–5," *The English Historical Review,* XL (1925), 34.

TEMPERLEY, HAROLD W. V. (*Continued*)
The Foreign Policy of Canning, 1822–1827: England, the Neo-Holy Alliance and the New World. London, 1925.

THOMAS, BENJAMIN P.
"Russo-American Relations, 1815–1867," in Johns Hopkins University, Studies in Historical and Political Science, XLVIII (1930), 127.

TUCKER, GEORGE F.
The Monroe Doctrine: a Concise History of its Origin and Growth. Boston, 1885.

TURNER, FREDERICK J.
The Rise of the New West: 1819–1829. The American Nation, a History (A. B. Hart, ed.), XIV. New York and London, 1906.

UNITED STATES. LIBRARY OF CONGRESS
A List of References on the Monroe Doctrine (H. H. B. Meyer, comp.). Washington, 1919.

VILLANEUVA, CARLOS A.
La Monarquía en América. 4 v. Paris [n.d.].

WARD, A. W., and G. P. GOOCH, EDS.
The Cambridge History of British Foreign Policy, 1783–1919. 3 v. Cambridge, 1922–1923.

WARD, A. W., G. W. PROTHERO, and S. LEATHES, EDS.
The Cambridge Modern History. 14 v. New York, 1902–1918.

WEBSTER, CHARLES K.
The Foreign Policy of Castlereagh, 1815–1822: Britain and the European Alliance. London, 1925.

WHITE, ELIZABETH B.
American Opinion of France from LaFayette to Poincaré. New York, 1927.

WHITNEY, EDSON L.
The American Peace Society: a Centennial History. Washington, 1928.

As noted in the Bibliographical Essay, the following works appeared after this book was written:

BEARD, CHARLES A.
The Idea of National Interest: an Analytical Study in American Foreign Policy. New York, 1934.

NERVAL, GASTON [RAÚL DIEZ DE MEDINA]
Autopsy of the Monroe Doctrine: the Strange Story of Inter-American Relations. New York, 1934.

SCHELLENBERG, THEODORE R.
"Jeffersonian Origins of the Monroe Doctrine," The Hispanic American Historical Review, XIV (1934), 1.

Index

Adams, John, President of the United States, 1797–1801, on Anglo-American relations, 61; refusal to join a Peace Society, 224

Adams, John Quincy, secretary of state, 1817–1825, character and experience, 208 and n. 2, 209–210; character and United States foreign policy, 207–208, 220 ff., 232–233, 249–250; training in European diplomacy, 122, 215–217; personal acquaintance with European diplomats, 216–217; self-analysis, comparison with Henry Clay, 210 n. 5; ambition, 213–215 and n. 13; idealism, 215; love of praise, 212–213; national spirit, 211–212, 225–227, 232, 235, 239–240, 249–250, 271; reflects popular sentiment, 241; sensitiveness to criticism, 210–213, 232, 240; tendency to overstate policies, 138 n. 80, 238 n. 58; opinion of foreign diplomats on, 214–215; relations with Stratford Canning, 236–240; Crawford's opinion of, 197; on Tsar Alexander, 55–56; on Calhoun, 213; on George Canning's proposals, 1823, 269; on Cuba, English policy toward, in 1823, 108–109; fear of English occupation of Cuba, 167 n. 89, 169; instructions to Nelson concerning Cuba, 175–179; on editors, 211–212; on England, growth of American hostility toward, 84; on England, attacks by, on America, 244–246; on England and the American Revolution, 241–243; on England and Europe in 1823, 146–147; on England, opposition to France in the New World, 108–109; on England and her policies, 219–220, 234–235; on Europe and America, 34, 218–219; on faction in American politics, 217–218; Fourth of July oration, 1821, circumstances, 241, content, 241–245, significance, 246–247, comment upon, 248–249; on France and England in 1815 *et seqq.*, 91–92; on Franco-American relations in 1821, 101; Jackson defended by, in 1818, 226–233; defense of Jackson, Jefferson on, 229; on Northwest Coast, 133; on Peace Societies, 224–226; on Russia, commercial treaty with, 122–123; on Russia and Spain, Florida, 125; on slave trade and English policy, 234–235; on South America, independent monarchies in, 98 n. 35; on principles of United States foreign policy, 227, 244–247

Aix-la-Chapelle, Congress of, 32, 126, 146

Alexander I, Tsar of Russia, 1801–1825, 1–2, 6, 113, 217; and American Peace Societies, 222–223; and the United States, 55, 135–136, 138

Ambrister, Robert. *See* Arbuthnot

American Revolution, J. Q. Adams on, 241–243

Anglo-American relations, 20–24, 26, 57 ff., 141, 181–182; in 1823, 253, 259–271; from 1824 to 1856, 280; basic factors in, 85; growth of hostility in, 81–84 and n. 102; lack of understanding in, 69–70, 247; commercial rivalry in, 21, 143–144, 183–184; naval rivalry in, 143–144; Cuba and Florida in, 157 ff.; cession of the Floridas in 1819 and, 160–163; English policy in South America, effect on, 151–153; slave trade and, 234–235; Stratford Canning and, 236–240; English reviews, effect on, 73 ff., 80–84; South American diplomats and, 154 n. 50, 159–160; Washington Irving's opinion of, 79–80

[305]